THE
BIG YANKEE

The Life of
Carlson of the Raiders

BY MICHAEL BLANKFORT

With Illustrations

LITTLE, BROWN AND COMPANY · BOSTON

LIBERTY BOOK CLUB EDITION
BY ARRANGEMENT WITH
LITTLE, BROWN & COMPANY

PRINTED IN THE UNITED STATES OF AMERICA

Evans F. Carlson
Recuperating from Saipan wounds. *La Jolla, California, October 1944*

To

THOMAS ALPINE CARLSON

His church and his country
owe him a greater debt
than they know

Contents

CONTENTS

THE BIG YANKEE

The Life of Carlson of the Raiders

Part One

▼▼▼

1

Prologue

It is a little like a good mystery story. You come on a man at fifty who has spent thirty-four years in the armed services — and he has done certain things. You wonder at them and you wonder at his life — and you ask: how did this come to be?

Many disconnected opinions face you all at once. Someone who had known him twenty years ago says: "He was ruthless; ambitious. All he wanted was to get ahead."

And then you read a report written for the War Department by a man who was trained to judge people accurately. "He made the observer . . . feel small in the constant self-comparison which goes on when one listens to a man like Carlson. Whereas the observer shows high interest in the concerns of self, family and friends in a limited section of society, Carlson seems to have a quite strong identification with segments at all levels of society but particularly with the ill-fed, ill-housed third."[1]

Is it the same man? you ask; or have the years made the difference? And, if so, how?

Where are the clues, what is the connection — in our times — between Peacham, Vermont, and Yenan in North China? Between the William Lloyd Garrison statue on Commonwealth Avenue in

---

[1] From the 1944 report of Professor John Dollard of the Yale Institute of Human Relations, onetime consultant on morale for the War Department.

Boston and a Nicaraguan patriot named Augusto Sandino? Between a widow who ran a grocery store in Portland, Maine, a Brooklyn boy, Vic Cassara, a journalist from the University of Missouri and Chiang Kai-shek?

Is it possible, we ask, for a man to get to know who his brothers are, if he tries hard for thirty years?

Where does Ralph Waldo Emerson fit into an American submarine called the U.S.S. *Nautilus* a half day out of Japanese-held Makin Island on August 16, 1942?

It's a little like a good mystery.

2

Prepared . . . for defeats

On August 9, 1942, two days after Marines of the First Division landed on Guadalcanal, a task group consisting of the submarines U.S.S. *Argonaut* and U.S.S. *Nautilus* slipped from their base in Pearl Harbor and headed west toward Makin atoll in the Gilbert Islands, 2500 miles and eight days away. On the subs were 215 men of the Second Raider Battalion, on their way to make a hit-and-run raid on Japanese-held territory, the first by Americans in the war. Their commander was Evans Carlson, son of a Connecticut Congregationalist minister; their executive officer, James Roosevelt, a son of the President of the United States.

Eight days later, in the dawn of August 17, they surprised the enemy by landing on a beach the enemy thought could not be landed on. In the next forty hours they killed the entire enemy garrison of 300, destroyed two small transports, two radio stations, two seaplanes, set the torch to 1000 barrels of aviation gasoline, refined by an American company, and burned and leveled all operating military installations. Thirty Raiders were lost.

In the United States, prepared since Pearl Harbor for defeats, the news of the Makin Raid stirred the hearts of the people.

The *New York Times* ran a half-page of pictures and a seven-column story. *Time* gave the story a page and a half, ending its account with a stanza of "Carlson's Raiders" to the tune of "Abdul the Bulbul Amir":

> They will sing of the sailor and soldier I know
> And tell of the deeds that were done,
> But Carlson's Raiders will sing for themselves
> And know how the battle was won.[2]

The *New York Herald Tribune* had a lead editorial, "Carlson of the Raiders":

> . . . those who knew him well will readily understand why he was chosen to lead the landing party on Makin and why he did such a thorough job and why the Marines sing about him.[3]

Eleanor Roosevelt in "My Day" wrote:

> I am deeply grateful that our son came through alive, but some did not. . . .
> Somehow I cannot free myself of a heavy heart which must keep companionship with the hearts of other men and women in our country and in other countries all over the world. With it goes a tremendous sense of the responsibility which must be carried by the older generation for the world we now face.[4]

And in the mail columns of the *Hartford Courant* was a letter headed "A Host of Heroes":

> To the Editor of the Courant:
> Your kind and discerning thought in sending the photograph of my son, Lt. Col. Evans F. Carlson, is deeply appreciated. We are naturally proud of the achievement, though a bit stunned by the wild publicity it has elicited.

[2] *Time,* Sept. 7, 1942.
[3] *New York Herald Tribune,* August 29, 1942.
[4] United Feature Syndicate, August 24, 1942.

What a great host of heroes we have, not only on that front but on every front. And thank God, it is not the courage of fatalism, but of a sound faith in what we preachers call, righteousness, in plain words, in an order of common sense and good will. Let us all pray God that politicians and self-interested poltroons do not wreck the order for which our fighting men are paying such a glorious price.

THOMAS A. CARLSON
Plymouth, Connecticut[5]

When the news of the Makin Raid came the hearts of the American people were lightened. The first completed action in the war against the Japs had been a success.

3

Seven faces

And now the Raid was over. The submarines were speeding due east from Makin atoll toward Pearl Harbor. In hot, tiny wardrooms used as operating rooms, MacCracken and Stigler, navy doctors, were completing an unbroken twenty-four hours of cutting and putting together the torn parts of wounded men. Elsewhere on the ship, comrades of the wounded lay stripped and exhausted in their makeshift bunks watching, with an odd kind of pleasure, oily sweat pour down their sides. They were alive — and they wanted to know it.

In the wardroom of the *Nautilus,* now crowded with men, Evans Fordyce Carlson, a bony, blue-eyed man of forty-six with a heavily lined face and a long nose that looked granite, was sitting by himself on a corner stool. He held a large white pad of paper on his

[5] *Hartford Courant,* Sept. 2, 1942.

lap, and in the side pockets of his open dungaree jacket were rolled-up official documents. He concentrated on the pad and held his pencil loosely in his long, tobacco-stained fingers. His face was in a frown of sadness that ill befitted its strength. An unlit pipe jutted straight out from between his lips, and glistening sweat dropped from his broad forehead onto his cheeks.

After a moment, he made a few scratches along the edge of the paper with his pencil; then wrote down the formal salutation of his battle report:

From: The Commanding Officer, Second Marine Raider Battalion.
To: The Commander, Submarines, Pacific Fleet.
Subject: Operations on Makin, August 17–18, 1942

Carefully Carlson underlined the words. Then he took the documents out of his pockets, glanced at them quickly, and, following the prescribed form, jotted down his References and Enclosures, and below them wrote in capital letters: NARRATIVE.

The really hard part was now to begin. A thousand details and reflections fought for supremacy in his thoughts. He knew, of course, that he would have to begin with the beginning, but where was the beginning? Did the battle really start at five forty five the morning of the seventeenth when the first enemy fire swept through his men, or did it start when he and his men had landed on the beach? How can battles faithfully be reported as commencing on a moment of time?

Suddenly into his thoughts burst the full essence of the sadness he had felt earlier, and he realized how much he had been putting down in himself.

He wiped his face and his long firm nose of sweat, and closed his eyes for a moment. The sub's engines beat a drum through the ship. At the chow tables, glasses and silverware made little homelike noises, and there were small sounds of men talking and laughing.

He would like to start his report with this: Total Japanese casualties — 300. Total Raider casualties — 30: eighteen by the enemy, five by their love of their comrades, and seven by stupidity, power, habit, prejudice. It was for these seven he felt sad. Their deaths were cruel because they were wasted.

One by one seven faces moved across his mind. Some he remembered better than others, a few he remembered little incidents about. He hoped that these seven dead would never be picked out by name from among the other casualties, for if they were, their families would be deprived of their last resource of consolation.

After a minute, he turned his mind away from the faces, disliking the self-indulgence of sadness. He believed that compassion must never be idle or passive.

He couldn't start his report with a statement of his casualties. The form required something else. His pad and pencil waited, and yet for reasons obscured he wrote nothing. He felt tired, depleted. Despite himself, he wanted to go elsewhere in his mind, to relax, to think back on other days.

And now he remembered a February day, nine months before, when it had seemed to him that all the threads of his life up to that time had come together.

It was on February 5, 1942, two months after Pearl Harbor, when Headquarters finally consented to establish a new kind of Marine Corps detachment — a Raider Battalion — with Evans Carlson as its commander.

On that day, Carlson wrote his father a long letter; and among other things he said:

> At last I have received a break. Today I was placed in command of a special unit with carte blanche to organize, train and indoctrinate it as I see fit. There is nothing like it in existence in the country. Naturally, I'm delighted. I will hand pick my personnel. Jimmy Roosevelt is to be my executive officer. . . .
>
> Things seem to be moving in a direction I have so long urged and had almost despaired of seeing materialize. But now I have been afforded the opportunity to practice some of the precepts I have been preaching these past years.

4

"Who the hell was Carlson?"

Word moves swiftly among men in jail or in a barracks. Word moved swiftly through the Marine Corps Base in San Diego, through the boot platoons and the regiments, and inland to Camp Elliot and up the coast to Camp Matthews. A new outfit was forming. Raiders or commandoes, rugged, suicide, the *crème de la crème,* the Marine of the Marines. You've got to have something on the ball to get in, men said. An officer named Carlson was going to be C.O.

Who the hell, they asked, was Carlson?

A few who knew had served with him in the Fourth Marines in Shanghai or in the Legation Guard in Peiping or in the *Guardia Nacional* in Nicaragua or while training in Quantico. Some liked him; some didn't; some said he was square, and some said he did everything by the book and was too tough. A few didn't know him but had heard of him. They had read a book of his about China.

When the men talked it over, some of them who were married and had children wanted no part of a suicide battalion. Others in the same situation wanted to get into the fight quick. There were a few who had fought against Fascism in Spain in the Abraham Lincoln Battalion. They were for volunteering. There were old-timers who had learned never to refuse an order, but never to volunteer, and there were other old-timers who asked: "What's the matter? You want to live forever?"

In a tent at Camp Elliot, a young boy from Chicago took out a brand-new fountain pen and a sheet of Marine Corps stationery he had just bought at the PX, and wrote a letter home.

DEAR POP AND MOM,

I just heard they are organizing, or as we Marines say, activating a new battalion like the British Commandoes. I'd like to volunteer. Please write me right away (or wire me) saying it's OK. I'm going to wait until I hear from you. . . .

In one platoon, fourteen volunteered in the afternoon and were given until the next morning to think it over, and only six came forth from the ranks in the morning. In another platoon, five men volunteered at first, and when they heard the sergeant warn them that Carlson's new outfit would be so tough that only real Marines could stand the gaff, the five remained in their places, and the rest of the platoon joined them.

Among the volunteers were old-timers and newly fledged boots, school boys and college athletes, forest rangers, ranchers, policemen, a preacher and a gardener from Beverly Hills; Sam Rodger Brown, an American Indian from Oklahoma; Victor Maghakian, called "Transport," a Fresno Armenian; Jack Miller from a Jewish home in Texas; Ken Merrill out of Arizona; Hermanek from Chicago; Thomason from Atlanta; Le François, Nelson, Peatross, Plumley, Lamb, Wygal, Jolly, Sebock, Craven. . . .

The volunteers were called for an interview; some by Carlson, some by Roosevelt, others by officers Carlson trusted.

"Carlson's eyes were stern. They made me feel like my preacher was looking at me," Private Al Flores said. "And yet he looked tough and hard-boiled like a typical, by-the-book Marine officer. Of course, after a minute or so he smiled and I felt a little easier. He had a helluva good smile. You felt he wasn't putting it on, but was really friendly."

With brown tobacco-stained fingers Carlson offered them cigarettes and asked what their names were and where they came from and what they had done in civilian life. And if he knew their part of the country, he would take a few minutes and talk about it. But, finally, when a rapport had been reached and the major's gold oak leaves on his shirt had retreated to their proper size, the interview began.

His voice was serious and his blue eyes searched out the face in front of him. "Why do you want to join the Raiders?" he asked, and waited anxiously for the reply.

"We want to fight, sir," they replied. Or, "We want to get overseas and come back quickly." Or, "We'd like to join a commando outfit."

He frowned at the answers, and asked his question a different way. "Why do you want to fight? What's the war about? What're we fighting for?"

Answers came to him in the patchwork of America; halting, uncertain, self-conscious, confused, but with good instincts. The men wanted revenge for Pearl Harbor. They wanted to teach the Japs a lesson. Only a few said something about democracy or Fascism or militarism.

In a sense, it was what he expected, though he hoped for more. But these answers were not enough. He must try to get behind them, into the mind. He must find out what they held dear enough to die for.

He dogged them with more questions: "What do you think of America? Why do you hate militarism? Do you think we ought to exterminate all the Japs?"

He had to know what they believed in. It was more important to him than his life, for it would mean his life and theirs.

"I won't take a man who doesn't give a damn about anything," he told Jimmy Roosevelt. "But if he has a deep feeling about wanting to fight, even for the wrong reasons, take him. I know I can shape him into wanting to fight for the right reasons."

Carlson never lacked confidence in himself when it came to men and things.

More questions:

"Why do you want to fight?"

"Because the war is righteous," a boy from New York replied with a fire that matched his own. "It's the will of God."

"Because we have no choice. But we've got to see that it don't happen again — or else . . ."

"Because the Japs attacked. . . ."

Those who didn't care or who wanted only adventure or were too old or had personal burdens that worried them, he thanked with kindness and let go. And for the others who believed in something, he had more questions.

"Can you cut a Jap's throat without flinching? . . . Can you choke him to death without puking? Are you willing to starve and suffer and go without food and sleep?"

And then he'd stand up, his six feet of strength and leanness towering high, his thin, New England face stern. "I promise you nothing but hardships and danger," he said. And if he sounded to them like doom speaking, that was the way he wanted it.

"When we get into battle, we ask no mercy, we give none."

Old John Brown had once said the same thing to his own sons.

Carlson tried everything he knew to frighten these volunteers. He felt he owed them something: a glimpse into the future, a chance to change their minds.

He wanted more. He wanted to know whether these men had confidence in their ability to do anything they *willed* to do.

"Can you walk fifty miles a day?" he would ask.

"I don't know, sir," they'd answer. "I never have. But I *think* I can."

"Not *think!*" he'd reply. "Do you want to? Do you *know* you can?"

Three thousand men volunteered. Roughly, two-thirds were acceptable, but only a thousand could be chosen according to Headquarters' Table of Organization.

One idea of Carlson's had so far been tested and found true. "Most Americans have deep and important convictions about something," he said. And then, after the long days of interviewing were over, he added: "Though, Lord knows, you have to drag it out of 'em."

5

Of dreams and plans

There was a lot more to do than getting a thousand men. It was a time of ordering up a new world with no seventh day of rest. A new theory of action had to be created, for the Raiders could not be like any other battalion.

Carlson's tired little office at Camp Elliot, California, smoky and bitter with a day's cigarettes and pipes, littered with manuals and mimeographed regulations, books and maps and old magazines and clothes and a sagging cot, became a general staff headquarters for the exchange of dreams and plans.

Tall, modest Captain Jimmy Roosevelt was there, and stocky First Sergeant Charlie Lamb from Snowhill, North Carolina, and Peatross and Davis and Plumley. They met at odd hours during the day and long hours at night.

The world outside was full of defeats; Hong Kong, Wake, Guam, Manila had fallen. The Japs were moving through Malaya toward Singapore — and no one could stop them. Burma was threatened; Alaska, Hawaii, California and Oregon were threatened.

"I expect to wake up any morning," someone said, "to find a Jap under my sack."

They laughed bitterly.

Carlson put a cigarette in his mouth and lit it. "We've got to get to work figuring how we're going to organize and train," he said.

"The battalion or the world?" Roosevelt asked with a grin.

"First things first," Carlson replied.

"We've got the regulation Table of Organization," Lamb said.

"I know," Carlson said, blowing a stream of smoke through his lips. "But I don't want to take it just because it's regulation. The mission of a military unit should determine its form."

Someone picked up a copy of the orders activating the Raiders and read from it. "Its mission is to engage in hit-and-run raids, to spearhead amphibious landings, and to operate as guerrillas behind enemy lines."

A voice drawled out of a dark corner of the room, "Anybody here think that can be achieved by a regulation battalion?"

The silence was his answer.

"The Japs are doing pretty good," the drawling voice remarked.

"Let's start with the Japs," Carlson said. He made an analysis of Japanese military tactics and showed how they were succeeding by the methods of flanking and infiltration. Too many British and American commanders were at a loss as to how to combat these tactics because they were trail-bound. They put too much faith in solid fronts, heavy artillery and unbroken communications.

"I've seen the Japs at work," he said. "Their flanking and infiltration tactics are good. But they've got a couple of important weaknesses — and we've got to take advantage of 'em. The Japs don't have much fire-power in their infiltrating groups. And, secondly, Jap commanders are so confident that their infiltrating troops will break through that they never provide enough security for their own camps and flanks and supply depots."

"If we can outflank 'em . . ." a voice started.

"And counterinfiltrate with heavier fire-power," someone else added.

"You've got something!" a third man concluded.

"But we're a light infantry outfit," came an objection.

"Exactly," Carlson said. "To carry out our mission we've got to have mobility and flexibility and heavy fire-power without sacrificing either."

First Lieutenant Davis rose from his chair excitedly. "We've got to figure out how to strike with a small number of men and give them the strength of weapons of a large number of men."

"What about our nine-man squad?" someone asked.

"Yeah — but the regulation table only gives 'em eight rifles and one automatic — a Browning."

"We need more than that."

"Sure — but how and where?"

"Doesn't it come down to this?" Carlson asked. "How can we use the conventional nine-man rifle squad in jungle and night warfare and yet maintain control of it?"

There was a silence that followed, each man creating ideas within himself, matching his wits and experience against the problem. Somewhere outside the room, beyond the sea that ranged against near-by San Diego, comrades of these men were falling back to Bataan, sick and outnumbered, helpless against the jungle and the enemy who was using the jungle as a weapon. Marines and soldiers were being cut down from behind by Jap sniper squads moving easily through our lines to blot out stragglers, to blow up ammunition dumps, to surprise command posts and disrupt lines of communication.

Someone in the room, thinking out loud, went over the regulation weapon strength of the regulation squad. "They've got eight rifles and one BAR (Browning Automatic Rifle)," he murmured. "Couldn't we add a couple more automatic weapons? Like another BAR or so?"

"How about a Tommy gun?" Lamb said.

Carlson straightened out in his chair and lit a cigarette from the glowing end of one he was finishing; then he ran his fingers through his close-cut hair. "Good!" he said softly. "We've got a nine-man squad now. Suppose we add a tenth man as squad leader. Then suppose we break up the nine-man squad into three groups of three men each." His forehead wrinkled as he tried to visualize all the possibilities.

"And how do we arm the three men?" someone blurted out.

"With a BAR, a Tommy gun, and an M-1," Carlson replied.

A long drawn out whistle came from the dark corner. "That's *real* fire-power," the men said. "Two automatics and a Garand!" He whistled again.

"Three men would have more fire-power than a whole squad did before," Roosevelt said.

And then everybody began talking at once and the idea flourished. "Let's call 'em fire teams or groups," Lamb said, or Peatross maybe, or Davis. No one remembered who said what at this point.

"The fire team has a thousand advantages. Small, mobile, flexible. Wherever a squad is used as a patrol or as security or as flankers, we use one of these teams."

"Wonderful for counterinfiltration!"

"In jungle fighting, you need small groups with lots of automatic weapons!"

"It's like multiplying each man by three."

"And it gives each man a chance to develop into a leader," Carlson said. "They'll live and work and train together. They'll get to know each other. They'll rely on each other, have confidence. They'll learn each other's weapons. It'll help 'em improvise in combat." He stood up, dodging the hanging lightbulb over him. "I think we've got something, boys."

"The Japs'll wish we hadn't thought of it," Davis said and they laughed.

"Yeah," the drawling voice remarked from the corner. "But what about Headquarters?"

"Uh-uh!"

"They've got to authorize the change, okay the additional weapons, and give us the right to promote our men to the ratings which they'll deserve as fire-team leaders," Roosevelt said.

Carlson was silent, clouding his face with cigarette smoke. "Let's get all this down in writing," he said finally. "We'll put through the request pronto — and see where we stand."

The request went through channels — and the reply came back through channels. Washington said "No!" The Tables of Organization and of Basic Allowances would not be changed.

Broken into its pieces, the "No" meant "Who the hell does Carlson think he is? . . . If he wants his Raiders let him work the way the rest of the Marine Corps works . . . Besides, the damned fire teams won't work!"

The general staff of dreams and plans at temporary Raider headquarters at Camp Elliot which had, in the interval, worked out the details of the fire team with increasing conviction of its great worth, felt as if their own Corregidor had been taken. They cursed Headquarters from bumper to bumper. Hotly, they talked of everything but outright mutiny.

But Carlson refused to give up. "Let's rewrite our request, saying the same things in different words. Let's use pressure through anyone we know. Let's pull strings. If we believe that the fire team will save lives and do our job, by God, let's don't stop at anything!"

They wrote memoranda through channels and outside of channels; they made trips at their own expense to Washington; they did everything that men driven by the strength of righteousness could do. And, finally, Headquarters spoke again.

"You will have to keep your present Tables of Organization and Basic Allowances," was said in essence. "But you can organize as you wish within the aggregate limits set by the Tables. We will even authorize the quartermaster to give you additional weapons providing he has them."

The jubilation at success was deadened only by this — that Carlson could not give promotions to men not authorized in the regulation battalions. Not one corporal or sergeant could be made regardless of what tasks he might be called on to do.

But the fire-team idea was saved, and it saved lives and killed the enemy, and to this day it has not been forgotten.

A time came after Makin and Guadalcanal when Carlson, burning with malaria, depressed that his Raiders had been taken away from him and he would never lead them again, heartsick at being "promoted" to a staff job to deprive him of direct command of men, received official word that not only the Marine Corps but the Army as well had revised its Tables of Organization and Basic Allowances to incorporate, with one slight change, the fire team and other innovations[6] which had had their start in the grubby Camp Elliot headquarters of the general staff of dreams and plans.

The fire team had become regulation. Headquarters does learn after all.

[6] These innovations were: (1) making the weapons platoon an integral part of the rifle company; (2) greater use of radio for control within and between small tactical units.

But he was not half as elated as the hundreds of letters from his men which told him how they had used the fire team in other outfits, and how it had saved lives and achieved objectives, and that through this they whom he had not been able to promote as their work and efforts deserved had won, in the Diaspora of other battalions, their rightful ratings and commissions by the uncompromising selection board of battle.

6

"The Star-Spangled Banner" . . . at three o'clock in the afternoon

February is the rainy season in California. Aleutian winds sweep the Pacific, piling up thunderheads, bringing rains that surfeit the parched lands.

In a wet muddy clearing surrounded by tall bitter-smelling eucalyptus trees at Jacques Farm, Camp Elliot, near San Diego, free for the moment from the downpour, a thousand men waited for the first speech by their commanding officer. They stood in their green uniforms a little stiffly and self-consciously, for they were volunteers and that gave them a slight swagger in the spirit and an uncertainty in the bones. Most of them had come from their interviews with an excitement tinged with an honest American skepticism. Carlson and Roosevelt had talked big.

There were a few among the thousand men who waited, but neither with excitement nor skepticism. They had an obscured and indefinable anger which they felt without understanding. Carlson had given them a choice where one decision might mean death, and another the loss of the right to live with themselves.

"Here he comes," someone in the front ranks murmured, and they all straightened up as if to brace themselves. A diffuse lemon sunlight warmed the air.

A jeep drove up from a back road near by and men got out of it carrying a portable loudspeaker set. In a few minutes, a microphone was connected with an amplifier and placed on top of a platform made from three ration crates. An enlisted communications man stepped to the mike, and asked if the fellows could hear him. They said they could.

A second jeep rolled in from the road, and Sergeant Major Charlie Lamb took a deep breath and shouted, "Attention!" Most of the men were at attention already. Carlson jumped down from the jeep and walked toward the platform. He was dressed in work khaki.

At the mike, he said in a relaxed and quiet way, "As you were, boys." Then he motioned them closer. "Come on up here. Let's get together."

The men broke ranks, moved forward across the muddy earth and crowded around him. He recognized some of them from the interviews and smiled and waved his hand. When they were as close to him as they could get he waited a moment, then he reached into his back pocket and took out a small harmonica, tapped it several times against his palm, put it to his lips and blew a C.

"The first thing we're going to do," he said, "is to sing our National Anthem."

His voice reached out in a warm, full tone. "O say, can you see . . ."

At first, his men followed him weakly, faltering. But slowly the song built strong and high, and a hundred yards away on the back road a 4 × 4 Recon truck stopped. Two Marines got out and, according to regulations, stood at salute, their faces showing confusion at hearing "The Star-Spangled Banner" coming from a distant eucalyptus grove at three o'clock in the afternoon.

7

"That day in China . . ."

Most of the thirty years of his military life as enlisted man and officer, Carlson had felt deeply the lack of communication between the commander and the men he led. He had evolved theories about it over the years, some good and some bad. But now, as he faced his men, he was certain that he had the answer.

He touched the microphone in front of him and began to talk through it.

"Boys, this mike and loudspeaker are the first things we asked the quartermaster for. We wanted it because we can use it to talk to each other directly. Me to you; you to me and to the rest. This mike is open for gripes and criticism." He smiled broadly. "You can say what you think about anyone — officers and yours truly included. And about the way we're doing things. Just so that you're honest about it — and that it's something which'll benefit the rest of us."

He looked down at his men, hoping that they would believe him, for he knew that at first they would doubt the possibility of freedom of speech in a military organization.

In the silence, raindrops pattered softly from the eucalyptus leaves. The men waited, listening on the tips of their minds, a little uneasy. The mike, the "Star-Spangled Banner," a C.O. with a harmonica, free speech . . . It was like walking into the wrong church.

Then he began to talk again, with none of the tricks of oratory, the change of pace or volume or pause for effect. Frequently, he gestured broadly with his two hands in parallel movement, an unconscious imitation of his preacher-father. He did not try to make his words simpler than was his custom, nor more impressive. He genuinely believed that although some of the men might not understand every word he used — his vocabulary was rather extensive and occasionally highfalutin — they would get the gist and the spirit.

But his words had a glow to them, and as he talked his lean face was illumined like a man with a dream in his head.

He told them that they all lived in a democratic country, and it was a contradiction for such a country to have an armed force that was dictatorial and undemocratic. Their battalion, the Raiders, would have none of it. The Prussian system of discipline which still influenced much American military thinking would not be tolerated. Yet, of course, there would be discipline. "But based on knowledge and reason — and not blind obedience. It's yours to reason why. In a democracy, men must be thinking human beings, not puppets."

Further, there would be no caste differences in the Raiders. Officers would be leaders by ability and knowledge and character — and not because they held the President's commission. They would give no unnecessary orders; they would not order a man to do what they themselves were not prepared to do with him; they would have no special mess or barracks or club. And there would be no unnecessary saluting.

"We'll live as you live; work as you work; eat as you eat; fight as you fight. We give up all our privileges cheerfully and willingly."

The ranks stirred like spring wheat in a breeze. They had just heard what seemed to them to be a violation of everything they had been told was the tradition of a thousand years of military life. Those words challenged the threats of their instructors at boot camp; the benevolent-despotic talks of old-time senior officers; the inbred legend and protocol of the Academies.

The enlisted men and junior officers fresh from Quantico and civilian life listened with singing hearts, their skepticism, for the moment, pinched away by a stirring hope that maybe what the Old Man was saying would actually be put into practice. A few old-timers thought the words sounded good but didn't believe Carlson stood a chance in hell. How could he change human nature? The Old Man had gotten some fancy ideas from somewhere. Well, he'd get over them.

A low-flying flight of planes from North Island came over, and as Carlson waited he wondered what the men were thinking. Were they believing him? If he could only, in an instant, project them all into the future to prove that he meant what he was saying.

The flight of planes arched into the horizon.

Carlson went on to describe what their training would be like. They would be hardened to march fifty miles a day without food or rest. They would learn to go without water and to get along with a few handfuls of rice. "A time will come when our only food will be what we take off the bodies of dead Japs." Day and night jungle fighting would be learned: patrolling, swimming, rubber boats, knife work, judo, marksmanship — "with every kind of weapon from every conceivable position." Each man and officer would be required to carry his rifle with him at all times while in camp. To sleep with it, eat with it; to take it apart until he could put it together blindfolded.

"Without this kind of hardening and training," he said, "we might lose five men instead of one."

What did he mean by constant training? Well, he meant that there would be mighty few hours a week when they wouldn't be on the go. Little liberty and less leave would be their lot. Even emergency leave. And what did he mean by hardening? Well, in addition to their hiking and physical conditioning, all men and officers would sleep on the tent decks; no sacks except in the sick bay; chow would be the kind they'd have in the field. Of course, an occasional traveling PX would come by; an occasional movie maybe; but most of their recreation would be sports, baseball, basketball, volleyball. Recreation that strengthened them.

And again he warned them as he had warned them before in their interviews. "The Jap is a wily and rugged enemy, experienced in hardships. And so I can promise you nothing but the toughest life while we're in the States and the toughest battles when we're overseas."

Now, his talk took a different turn. He seemed to the men suddenly to become less stern, almost less driven. His tall, gaunt body leaned forward. He admitted that what he was asking of them and of himself would not be easy. It required even more than physical stamina or the discipline which comes from mutual respect and understanding. The Raider Battalion needed a spirit, something that would make bearable all the hardships to come.

He told them a story, a part of his life. . . .

"In 1937," he began, "when I was in China with the Fourth Marines, Admiral Harry Yarnell, at that time Commander-in-Chief of our Asiatic Fleet, assigned me to Naval Intelligence and ordered me to make a study of how the Chinese armies were fighting the Japs. I watched the Chinese around Shanghai for awhile, and then I heard of another Chinese force up in the North. It was called the Eighth Route Army. I heard they were very successful and that they had worked out a new kind of battle strategy and guerrilla warfare. I was also told that they had a different kind of army organization. And so I went up to join them. From then on I had a lot of experiences with the Eighth Route Army, and I'll probably be telling you quite a few of them as time goes on. But there's one I want to tell you now. . . ."

. . . It was morning and he was with the Eighth Route Army — about 600 of them on a forced march in Shansi Province, with orders to head off a Japanese column. The terrain was the roughest he had ever seen: deep gorges, thick forests, swift and bitterly cold rivers. The days were blasphemous with cold. And through it they had marched steadily for twenty-four hours without rest, and had covered fifty-eight miles. Most of the way the Chinese soldiers had been singing but now the column was silent. Only the sounds of panting men and the ceaseless shuffle of sandals or bare feet against the rock and the earth could be heard. Every face in the morning light was marked with the stigmata of exhaustion — bulging eyes, slack jaws, cracked and dried lips.

To Carlson who marched with them, the fifty miles had been an accumulation of miracles. Not merely had men endured an enormous trial of strength but of the 600 who had started, *not one* had fallen by the way and dropped out. In his own country on maneuvers, he had led men on marches of similar duration and intensity; in Nicaragua he had marched against the "bandits" and the going had been almost as strenuous. But there, as always, some few men had given up, had deserted or had surrendered to fatigue.

He looked at the Chinese soldier next to him, watched his face, listened to him pant, and wondered what it was that made him endure.

Far ahead in the column they were beginning to sing again. The song moved down slowly like ripples on a mill pond.

The soldier next to Carlson noticed that he was being studied — and smiled.

"A long march," he said in his own language.

Carlson nodded. "Tired?" he asked, his breath hurting.

"*Tsan T'san*," the soldier said slowly between gasps. "If — a man — has — only legs — he gets tired." . . .

"That day in China," Carlson said, "I saw in practice the secret of the Chinese Eighth Route Army. Two words — 'ethical indoctrination.' Those are big words, boys, but let me tell you simply what they mean. The reason those 600 men were able to endure such hardship was because they knew *why* it was necessary for them to complete that march. But more than that, they knew *why* that march was important to the whole series of battles they were fighting; and they knew *why* these battles were important to the whole war against the Japs. And the war against the Japs was one they understood and believed in. In short, they understood why the efforts of every single one of them was necessary for the victory of the whole Chinese people. That's ethical indoctrination. That's what you've got to have besides 'legs.' That's why 600 average Chinese men did what 600 average Americans might not have been able to do — march fifty-eight miles in twenty-four hours without rest and without one man falling by the wayside."

He explained carefully how out of ethical indoctrination men grow to have confidence in themselves and in their officers; how when every man knows his efforts count, whether officer or cook, general or quartermaster coolie, no one thinks of himself or his job as being more or less important than anyone else or anyone else's job; and each man has respect and confidence in himself and in the others. Out of this mutual respect and confidence, comes the ability of men to work together wholeheartedly, without fear or favor or envy or contempt.

He trembled a little inside him as he spoke, for if ethical indoctrination was the key of the Raiders, it was also the star by which he finally had come to steer his own life. This battalion, these thousand men, was the test of himself.

"The Chinese have two words for 'working together,'" he said. "*Gung,* meaning 'work'; *Ho,* meaning 'harmony.' *Gung Ho!* 'Work Together!' That is the end result of ethical indoctrination."

He went on to explain that Gung Ho was important to all of them, because they were Americans — for it gave them the chance to practice the democracy they believed, where no man should have privileges over another man and where discipline comes from knowledge. It was important because they were fighting men, and it would give them confidence in themselves and in their comrades — a confidence that creates initiative and daring in battle. And that out of this would come greater damage to the enemy at lower cost in lives to themselves.

"We will strive," he said, "for ethical indoctrination, and so I propose that Gung Ho be the spirit and the slogan of our Raider Battalion."

He paused and moved closer to the microphone. "It's a good slogan, boys. Let's hear you say it." He raised his voice and shouted, "Gung Ho!"

There was a split-second silence in the ranks. Then the reply came, not in unison, for some men spoke or self-consciously whispered the phrase and some shouted it in a burst of elated appreciation. But the words came, and the grove of eucalyptus trees in the middle of San Diego County heard a thousand voices say a strange and foreign phrase that, in the necessary coincidence of human history, was as American as it was Chinese.

8

"It was never finished"

Professor John Dollard, in his study of Carlson and his Raiders, wrote: "Ethical indoctrination is concerned with achieving consent to the mechanisms of control, volition for the common ends, and arousing guilt concerning differential privilege."

That was the sociologist's way of summing it up.

Dr. Kurt Lewin of the Massachusetts Institute of Technology, director of its research in group dynamics, said of Carlson's Raiders that "they received their status by a high level of aspiration. 'We' thinking in battle reduces the sense of personal danger . . . and when the level of free expression goes up, leaders can demand more from their followers. The men were given moral stamina . . ."

And that is the psychologist's way of analyzing the great experiment.

Carlson says: "In a military sense ethical indoctrination requires knowing the issues of the battle and the war, and believing in the justice of the cause for which a man fights. In order to be fully effective, however, ethical indoctrination requires a system of life in which men can believe — a system where people, regardless of color, creed, or national origin, are equal before the law, and where none are exploited for the profit of others: in short, where there are no unearned privileges.

"In part, we were able to create ethical indoctrination in the Raiders because the real promise of our country and our cause was worth fighting for. Without this real promise no amount of indoctrination could long sustain the belief of men.

"In the Raiders it was a long and hard job and we had to work at it every minute; it was never finished."

9

By touch and feel

The training was as hard as he had warned them it would be.

In the thicketed high hills of the Camp Elliot boondocks, a sergeant from Atlanta, Georgia, Clyde Thomason, found a minute at chow time to write a quick note to his friends in the Atlanta office of the Fire Companies Adjustment Bureau. Claim adjusting was Clyde's first job — found in 1939 when he was twenty-five, after he had graduated from high school, jalopied all over the forty-eight states and had one five-year hitch in the Marines. The boys and the office manager of the Atlanta office promised Clyde they'd keep his desk for him, and he in turn promised to write regularly and send them souvenirs from Tokyo.

"We're bivouacked out in the mountains away from anywhere," he wrote late in February 1942. "There's been nothing but manual labor — marching five, eight, ten miles and calisthenics to get into shape. Twice a week . . . a thirty-five-mile hike, and once a week a seventy-mile overnight hike. We never ride. Every man will be a walking arsenal, including . . . a knife which we are learning to throw. Hope I haven't bitten off more than I can chew. We all have crew haircuts. O, my beautiful waves!" [7]

A month later he wrote more about hikes and firing practice, close combat fighting, demolition work and rubber boat handling. "We're about to get rounded out into a pretty good outfit. And it wasn't over any smooth, straight highway . . ."

Clyde Thomason and the other nine hundred and ninety-nine Raider men and officers learned the science of killing and the art of saving their own lives. Nothing was omitted. Patrolling, scouting, compass work, communications, food and water discipline, judo,

[7] *Eastern Underwriter,* Sept. 25, 1942.

camouflage, stalking, fire-team tactics, first aid, swimming, handling of rubber boats. They worked at day and at night and in the times of the month when the nights were darkest. They made practice landings on San Clemente Island off Southern California and later on Barber's Point off Oahu. They learned to fight the surf, the same men each time in the same boats so that they could learn to work it together and what to give and what to expect from each other.

"Training and Gung Ho is everything," they heard their Old Man say over and over again.

Of the two, the training was easier to get, for Americans have a native desire for physical competence.

But no one became Gung Ho in a day or a week or in months. Neither the Chinese, nor the men and officers of the Raiders. It had taken Carlson himself three wars and thirty years.

The American is a man who's willing to give an ideal an even chance. At first, everybody was enthusiastic and tried hard. Self-consciously, men and officers tried to forget caste and rank, and sought the things which would create respect for each other. Men, among their comrades, found ways of showing their willingness to work together in the thousand ways of camp life. They puttered around each other's rifles and packs, offering help and suggestions, volunteering to take on burdens and duties, and striving strenuously each to be more brotherly than his neighbor.

But old habits of thought and thoughtlessness are as tough as crab grass. Slowly, almost without willing it, men began to take advantage, to see how much they could get away with; officers began to use their rank as a decisive argument; old prejudices — the smoldering fires of American life — blurted flame-like out into the open. Many Americans can live a lifetime without being tested as Americans. This was a test — and there was confusion.

Carlson saw what was happening, and he was sorely beset. He talked with his men and officers, exploring their ideas and his own. He lay awake nights, trying to find clarity in the puzzle of human behavior. He realized that after the first enthusiasm had died away the Raiders would come to know that to live Gung Ho would mean a self-discipline and self-abnegation which they had neither been conditioned nor educated for. And they would fall back on self-interest. Self-interest was a primary human urge. But wasn't self-interest better served through co-operative effort than by direct individual action? Could he make his men see that? He began to re-examine his own convictions about men. Did he believe in their basic good sense and intelligence? Yes. Did he believe in their willingness to use these for the advancement of their combined welfare? Yes. This is what he believed about human beings. But what stopped them from seeing their self-interest? What were the elements which helped them see it?

He pondered this question, going back into his own life, and there seemed to him to be but one answer: leadership and information.

First, he examined "leadership." He had a military task in hand. He was a military leader; how must he act?

He knew from experience that a leader has the respect of his men when he shares their privations and dangers. In his opinion a leader's success with his men is in inverse ratio to the degree to which he uses his authority to increase his own comfort, convenience and security.

The leader, in the interval between battles, or as he now stood, before the first battle, must create the spirit of co-operation by his own co-operative attitude. He must discipline himself to abide by the rules he lays down for his command. He must grapple endlessly with the problems of the relation between individual initiative and the essential control from above. And as for informing his men — he must never cease explaining, teaching, preaching, practicing.

Carlson knew it was always slow and tragic, the practice of common sense. But he also knew if a man doesn't believe it can be done, he might as well die right now in a dark corner of a dark closet.

Of course, from the very beginning, he policed his own quarters, slept on the tent floor, waited in line for chow taking his turn when it came. He lived out in the boondocks with his men, hiked with them, with full pack and weapons, made his own fire, cooked his own chow. If they worked seven days a week, as they did, so did he.

With his men he was considerate and patient. He treated them as equals, on duty and off. His time was open to them, their complaints and suggestions. He encouraged them to come into his office and talk.

With every order he gave, he asked himself: Was it necessary? Was it just? Would he do it himself? Or was it like so many orders he had known in the past, humiliating to the man who gave them and the men who had to obey? He insisted to his officers that they give few orders, for he knew that men who received too many orders were inclined to wait for more when they met perplexing problems in the field. The service tradition of demanding uniformity in all things was a curse that not only impaired initiative but helped the enemy predetermine our habits and probable reactions.

He was strict with himself.

One day his son, Evans, Jr., a Lieutenant, presented himself in the office as a volunteer.

He stared up at this boy who looked like him. They had had very little of a life together. Carlson was proud of his son's Marine record. He would have wanted to be close to him in the warm comradeship of work and battle. But he pushed the thought away and refused to accept him into the Raiders.

He couldn't take the chance of being accused of favoritism. It would be better for the battalion not to have his son a member of it.

When his officers heard about this, they tried to persuade him to change his mind.

He explained why he did it.

"But," they argued, "we don't think you're capable of favoritism."

"I don't want to give anyone the opportunity of thinking so," he replied.

The debate lasted a long time, on and off for several months, even up to the time the battalion had shipped out to Hawaii. During that time, Evans, Jr., had volunteered four times — and was four times turned down. Finally, on the eve of the Guadalcanal campaign, Carlson's officers won — and he accepted his son.

"Expect no favors," he said when Evans, Jr., for the fifth time,

presented himself. "If anything, I'll be tougher on you than on anyone else. I won't mean to be, but that's what I'm sure will happen."

"That's all right with me, sir," Evans, Jr. replied happily. To be
with his father was a boon he'd accept under any condition.

If he was strict with himself, he was strict with others.

One of the Raiders came into his office to ask for emergency leave.
His mother was very sick.

"I'm going to leave it up to you," Carlson said. "I know how
much it means for you to be with her. My own mother died not so
long ago. But your mother is in Georgia. You will be away fourteen
days. During that time you will miss a great deal of training. You
may miss something that might save your life some day or your
comrades' lives. Think about it. Come back in a couple of hours
and tell me what your decision is. If you decide to go — you have my
permission. If you decide not to go, I know it will be a great sacrifice for you. But ask yourself — is our cause worth making a
sacrifice for?"

When the boy left the office, Carlson wondered whether he'd
done the right thing. Had he been too harsh? Was he expecting too
much from human beings? Where does a man draw the line on
sacrifice?

And while the boy thought it through, he, too, thought it through.
The war, which he believed in, demanded the sacrifice of life. There
can't be any lines drawn anywhere. When a man believes in something, he's got to live it one hundred per cent, twenty-four hours a
day. Though he felt the boy's sadness, he knew that what he had
asked him to do was right.

That evening the boy returned and said that he had decided not
to go home and would telephone instead. "And would the Major
speak to my mother," he asked, "and explain to her why?"

But Gung Ho didn't come in a day.

"We've got to seek every means to inform our men and ourselves
as to why we are fighting," Carlson told his officers.

And so they had weekly Friday night open forums which began

with a song, the "Marine Corps Hymn" and the slogans, "Ahoy, Raiders! Hi, Raiders! Gung Ho!", and ended with the National Anthem. And in between there would be a harmonica piece by Carlson, or the whole battalion singing "Carlson's Raiders." But the important part of the meeting would be a talk by Jimmy Roosevelt about the war and the world they lived in.

The tall, lanky son of the President, Gung Ho in his own right, conscientiously put together the little pieces of world history which made the mosaic of our times.

"This is why we are fighting," he would say. "In 1931, the Japs moved into Manchuria . . ."

He told them the sad and essential story with maps and figures and experiences: Czechoslovakia, Munich, Chamberlain, the non-aggression pact, China, our neutrality, our mistakes, Ethiopia, Spain, the one world, the one war, the one indivisible peace. . . . He explained what democracy meant, and Fascism, militarism and imperialism. . . . And they listened, some of them hearing new words and thoughts and getting new meanings.

It was slow going. The question and discussion periods lay empty and fallow week after week. But after a while questions would come: Can we trust Russia? Why did we sell oil and scrap to the Japs if we knew they were going to attack us? Is it true that Fascism is only against the Jews?

There were other Friday nights when Carlson would do the talking. He talked Gung Ho. "You just can't drift and get along with people. You've got to make a conscious effort."

He'd tell them about China and the Japanese way of fighting. And he'd explain that this wasn't a race war or a war of color against color. "The worst thing that can be said of a man," he said, "is that he hates another man because of his color or religious creed or the place of birth of his father."

"Major," some one yelled during one question period. "When you say we should have no prejudices, does that apply to the dog-faces, seabees and swobbies?"

The battalion roared with laughter, but Carlson answered with great seriousness. "Soldiers and sailors are Americans, too! It's all right to have jokes about them but you'll be damned glad to have 'em around when you get into battle."

He preached Gung Ho until the phrase became part of their living. Men loading a truck would yell to a Raider passing by, "Hey, Mac. How about a little Gung Ho on the box?"

He had his times of great elation, in which he could tell the idea was catching hold, like once when he overheard a Raider say that his ambition was to be a Gung Ho citizen even after the war. But his hours of faltering and despair were even more frequent. Yet, stubbornly, he believed that Gung Ho would work. The final test of it, of course, would have to come in battle when with every consideration but life and death dissolved out of his men, their natural urge to co-operate would find a reservoir of specific experiences to draw upon. These talks at camp, these examples, these ceaseless reiterations of principles would be, with their training in arms, a pattern transfer on their hearts and minds. Battle would be the hot iron. The pattern was bound to come through.

In battle, his men would know Gung Ho, and how to fight by touch and feel, if by no other way.

10

"... the softness of Americans ..."

In April, Clyde Thomason told the boys in the Atlanta office that he expected to be on his way soon.

> Just to give you an idea of how complete our equipment is, we have belly bands (something like corsets to prevent intestinal disorders), wrist watches, flashlights, polaroid sunglasses and theatrical make-up for night work. . . . It won't be long now. Had a farewell speech by Admiral Brown. Also by General Vogel (Marine). Sunday, a week ago, there was

a speech by Secretary Knox speaking for the President. And previously, Eleanor herself had talked to us. By the way, I like her a lot. . . . For such a small outfit we have been getting quite a lot of attention. I'm really thrilled I've gotten into this outfit. . . .

The transport U.S.S. *J. Franklin Bell* moved out of San Diego to take her place in a convoy for Pearl Harbor. May is a good month to cross the Pacific and the Raiders aboard, after four months of training, enjoyed doing nothing for a change.

In his cabin, Carlson, now a newly promoted Lieutenant Colonel,[8] was writing Battalion General Order 5-42. He did not know what his battalion would be asked to do after it reached Pearl. He was sure only that it would be used, and that the using would be hard and bloody. In preparing his Battalion General Order, he was seeking for something that would sum up their months of training and strengthen the spirit of his men for the task that lay ahead.

Several days after leaving San Diego, he finished writing it, and ordered it to be read on board at formation by each company commander to his men, and then to be posted on company bulletin boards once a camp site had been established.

The solemnity of the time in which it was read was scored by the fact that it was so pitifully early in the war and that the Raiders would be among the first, if not the first, to move offensively against the conquering enemy.

"Battalion General Order, Number 5-42, The Task that Lies Ahead," the Company Commanders read. "This battalion is now headed for the theatre of operations in the Pacific. . . . We become the first of our land forces of our nation to carry the war to the enemy."

The hollow drums of the blowers sounded like distant guns.

"During the course of our training there are a few points on which I have placed unusual emphasis. I want to emphasize them again for they have a vital bearing on the accomplishment of our mission. First: a deep-seated conviction on the part of each in-

---

[8] Notification of his promotion did not come to him until he reached Pearl Harbor.

dividual of the righteousness of the cause for which we fight.

"We are striving to build a society wherein the members will be able to enjoy the four freedoms. . . . If we do not produce the courage, the sinews . . . to defeat Japan, our people, too, will become slaves. . . ."

The ship's crew hung over the toprails listening.

"The enemy . . . is fully aware of the softness of Americans and on this factor alone he banks to give him 75 per cent of his victories. . . . We must constantly keep in condition . . . moderation of eating and drinking and the avoidance of venereal disease. . . .

"The Gung Ho spirit . . . Know the tools with which you work. . . . Study terrain at every opportunity. Learn how to use it to gain cover and to sneak up on your opponent. Keep contact with your fire group leader. . . . Reflect daily on these precepts. . . ."

The voices of the company commanders sounded clearly over the boom of the wind in the rigging. The ranks held against the slow roll of the decks.

"By our faith, our energy, our courage and our intelligence — perhaps most of all by our willingness to sacrifice comfort and convenience — we shall march on to victory. Even more important, we will set the pace and blaze the trail for those behind, inspiring them with confidence and showing them that we Americans have what it takes to win battles. It means work and sacrifice, Raiders, but let's go."

The ranks broke up on order and the words went silently away with each man. The ship raced ahead across a bright and unruffled sea.

They went into camp in the boondocks of Oahu and continued their training and their ethical indoctrination. The hikes were longer and harder, the rubber boat and swimming were against a tougher surf; and the Friday night forums were keener and livelier.

"I remember," Lieutenant Victor Maghakian said, "sitting out in the open when some of the men started yelling for Carlson to sing, and he blew his old harmonica to give himself the pitch and sang the Chinese Partisan song and 'Darling, I Am Growing Old,' and 'Abide with Me.' And then he'd do some talking. Lord, I loved to hear him talk. He spoke about religion a lot — not just going to church, but living it. He was the most religious man I ever knew."

"I remember," Lieutenant Tom Jolly said, "that we were so keen to train at Oahu that one day after we came out of submarine school someone passed some crazy scuttlebutt around to the effect that the Old Man was starting a catapult school to teach us how to catapult over the Jap lines. We took it so seriously fifty men went right over to the First Sergeant to volunteer. He hadn't heard about it, but he said he'd ask the Old Man."

Private Al Flores remembers: "We took pride in the fact that our training was tougher than anyone else's in the whole Marine Corps; we even took pride in getting less liberty than anyone else. The Old Man showed that he admired and respected us, and we saw that there wasn't anybody who loved our country more than he did — and that's why we loved him."

But Oahu on the Islands wasn't war.

Carlson's Raiders was the only land force personnel attached to Admiral Nimitz, and Nimitz could order it into action without going through the conventional chain of command. The Raiders were called "Nimitz's personal army."

"What's your idea of how to best use your Raiders?" Nimitz asked Carlson when he first saw him in the crowded corridor of Navy Headquarters.

"Hit-and-run Jap-held territories, sir. Using submarines for transporting the men."

"Toward what end?"

"To work out the Jap pattern of defense and to do as much material damage as we can. If we hit a half a dozen different spots at different times and places we can tell what places he'll defend at all cost, and what places he won't. We can tell where he'll get his reserves from. This'll give us his probable reaction in the future when we make our main drive."

"How many subs do you think you'd need?"

"Twenty."

Nimitz laughed. "I can let you have two to practice landings from."

"That's all right for a starter."

"You're lucky you can have a real sub to practice with instead of a mock-up," Nimitz said with a quiet bitterness. He looked out of a near-by window. There was a disciplined yet desperate frenzy in the view, naval and marine officers hurrying from one office to another, and beyond, in the repair base, the mosaic of sounds rising from the drydocks where half-ships being made whole lay like wounded men. Time was defeat at Pearl in those feverish days of 1942.

"Carlson," Nimitz said softly. "We're short of men, short of ships and short of planes. Your ideas are sound enough but find out what you can do with the subs, and I'll take up the question of hit-and-run raids with the staff."

Carlson and his men found out that they could disembark with their weapons from subs into rubber boats and undetected make a landing with the help of outboard motors whose noise was blanked out by the greater sounds of the breaking surf. A demonstration for Admirals Nimitz and Spruance and Marine Brigadier General Harry Pickett proved this, for the Raiders had made a landing on a moonless night and came within fifty feet of these officers before being heard or seen. It was obvious to them all that surprise could be achieved with such raids, and that they were worth trying.

But Carlson and his men were worried. In order to make a beach with rubber boats and then to leave it in any kind of order and with any timing, outboard motors were essential. But the A motors they were using were not doing the job, for their coils and generators were exposed and easily water-logged and made ineffectual. Another motor, the B, had these vital parts enclosed and Carlson pleaded with the quartermaster to buy them for the Raiders. But Headquarters in Washington replied that A had already been approved and purchased in quantities and nothing could be done. Carlson and Roosevelt tried every way they knew to change this, but the war caught up to them too quickly.

From Nimitz and the staff came ideas on where to use the

Raiders. Carlson was ordered to investigate the possibilities of hit-and-run raids on Wake, Tinian, Hokkaido, Tulagi and Attu. In each case something came up to change the plans. During this time, however, two companies of the Raiders were transported to Midway, where, during the battle from June 3 to June 6, they manned anti-aircraft batteries.

By the beginning of July, Nimitz's headquarters, trying to fit Carlson's plan into the general strategic scheme, decided on Makin Atoll in the Gilbert Islands.

"This time, Carlson," Nimitz said, "it sticks. We don't know much about what the Japs have there. Tarawa, near Makin, doesn't seem like much — yet. From reports Makin is their headquarters in the Gilberts. They've got a seaplane base and a great deal of supplies. As to how strong a force defends the place — we haven't much definite dope. You'll have to make your own estimate. We're allowing you two subs. That'll mean a force of about 200 men."

Until the time of the Raiders' departure from Hawaii only six officers knew the destination. Yet when the Raiders reached Makin, Gilbertese natives told Carlson that the Japs knew they were coming, and even knew within two days of the exact landing date. So much for Japanese espionage!

For Makin, plans were composed with endless care. A mock-up of the atoll was built at Barber's Point with roads, wharves, houses and stores just as they were placed on the aerial photographs of Makin, itself. Countless practice landings were made from the subs in the dark of the month of July until the Raiders knew by heart the terrain and its features, the position of every house and direction of every road. They could take the atoll in the night, blindfolded.

The only thing left was to move on to the real thing.

11

Clenched tightly in a Japanese fist

When the Raiders left Pearl Harbor for Makin, on August 9, 1942, maps and aerial photographs were distributed, and the men were told their destination. Every man recognized the tiny, thousand-yard-wide Italy-shaped atoll as the mock-up on which they had made so many practice landings on Oahu. Someone yelled: "Hell, I know this atoll ass-backwards from the king of spades." It pleased Carlson that their training had been so effective and, as a result, their confidence so complete.

En route, they studied the maps and photographs under magnifying glasses, and learned by heart the schedule of their raid. They were to disembark from the *Nautilus* and *Argonaut* at three o'clock the morning of August 17, assemble alongside the subs until the companies were organized, then move into Butaritari, the main island of Makin atoll. The landing had to be made by 5:30, a few minutes before daylight. Company A under Lieutenant Plumley would land at Beach Y, and Company B under Captain Coyte at Beach Z. The mission of the raid was to destroy enemy forces, installations, capture prisoners and documents. Withdrawal to the subs must be made no later than by 9 P.M. (2100) of the same day. If for some reason they had not reached the submarines by that time, it would be up to the discretion of the task force commander, Commander John Haines, whether to wait any longer or to make his way back to Pearl without them. And if everything went well, another island, Little Makin, would be raided the next morning.

From the very beginning, almost every one of his plans for Makin had gone awry.

On Sunday night, August 16, the *Nautilus* and the *Argonaut* lay off Makin. Commander Bill Brockman, a big muscular man for a submariner, came down from the conning tower of the *Nautilus* wiping his face of sweat and the sea mist.

"Colonel, I've got some bad news for you," he said. "Squalls above. Heavy swells and an onshore wind. It's going to be touch and go gettin' off the subs and gettin' onto the beach."

Carlson went topside to look for himself. The moonless dark of the night kept him blind for a moment and the fresh air relief went unnoticed. His first thought was the unreliable outboard motors. The best his men had been able to do was to construct makeshift coverings over their exposed parts. Would they stand up against the high running seas?

He stared into the darkness in Makin's direction. As he heard the waves bang against the sub he could understand why the Japs were so certain no one could possibly land on the seaside of the atoll. Aerial photographs had shown that all their defenses had been placed to face the quiet lagoon within. If everything else fails, he thought, at least he could still count on the element of surprise.

The time had come for disembarking, motors or no motors, high seas or no high seas. He bit on his unlit pipe and passed the word along. Up through the hatches camouflaged men and rubber boats and weapons came swiftly from long practice. Air hoses were run out on the deck to inflate the rubber craft. Weapons, ammunition, signal equipment were lashed in place.

The sub rose and fell and drifted toward the beach.

From the dark sea came voices calling from the boats the *Argonaut* had launched:

"My motor's out!"

"Mine too! I can't get headway."

"The sub's moving!"

"God-damned ocean!"

"Oh you friggin' motor!"

Black silences were broken by the voices and the despairing, ineffectual coughs of half-drowned motors.

His own boats from the *Nautilus* had not yet been launched and he knew with certainty that they would meet the same fate. His plan of landing would have to be changed.

Brockman came up to him. "The tide's movin' us in toward the reef, Colonel," he said. "We've got to start backing away before we pile up. That's what's happening to the *Argonaut*."

"We won't be able to assemble our boats alongside then," Carlson said quickly.

"Right."

"That means my company commanders'll lose control."

Brockman said nothing.

"If you have to get the sub moving — move," Carlson said. Everything now would have to be changed. Swiftly!

Carlson checked alternatives. But there were no alternatives. The landing, of course, would be made although he would have to abandon everything but his confidence in his men.

Yet, these men of his whom he trusted had to have every break. They must not be permitted to land in small groups easily outnumbered. They must not be left isolated, out of contact with each other, and alone against an enemy in defense and well co-ordinated.

Somehow they must be brought to the beach, any beach in an organized way.

The dying motors choked and were silent. He heard in the darkness his men cursing.

The hilly sea, now ally to the enemy, thrust the sub away from it, sucked it back, swirled around and over its deck. The rim of darkness beyond lay cavelike. Seconds had passed.

Quickly, he shouted an order, "Disembark and follow my boat to the beach!" That was all he could do now!

Men pushed boats past the deck onto the breasting sea. As a man held the stern rope, other men jumped in, took the other end and held the bouncing craft against the slowly moving sub until the rest of the crew boarded. The motor was started. It turned over a few times when a wave smashed into it and it died.

From the deck of the *Nautilus,* men whose faces were painted as dark as the night jumped into the bobbing boats uncertain whether they'd land on them or in the sea. Carlson was the last man to leave the sub. He had to leap across several feet of raging water. As he fell into the boat he smacked his right cheekbone near the eye against the butt of a rifle. During the ensuing battle, half his face was swollen as if with mumps.

Across the dark water, he and his men yelled the new plan to the *Argonaut's* men. "Follow us! Follow us!"

The yell was passed from boat to boat.

The noise of shouts and the beating of the boats against the sub made it seem certain that the Japs could hear them.

Finally, gathering as many boats as he could reach, Carlson led his men toward Butaritari, specifically in the direction of the ocean beach opposite Government Wharf which jutted out from the lagoon side of the atoll.

The column of boats moved slowly. The sea smashed against them roughly, twisting them, pushing them up on their ends, whirlpooling them around until all headway was lost. But the men had worked in surf like this before — and they had worked together. Paddling with all their strength, they knew from the instinct of long practice, where to throw their weight to keep the bow headed straight. They were helped by the tide moving in, and after about an hour of exhausting effort they heard, jubilantly, the surf thundering. The dawn bloomed slowly behind the atoll and the outlines of the tops of palms could be seen. Breakers fought to upturn the light craft but again the pattern of practice came through — and by 5:30 the landing was made.

On the beach, it was still dark. The panting men tried to find their outfits. Both companies were badly intermingled. Slowly, in the stumbling darkness, names and commands brought order. Fifteen of the eighteen boats had landed. Men previously designated carried their rubber boats to the underbrush fringing the beach and concealed them with sand and palm fronds. Others swiftly oiled their wet weapons.

So far, there was no sound from the enemy. The men heard only the shuffle of their own wet shoes over the beach, the surf booming, the breezes of dawn on the palm tops.

Carlson felt good. His men had made it, and surprise was still his; an unapproachable beach had been approached and landed on despite the failure of his motors. Suddenly he heard a ripping blast from a BAR. Carlson ran long-legged through the gray-streaked light toward the sound. A Raider saw him and thought how even in the dark the Old Man's face glowed insanely.

"Japs?" he called.

"No, sir," replied a despairing voice. "One of the boys accidentally discharged . . ."

"Japs heard it too, then!" Carlson said. But he forced calmness into his voice, called for Plumley, commander of Company A, and ordered him to move his company across the island. "Find the road on the lagoon side and send a messenger back when you find it. I want to know where we're located in relation to Government Wharf."

Plumley sent a patrol ahead, Sergeant Clyde Thomason in command. Squads led by Corporals Pisker, Debosik and Wittenberg followed.

A haze over the island slowly lifted.

In fifteen minutes, Plumley sent Le Francois back to Carlson's Command Post, which was in a little taro patch near the beach, about fifteen city blocks away.

"You hit the nail on the head, Colonel," Le Francois whispered. "Where you are now is right opposite Government Wharf. Plum has some men on it, and we've taken Government House without opposition. Haven't seen a Jap yet."

Orders and questions were spoken swiftly. Carlson wanted to keep the Japs as far away from the beach as possible. Plum was to advance South to see how far he could get. Company B, under Coyte, would remain in reserve and protect the left flank. Were the anti-tank rifles set up on the lagoon road to stop any Jap mechanized force?

In the Command Post, Roosevelt was talking via radio to the subs, keeping Task Force Commander Haines informed of the situation.

From across the island, shotguns and rifles suddenly blattered into the silence.

Over the walkie-talkie came news. A platoon of Plumley's men

surprised some Japs near a native hospital. Three truckloads of
Jap reinforcements had been forced off the road by the anti-tank
rifles.

Another message: "Two small Jap transports entering the
lagoon."

The firing continued on the lagoon side. Plum's men were really
at it.

Three Gilbertese natives, brawny and dark, and with dignity,
came stalking through the underbrush.

Carlson and Roosevelt welcomed them gravely. A few yards
away, armed Raiders remembering that Gung Ho meant treating
natives kindly, fingered M-1's and Tommy guns — just in case.
In broken trader English the natives welcomed the Americans.
Carlson shook hands with them.

"We knew you come," a native said. "Jap in trees three days.
Food in trees. On lagoon."

Carlson smiled.

"You fly here?" the native asked.

"How many Japs on the island?" Carlson asked.

"Two hundred — three hundred mebbe."

"Tanks?"

The natives didn't know what tanks were, and obviously there
were none.

"Where are Japs now?"

"Plenty Japs on On Cheong's Wharf and Ukiangong Point."

Carlson raised the subs on the radio and requested them to surface and fire their six-inchers across the island onto On Cheong's
Wharf and the causeway leading from Ukiangong Point.

A few minutes later, the whistle of shells arched overhead and
burst beyond. Though there could be no spotting from the shore, the
subs' gunners were extraordinarily accurate.

Roosevelt remained at the CP, and Carlson moved up to the lagoon road to observe how his men were doing. This was their first
combat. He had to see with his own eyes.

The firing was heavy when he reached Plumley's CP.

"I'm worried about those transports," Plum said.

They crawled to the edge of the lagoon.

"Those ships've got men," Plum said.

Two ships moved in slowly toward them: a transport of about 3500 tons and a gunboat of about 1000 tons. Men on the decks were visible.

Carlson called his radio man. "Can we reach the *Nautilus* from here?" he asked.

The radio man started calling. There was no answer.

"What's wrong?" Plum asked.

"Can't reach 'em from here, sir."

Carlson took a bearing on the ships, then ran back to the ocean beach.

The sun was higher now. The sweat wet his face and hands. His shoulders slithered against his wet shirt.

At the CP, he saw Roosevelt's bald head shining and moist in the sun. He was helping the wounded to a first aid station.

" 'Transport' Maghakian's shot!" someone yelled as Carlson came up. "He was waving his arms around directing his men and a Jap sniper caught him in the right arm."

"He ought to learn not to use his hands," someone else said and laughed.

"Where is he?" Roosevelt asked.

"He wrapped it up — and he's waving his left arm now."

Carlson was talking to the *Nautilus*. "Two ships in the lagoon," he said. "Bearings as follows . . ."

The crew of the sub heard about the two Jap ships almost as soon as the skipper.

Said the submarine gun captain: "Skipper, shall we man the guns?"

Said the skipper: "Man the guns."

Said the gun captain instantly and without moving an inch: "Sir, the guns are manned."

Said the skipper, grinning: "What the hell goes on here?" [9]

The Jap ships in the lagoon were out of sight but the gunners scored direct hits.

Over on the lagoon, the men fighting the Japs along the road and

[9] W. S. Le Francois in his report on Makin. *Saturday Evening Post*, Dec. 4, 1943, and Dec. 11, 1943.

on the wharves heard the shells and someone shouted what each of them had feared most from the start: "The Jap fleet is here!"

At the Command Post on the ocean side, the men saw two plumes of smoke from the direction of the lagoon rising over the palm tops.

"Direct hits," came over the walkie-talkie from Plumley. "The ships are on fire. Lots of Japs drowning."

Suddenly men from two of the missing boats who had landed in the darkness a mile north came running out from the fringing shrubs yelling "Ahoy, Raiders!" They reported to Carlson.

"Isn't Peatross with you?" he asked.

"No, sir."

"What happened to him? He had eleven men."

"The last we saw of Pete and his boat was just after he left the sub."

Le Francois was back in the fight and four Jap machine guns crossed their fire on him. He fell with five bullets in his right arm and shoulder. After awhile, they brought him to the dressing station on the beach where the corpsmen and doctors were working.

The dressing station was in a half-ruined warehouse with an arched roof. Jap snipers tried to pick off the wounded from the trees outside.

Le Francois lay on a bloody mat. In a daze, he remembered Clyde Thomason.

He remembered him running up and down the firing line seeing that the men in his squad were well placed. He could see, as on a red-green-sandy screen in front of him, a line of Japs creeping toward them through the trees and brush. Then, in recollection, came the hollowed, feverish cry of Thomason's, "Let 'em have it! Gung Ho! Raiders!"

Thomason looked funny, his make-up streaked with sweat, his fine face screwed up and his tongue stuck out in excitement like a boy's on the Fourth of July.

The creeping Japs died as they lay. From behind Le Francois's men there were Jap snipers working from cocoanut trees.

There was the baby-cry sound of a light sniper's rifle.

A Raider turned to Le Francois and said, "That one got Thomason."

Le Francois crawled over to the boy and felt his pulse. There was nothing. The pulse was silent. The heart was silent. The tongue still stuck out. The boys in Georgia would receive no souvenirs. But later his folks were sent Clyde's Congressional Medal of Honor.

By 0700 the pattern of the enemy defense was apparent. It was built around four machine guns, two grenade throwers, automatic rifles and flame throwers. A corps of snipers operated from the tops of coconut trees. They were cleverly camouflaged and their fire was extremely effective. By 1130, our line was able to move forward but the snipers continued to be a problem.[10]

To Carlson, the four hours between 0700 and 1130 were a series of movements and events which crossed and recrossed each other like an intricate maze, but with each line clearly established and meaningful.

During much of those four hours, he was trying to anticipate next steps. The Makin radio had not yet been knocked out. The Jap-held atolls of Mille and Jaluit, approximately two hundred and fifty miles away, had been undoubtedly informed of the raid. Enemy seaplanes were probably on the way now to bomb and strafe Makin and to bring reinforcements. Even if the Raiders could prevent them from landing in the lagoon, they could drop paratroopers. He calculated his strength and chances against fresh Jap troops if they numbered a hundred or numbered a thousand, if they landed in the south or north. Mentally he prepared positions of ambush, attack, defense and withdrawal.

Against any eventuality, he fought to be prepared, to anticipate, to have alternatives for alternatives.

As he worked on this level of his mind, his long legs took him all over the firing front. He checked with his company command-

[10] Carlson's battle report. All italicized quotations in this section are from the same document.

ers, with their platoon leaders, and even with the squad leaders wherever he could. He moved ceaselessly, getting reports, offering suggestions, giving orders.

"It's funny," a Raider said later. "It happened a lot of times when I was scared. I'd turn around and there was the Colonel, calm as hell, smoking that stinkin' pipe of his."

" 'Hya Raider,' " the Old Man would say. " 'Hya doin'?' "

"It happened a lot of times," the Raider said. "It helped you feel not so scared, his being right up front with you."

Carlson was everywhere, and his men came to expect him; few missed him. He had told them often enough that a commander must share what his men are enduring.

But beyond that, beyond giving his presence to the alleviation of the awesome loneliness of battle, he needed the presence of his men, to see what they were suffering, what they were doing or not doing. He needed to see for himself the terrain and the obstacles confronting his men. "You can't issue orders from a map," he had warned his junior officers.

A little before noon, one of the things he anticipated happened.

Planes!

Two Jap Navy reconnaissance planes came over and circled the fighting area for about fifteen minutes, dropped two bombs that did no damage — and departed.

"They'll be back," Carlson said to Lieutenant Lamb who only a few weeks before had been a Sergeant Major. "Tell your men to lay low and find cover when they do."

"They'll be back," thought Wygal and Brown and Pisker who fingered a little red rag he always carried with him because his mama from the old country told him that a piece of red on his uniform would keep away blood.

The wounded too knew that the planes would be back as the Gilbertese natives, men and boys, carried them from where they lay to the first aid station on the beach.

For a moment, a throttling terror choked Raider hearts. With the planes the full impact of their isolation hit them. They were on an island, a tiny island 1000 yards wide and 10 miles long, in the middle of the Jap empire. Only two slim subs, easily vulnerable from air and sea attack, were their life line home — eight days away — while Jap help was only an hour's flying time distant. From Makin there was no place to go, no terrain into which they could disappear, retreat, withdraw, get new weapons and forces.

Shrill, treble notes of a Japanese bugle sounded. A line of about a hundred green-uniformed men yelling "Banzai! Death to Roosevelt's Bastards!" charged en masse down the center of the island. They ran ahead passionately, fanatically, like men loving death, with fixed bayonets and flame throwers at the ready.

Oddly, the Jap attempt to terrorize dissolved the terror the Raiders had just felt, and they waited patiently almost until the enemy was on them.

"Roosevelt's Bastards!" the Japs yelled.

"Gung Ho!" came a reply, and the Raiders fired and fought carefully, thoughtfully, almost scientifically, like men hating death.

At 1:30 twelve planes came over, Zeros and seaplanes.

Carlson had already ordered his anti-tank rifles to be moved as close to the lagoon as possible. If the seaplanes were to land, he wanted to knock them out.

For seventy-five minutes, the planes bombed and strafed, and the Raiders lay motionless in their positions under palms and dead leaves — and none were touched.

One Kawanishi four-motored and one light seaplane landed in the lagoon and discharged about forty reinforcements. From the fringing land, Raider rifles and machine guns set the light plane on fire and damaged the huge Kawanishi lumbering across the lagoon. Tracers, anti-tank .55 caliber bullets, light machine gun .30's fought to find her. She circled three times to take off. Finally, the javelin of bullets speared her, and she dove her head into the water and disappeared. The other planes, now emptied of bombs, headed toward Jaluit and the Marshalls.

"Come on back," the Raiders yelled.

They were defiant now.

A cry of "Gung Ho!" came out of the bushes. A Raider, trembling with excitement, ran across the beach toward the CP. "Where's the Colonel? Where's the Old Man?" he yelled.

Carlson strode up to him.

"I was with Lieutenant Peatross," the boy said, his lips shivering and his face streaked with sweat.

"Pete landed!"

Men came running up to hear better.

"Yes, sir!" the boy said proudly.

"Where is he?" Carlson demanded.

The boy pointed south. "About a mile or so. The current took us. We been ashore since seven o'clock, cutting up Japs no end. We knocked over a small radio station near the trading post. It's on the map. We lost three men." He stopped. "Three good men!" His voice fluted to a shout. "Three God-damned good men! We killed over twenty though, burned the houses, burned a Chevvie truck. We heard you firing up here but we couldn't get through. The Japs is between us." He paused to catch his breath. "I got through. Pete told me to get through. I'm here, ain't I?"

"Good old Pete," a man said.

"Thanks, son," Carlson said. "Get over under that palm and take a rest. You've done a great job."

Peatross had obviously used magnificent initiative; not going back to the sub, not waiting to get a messenger through for orders, but relying on himself. Carlson knew that Peatross and his men, by the accident of landing behind the enemy lines and attacking, had made his own job easier.

Carlson spoke to Roosevelt. "More planes are going to bring back more reinforcements next time."

"If we could keep knocking off those seaplanes," Roosevelt said hopefully.

Carlson glanced at his watch; then took a cigarette from a small metal box — a Japanese surgical kit he had found earlier. He rolled the cigarette thoughtfully.

"Three o'clock," he said.

Roosevelt, out of habit, checked his own watch.

They had been on Makin eight-and-a-half hours.

.

"We've got another two hours before it's time to get back to the subs," Carlson said, glancing out to sea. He was worried by the waves that pounded roughly against the coral and sand beach. He hoped that by sundown they would not be so high.

From the Jap trading post across the island, came a sound checkerboard of rifles and machine guns and grenades.

He stared into the ocean. No amount of planning and foresight could reduce the size of one wave. His eyes moved into the sky. "The planes'll be back soon." Then with sudden decision, he said, "Jimmy, let's go up front and take a look."

They found that the center of the Raider line was in an area thick with foliage providing excellent cover for Jap snipers. It wasn't a healthy situation for the Raiders.

Carlson bit into his pipe and looked around. Near him lay a man from Company B sighting an M–1 at a tree beyond.

"Hya Raider," Carlson said in a whisper. "Hya doin'?"

"Hya Colonel," the boy said without taking his eyes off the sights.

Bullets from Jap snipers spattered in the grass.

"Get the hell outta here, Colonel," the boy said. "Ya gotta get us off this aye-toll."

He and Roosevelt moved along the flank toward the Company Command Post in the center. They stumbled on a dead Jap. They looked for a moment at the face angry in death.

"I hope the boys remember what I told them about not disfiguring the Japs," Carlson said.

When they reached the Command Post, it was even more apparent that the Raiders were not advantageously located in the heavy brush. Their field of fire was circumscribed by the thick growth.

Roosevelt suggested that the men ought to be pulled out of the area — to a position where the field of fire would be greater.

Carlson nodded; then calling the Company Commanders, he ordered them to pull the men on the right flank back to clear ground. "Leave the left flank where it is," he said. "When the Japs find we've moved out of the area, they'll move in. Then the boys on the left can pick 'em off as they advance."

"It is just barely possible," he told Roosevelt, "that when the planes come back, they might bomb the area we just evacuated thinking we're still there."

Roosevelt grinned.

"And it's just barely possible that at that time the area might be filled with Japs moving in."

Roosevelt smiled broadly. "It's just barely possible."

At 4:30 more Jap planes flew over and, while the Raiders looked on triumphantly, the planes bombed the recently evacuated area for half an hour, killing many of their own troops.

"It's not only possible, Jimmy," Carlson said exultantly as they watched the bombing. "It turned out to be probable."

At five o'clock Roosevelt said, "Time to start our men back to the beach if they're to make the subs on time."

Carlson nodded. "We haven't done everything we set out to do."

Roosevelt was silent.

"The question is," Carlson said quietly, "whether we withdraw now — or later." He started to walk toward the firing front, putting his pipe away, lighting a cigarette. "Let me think it through a minute, Jimmy," he said. "I want to see what it's like up there."

A time comes in every battle when a commander senses that his next decision is make or break, that the climacteric has been reached when the battle with its infinite potentialities passes from one life to another.

Military academicians have drawn up long lists of factors and values which must be considered in an "estimate of the situation" — time, terrain, disposition of enemy forces and friendly forces, and so on. Despite this, to arrive at an "estimate" is no more a scientific process than the process of mind which made Debussy's "Reverie" or Keats's "Ode to a Grecian Urn." The poet uses hard, definable words, the musician, calculable and finite mathematics of sound, but as the sum of their "facts" is not science but art, so it is with the sum of military facts. Intuition, a grasp of wholeness, perceptivity, imagination, or lack of these — in short, a commander's entire life and character, as with the artist — comes to a flood tide in the creative act of making an "estimate" and deriving a decision from it. For this reason, the commander's soul, the total of his experience, military and personal, is the most important fact of all.

It was in the light of his total experience that Carlson, walking warily across the island, marshaled the facts with which he could "estimate the situation."

FACT: His immediate mission had been to destroy enemy forces and vital installations, to capture prisoners and documents. It had not been accomplished, despite heavy damages inflicted on the enemy, two planes and two ships destroyed.

FACT: It was now five o'clock.

FACT: His orders were to get his men off the island and back to the subs by 7:30 that night — no later than nine.

FACT: His orders were to raid Little Makin next morning.

FACT: His casualties, though lighter than he had hoped for at best, were eleven dead and twenty wounded.

At the firing front, he talked with his Company Commanders. They gave him more facts — facts he could see and confirm with his own eyes. In terms of his character, this personal investigation was essential.

FACT: The enemy was still strong and fighting with great violence. His men were advancing very slowly.

FACT: The terrain was not conducive to rapid flanking or infiltration maneuvers.

And with these facts in mind, he asked himself, should he withdraw now — or later?

Carlson went from fact to deduction. The time factor, one hour and a half to two hours, was not enough to permit his forces to complete much more of their mission. He knew also that the toughest and most difficult military maneuver is withdrawal from combat quickly. Usually time was gained at the cost of lives or lives at the cost of time. If he took the chance to wait for the last minute to

withdraw in the hope that some "break" would bring completion
of his task, would not the risk be too great for the gain?

He decided that it would. He consulted with his battalion staff
and told them that in his opinion to wait would be a mistake and
withdrawal should begin immediately.

They agreed with him — and orders went out to the companies.

12

"The spiritual low point"

*The hour of 1930 (7:30 P.M.) had been selected for the retirement
because darkness would have set in and the tide would be high, en-
abling boats to get over the reef. The surf didn't look tough, not
nearly as tough as other surfs we had worked in, though rollers
followed each other rapidly. No one was apprehensive of getting
through. However, I had failed to take into account the speed of
the waves and the rapid succession in which they followed each
other. The following hour provided a struggle so intense and so
futile that it will forever remain a ghastly nightmare to those who
participated.*

The withdrawal from combat had been orderly, the boat crews
had been sent back to the beach to prepare their craft and check
the motors, the stretcher wounded were given a final once-over by
the doctors.

Carlson and Roosevelt said good-by to the natives who had
helped them. Joe Miller, the chief of native police, and William, his
brother, promised to find and bury the Raiders who had been
killed. Carlson gave them and their men some shotguns and ammunition. The Gilbertese were sad to see the Marines leave. They

had hoped they had come there to stay, to free them from the Japanese slavemasters.

By seven o'clock the bulk of the Raiders were on the beach. Only a covering force remained engaged, and they were placed so efficiently and were doing their job so well there were no Japanese charges or infiltrations. At 7:15 all the boats were lined up, and the ones at the extreme right and extreme left entered the water first. Others followed working toward the center. The center boat, which was Carlson's and the squad that covered the withdrawal, took off at 7:30 after all the other boats had left.

The darkness hid the beach from the enemy, and hid the boats from each other.

Out beyond the tumbling, ragged surf lay the *Nautilus* and the *Argonaut,* lay safety and home. Only a few thousand yards away.

With a bullet in his head, a Marine named Lenz was in the first boat to go. Dr. Stigler was with him. If they could reach the sub in time, Lenz might live.

Losing blood from five bullets in him, and half-conscious, Le Francois was in the second boat to go. A corpsman was with him. They'd have to get to the sub quickly.

Lieutenant Charlie Lamb, wounded twice, was in the next boat. The taste of blood in his mouth made him vomit.

The boats were filled with exhausted men, a battle behind them, their trembling nerves hungry for a moment's rest.

But the night hid the boats from each other, and the thundering waves hid the sounds of men from each other.

The experience in my own boat was typical. We walked the boat out to deep water and commenced paddling. The motor refused to work. The first three or four rollers were easy to pass. Then came the battle. Paddling rhythmically and furiously for all we were worth we would get over one roller only to be hit and thrown back by the next before we could gain momentum. The boat filled to the gunwales. We bailed. We got out and swam while pulling the boat — to no avail. We jettisoned the motor. The boat turned over.

Our weapons, compass, radio, ammunition were lost. We righted the boat and continued the battle.

"The God-damned ocean."

"The friggin', sonuvabitchin', ocean!"

The curses bounced against the waters like pebbles against the Chinese Wall. The men were answered with stinging salt water in their mouths. Gigantic waves crushed them, threw them back, squeezed the life out of them. If they could only shoot the ocean, judo it, throttle it, plant a sharp Raider knife in its back, kick it in the crotch, thumb its eyes out.

Or if only the motors worked!

The ocean roared back at them.

Three times, Lenz with the bullet in his head was turned over into the water. Three times, Dr. MacCracken dragged him onto the beach and pumped the water out, keeping the brain and the man alive.

Le Francois, wounded and weak, couldn't paddle with the others in his boat and was a burden to them. When the tide and the waves had thrown his boat back on the beach, he asked his friends to leave him there and to go on without him. They refused. They tried five times — and gave up.

Someone saw Little Smitty swimming toward the *Argonaut* — and that was the last they saw of Little Smitty.

Charlie Lamb lay with his head in the water and his feet on the beach. They thought he was drowned and they pulled him out to save his body. He looked up with water-soaked eyes, and was silent, without saying thanks.

All this time I thought ours was the only boat having this diffi-culty, for the others had left ahead of us.

Carlson yelled encouragement to his men, and blessed the months of training back in the States and the months on Oahu when he had fought to make himself and his men strong.

The waves swept him down. He heard a man cry, "God in heaven! God in heaven! What am I doing here?"

After nearly an hour of struggle, men swam up to our stern and reported that their boat had gone back because the men were exhausted. They intended to rest, then walk the boat up the beach and try another spot. Our men were equally exhausted and I directed our boat be returned to the beach. On my arrival, I found that over half the boats were there and that all men were in a state of extreme exhaustion. Most of their gear had been lost. The wounded of whom there were four stretcher cases and several ambulatory were particularly helpless.

"Take it easy now, fellows," they heard the Old Man's voice. "Rest. Go to sleep if you can. We'll get off the island. Don't worry."

There were 120 men on the beach and others perhaps had landed elsewhere. With such arms as could be scraped together, guards were posted.

One of the guards was Jessie Hawkins from South Gate, California. He had told everybody that South Gate was tough and that nobody from there ever died. He was shivering with cold at his post. His body and clothes were kept wet by a drizzle of rain. He wondered what the hell they were doing in South Gate that night. The seventeenth of August. He must remember the date to ask what the hell they were doing.

Then he saw or heard footsteps and he saw eight forms moving slowly toward him on both sides. He picked the forms in front of him and fired. The forms on his right and left fired back. Bullets entered Jessie's chest from two sides but he kept firing at the forms until three stopped and lay where they stopped, and five ran away.

They brought Jessie back to the beach.

Dr. MacCracken looked at the open, blood-flowing chest, while Carlson and some men went looking for the Jap patrol. They found the three that Jessie said he'd gotten. But they didn't find the five. And MacCracken concluded that Jessie didn't have much of a chance to live.

MacCracken bent over Jessie and took his hand. "Okay, Jessie?"

"Sure. I'll live. South Gate . . ."

"You'll be okay, Jessie," the doctor said.

"I'll be okay if I can get out to the sub," Jessie said, and fell asleep from the morphine.

Carlson asked if anyone saw Roosevelt and someone said they saw him about a quarter of a mile away.

The next thing to do was to make contact with the subs. Would Haines wait for them? How long would he wait?

He inquired for his communications men, and found that none of them were around. Either they had made the subs, or had been lost in the surf, or were somewhere else on the island. Someone brought him a radio but it was filled with brine and water. The only thing left was to use blinker lights but they, too, had been lost. Did anyone have a flashlight? After a few minutes, one was found. Now who knew the Morse code?

One of his men came up to him. His name was Craven.

"Colonel, I know Morse," he said, almost with reluctance.

"Are you a communications man?"

"No, sir. But I used to be."

Carlson gave him the light. "Tell them we couldn't make the surf. Ask them if they'll wait until morning."

Craven moved to a hillock of sand and flashed the message. All eyes searched the black borders of the sea. There was no answer. Craven repeated the message.

A pinpoint of light showed, blinked off and on. Craven read out the message.

"We will stay until you get off. Try to make it before Christmas."

"Hurray for the Navy," someone whispered. No one knew how many Japs were around — or where.

Carlson put his arm around Craven. "What's your name, son?"

Craven hesitated, and backed away a step. And then as if he

thought it over, he said, "Colonel, can I say something to you—
in confidence?"

"Certainly."

The boy moved closer and whispered. "I'm an Army deserter,
Colonel. That's where I learned code. I'm AWOL about two years. I
deserted to join the Marines. I always wanted to be a Marine. My
name is Craven. I don't want Headquarters to get my name. They'll
check up and I'll be in trouble."

Carlson smiled. "Okay, Craven. Let's talk this over when we get
back to Pearl. Maybe we can fix things up. Until then—many
thanks."

In the darkness, he strode off down the beach to look for
Roosevelt.

While he walked, he tried to gauge his situation. The appearance of the Jap patrol indicated that the enemy was still strong,
and probably at the moment was concentrating its forces for a
charge during the night or early morning. From all reports he had
about a hundred and twenty men on the beach with perhaps twenty
working rifles and no machine guns. By morning Jap planes from
the southern Marshalls, from Mille and Jaluit, would certainly continue their raids and attempts to bring fresh troops.

Was there anything that could be done immediately? They
could try the surf again until they were either all drowned or had
reached the ultimate of human endurance. No. It would be better
to keep what strength they had, and to wait until morning. Then,
they might be able to augment their supply of weapons and food by
capturing them from the Japs. In the morning, they could reach
the natives again and get outrigger canoes. By morning, the surf
might have subsided.

He passed a group of men huddled against the base of a palm.

"Hya, boys," he called softly.

"Hya, Colonel."

"Get some sleep. Try anyway."

"We're in a spot, ain't we, Colonel?"

In the darkness, they could see the white of his grin, remembered under other circumstances.

"Don't say I didn't warn you, boys. I told you it would be tough in the Raiders."

"Who's complaining?" someone said.

"It still ain't as tough as you told us it might be," someone else said. "I got a half a bar of chocolate left."

"Gung Ho, Colonel," a voice said.

"Gung Ho! And don't worry. We'll be at Pearl next week this time."

He walked away, feeling warmed by the talk. And the men, too exhausted to think much more, moved close to each other to get some body warmth against their wet clothes and the rain.

The beach was hard and cold and dark and he stumbled on a man sleeping. And then he saw another small group and heard a man say hysterically, "Let's surrender! Goddamit, what are we waiting for? Let's find the Japs and surrender!"

"Shut up!" another voice said, and he recognized it as "Transport" Maghakian's.

Carlson waited.

"The subs have left us and we're thousands of miles from help," the hysterical voice went on. "There're only about a hundred of us. And maybe five hundred Japs. And more tomorrow. Let's surrender!"

"Shut up!" Maghakian said.

"I won't shut up! I'm going to find the Colonel."

Then came the sound of men moving in the sand and a series of short slaps.

"I told you to shut up," Maghakian said. "I warned you."

The other man was sobbing softly. "You can't stop me from thinking," he said between sobs.

"Shut up," Maghakian said.

There was silence.

Another voice said, "What the hell! This's gonna be a long war. If you don't get it at Makin, you'll get it somewhere else. I'm not surrendering to any friggin' Jap."

"And don't worry," Maghakian said, "Carlson and Roosevelt

aren't either. Did I tell you what the Old Man told me before we left Pearl? He told me . . ."

Silently, Carlson moved away. Surrender? He was sure that everyone on the beach was thinking of *that* possibility. He, himself, had thought of it before this night, before they had even left Pearl. It was something you had to anticipate — and his decision had long been made. Courage to die had meaning only in relation to what men offered their lives for. If nothing could be gained, tactically or strategically or morally by an all-out, suicide last-ditch fight, he would surrender his men. But the estimate of the gain would have to wait until the facts were before him. Right now his hunch was that the enemy was still quite strong, but he did not yet know how strong his own men were.

After a while, he found Roosevelt and was much relieved.

They talked over their situation — and decided that there was nothing that could be done until daylight.

"Let's get some sleep then," Carlson said.

The rain and the night-cold swept the beach. From the sea, waves slammed angrily against the coral sand.

Carlson hollowed out a little hummock for himself and curled up and closed his eyes.

For a moment, he permitted himself to think of his home, his father, his sister, his brother and his son who was waiting with the rest of the battalion on Oahu. And then he retraced the steps of the day. Suppose he had not made the decision to withdraw and had waited? Would it have mattered? The sea would still have been too high. Suppose there had been no definite time set for withdrawal and it had been left to his discretion? That would have been better. Suppose they had had the enclosed B motors and not the Headquarters-approved A? Ah, that would have been much, much better.

He hoped that no men were drowned in the surf, but he knew, even as he hoped, that lives must have been lost.

This was no time for "ifs," he told himself. This was the time for rest, for gathering back the strength lost so as to confront the facts that would come with day.

For the moment, he had done all he could.

Elsewhere on the beach, his half-naked men huddled together trying to keep warm, trying to keep from their thoughts terror and loneliness. They dared not think that perhaps the subs would leave them. Or that the Japs still outnumbered them. Or were, at this moment of darkness, landing reinforcements.

The sea pounded, the night moved on slowly. The guards watched with their hearts in their eyes.

Rain and the fact that most of the men had even stripped themselves of their clothes in the surf, added to the general misery. This was the spiritual low point of the expedition.

13

Who followed my father . . . ?

Shortly after daylight, one group of men requested permission to make another try through the surf. After a terrible battle, they made it. Another group was organized and succeeded, but the struggle was too much to send the stretcher cases.

Carlson directed Roosevelt to return to the sub and take charge of the men aboard. Roosevelt's boat left the beach toward the subs that, now that day was here, had surfaced and had moved in as close as possible to the shore. A few minutes later a boat with five Marines left the *Nautilus* for the beach. These five men, visualizing the hardships of their comrades ashore, had volunteered to bring them supplies, weapons and ammunition.

As the two boats, one going out and one coming in, bobbed in the sea, a flight of Jap seaplanes, hedge-hopping from the lagoon side of the island dove toward them, strafed and bombed the boats

and subs. Roosevelt's boat reached the sub a few minutes before
the bombs bracketed it. Mountainous geysers hid the scene from
those who watched. It looked as if the sub had been hit.

"Poor gobs," Le Francois heard someone sob.

"There goes our transportation."

When the geyser subsided, the subs had disappeared and all that
was left on the surface was the one rubber boat with the five volunteers. The planes concentrated on the boat, criss-crossing it with
lines of bullets. It overturned. Men started swimming away. Bullets from the screaming, zooming planes sought them out. One by
one they sank beneath the sea to stay, and then men on shore yelled
in fury and frustration.

Five men gave their lives for their comrades: Sergeant Allard
of Woodside, Long Island; Sergeant Dallas H. Cook of Redjacket,
West Virginia; Private First Class Richard Olbert of Durango,
Colorado; Private John L. Kerns of Cooper Hill, Tennessee; Private
Donald Robertson of Franklin, Louisiana.

There were now seventy men left on the beach, and when the
air raid was over they thought they were there for good, for it had
seemed to them that the subs had really gotten hurt.

Carlson gave his men no time for wondering but sent out patrols
to bring him the answer to the prime question: how many Japs
were left? Word came back shortly that a patrol at the north end
of the island had uncovered two Jap marines and shot them, and a
patrol on On Cheong's wharf had killed another. On the whole of
Makin no other enemy was found. It was like the bursting of a big
balloon. The anxiety blown to monstrous proportion by the night of
uncertainty collapsed.

The men were too tired and hungry to celebrate, but a few started
singing. They had won Makin; it was theirs!

For the first time they felt the sun, smelled the scented coral air.
For the first time since they had landed, they looked around and
felt alive.

But there was no getting off the island yet. The fate of the subs
was uncertain; Jap planes would be coming back and the surf was
higher than ever.

Carlson led a patrol to collect food and ammunition for his men, to inspect his own dead and the enemy dead, to search for papers. He found altogether about two hundred enemy dead. Natives brought him word that they had picked up three survivors from the Jap transport that had been sunk in the lagoon by the *Nautilus's* guns. About a hundred Jap marines had been aboard; most had been killed by the direct hits, a few had drowned, and the survivors were probably the men killed by the patrols that morning.

His own dead numbered eighteen, not counting the five volunteers and the seven presumed to have been drowned in the surf during the night. But Carlson didn't know about these seven yet.

He found the dead Raiders: Jerry Holtom and Clyde Thomason, I. B. Earles, Dan Gaston, Harris Johnson, Ken Kunkle, Big Ed Maciejewski, Bob Pearson, Ashley Hicks, Norm Mortenson, John Vandenberg, Bob Maulding, Frank Nodland, Mason Yarborough, Vernon Castle, Bill Gallagher, Ken Montgomery, Charlie Selby.

Carlson turned each man on his back and said a prayer. He would have buried them but the coral was too hard and he had no instruments with which to dig. Moreover, time was going fast.

He reminded Joe Miller, the native police chief, of his promise to bury the dead, and gave him fifty dollars in addition to what he had given him the day before. Miller solemnly agreed.

Later, a year and four months later, on November 21, 1943, Roosevelt landed again on Makin with part of the 165th Army Combat Team, part of the 27th Division, this time to take and to hold the island. He sought out Miller, who showed him the graves. They had been well cared for; they had little headstones and palm fronds and a few flowers over them. "It be done," Miller said.

By late afternoon, there were three more air raids, and by the actions of the planes, it seemed as if the enemy was completely confused. Butaritari was bombed, but also Little Makin, and all the other islands of the atoll. If there were Japs hidden on those islands, their own planes either kept them hidden or killed them.

The day had given Carlson the time he needed to complete his mission. Every installation was burned, the Jap Commandant's papers were seized, and 1000 barrels of gasoline were fired. Only one thing was left undone — the taking of prisoners. But there were none to take.

All day, he had been worried about the subs. He had decided not to attempt the ocean again but to get out through the lagoon. Natives and his own patrols had assured him that no enemy guns had been emplaced on the land bordering the lagoon. But were the subs still around? Had they been damaged or destroyed by the air raids? Or had they remained submerged all day for safety's sake? He would have to wait until night to know. In the meantime, he directed that four rubber boats — all he had left — be carried over to the lagoon and their motors worked on. And from the natives he got an outrigger canoe big enough to hold the rest of his men, including his stretcher wounded.

When night came and the last of the enemy planes had disappeared, he ordered his men to board the canoe and the boats while he and a small patrol, including Craven with the flashlight, remained on the ocean side to try to reach the subs.

It was dark, and Craven walked to a high point and flashed his light on and off. MEET US OFF FLINK POINT AT END OF LAGOON, he signaled. MEET US OFF FLINK POINT AT END OF LAGOON. MEET US . . .

No answer.

MEET US OFF FLINK . . .

From the night sea came a light.

Craven read the letters aloud, "W-h-o? W-h-o?"

"They think the Japs are trying to trap them," Carlson said. "Tell 'em it's Carlson's Raiders."

Craven blinked out the words.

The answer came back: WHO? WHO?

"Tell him my name is Evans Fordyce," Carlson ordered.

But again the answer was WHO? WHO? WHO?

Then darkness.

And out of the darkness came another message.

WHO FOLLOWED MY FATHER AND ME FISHING?
WHO FOLLOWED MY FATHER AND ME FISHING?

"Now, what the hell?" Craven said.

"Colonel, did you get into an argument about fishing with any of the fellows on board?" Craven asked.

"No. . . ." Carlson said. He pondered the question. "Fishing?" It didn't make sense. "Who followed my father and me fishing?" Whose father? He went over the men on board whose fathers he knew. Brockman? Pierce? Haines? Ah, Haines!

Then it suddenly came to him. He had known Commander Haines's father when he had been the Adjutant and Inspector of the Marine Corps. On board, he and Haines had had long and friendly arguments as to who had succeeded Haines's father in the job. Haines had insisted that it was Rufus Lane; and Carlson said it was "Squeegie" Long.

"Try this, Craven," Carlson said, fighting to keep his voice calm. "Try this. Just flash '*Squeegie.*'"

"Spell it, Colonel."

Craven blinked out S–Q–U–E–E–G . . .

The blinker from the sub interrupted.

ROGER, the light said.

And it was welcome.

The little party hurried across the island.

"The colonel and his detail were the last men to reach the boats," Le Francois reported later. "He was tall and gaunt and sinewy, a man with a tremendous amount of endurance and a trigger-fast mind that made the right decisions in a split second. His men had followed him into this dangerous mission because they believed in him." [11]

Carlson wanted to make certain that all his Raiders were accounted for. Quickly he asked the help of his men to ascertain whether everyone who had been seen on the island during the day was in the boats. He knew that once he had left Makin for the subs there would be no way of determining who was missing until

---

[11] *Saturday Evening Post.* Op. cit.

he reached Pearl Harbor, for between the subs there could be no breaking of radio silence.[12]

The men reported that as far as they knew all who had spent the day on Makin were aboard.

Carlson gave the order to start the motors.

The Raiders waited hungrily for the first "sput." It came — and it died, and when it came again and kept going the motors sounded like Handel's "Hallelujah."

The word was passed back to the coxswain. "The Colonel says keep headed for the star."

There was a star, way out ahead of them, and they moved toward it slowly.

The motors stuttered and stopped, and men cursed and paddled. Behind them, came the whipthong sounds of shots, perhaps from the natives. Ahead, past the black jutting cliffs of the lagoon walls, rose a red flare burst.

[12] On May 22, 1946, an A.P. dispatch from Guam stated that nine United States Marines — all from Carlson's Raiders — were beheaded to celebrate a Japanese holiday. This was revealed by a defendant at the war crimes trial. The victims were supposed to be from among Raiders stranded on Makin after the raid. Commenting on this report, Carlson said: "You have my account of what happened at Makin. You have also interrogated numerous Raiders who have also participated in that raid. My official report contained the basic facts as I knew them. You remember that there were twelve men whom I reported as 'missing.' Of this number five were the crew of the rescue boat which was strafed by Japanese planes on the morning of the eighteenth of August. None of the twelve were seen by the seventy of us who spent the second day on the island. I was the last Marine to leave the beach, when we attempted the evacuation on the night of the seventeenth of August, and when we succeeded in getting away on the night of the eighteenth.

"There can be no question about the eighteen that were killed in action, for I checked their bodies. The twelve 'missing' were presumed to have been lost in the surf during the first night attempt at evacuation and during the strafing of the boat the following morning.

"It is entirely possible that some or all of the twelve whom we listed as 'missing' men had reached the shore of an adjacent island, or of the southern tip of Butaritari. This is the only explanation I can offer for the A.P. dispatch from Guam. If I had had knowledge that any Raiders remained on the island at the time we left, I would either have evacuated them or remained with them."

"Jap destroyers," Charlie Lamb muttered.

"Maybe it's our Navy," some one said.

"What do we do, Colonel?" the coxswain called.

"Keep headin' for the star," the reply came.

Near the mouth of the lagoon, the water roughened and waves curled over the outrigger and rubber boats. The men at the stern spread themselves out over the motors to keep them dry. The sound of *sput, sput,* was their reward.

It took them three hours to reach Flink Point, and every minute of it they expected to be attacked by Japs from a shore ambush or, what at this time their minds told them would even be worse, to have their raft sink under them.

"We hung on to one another and to the raft," Le Francois wrote. "It pitched and tossed, and the rubber boats groaned as they beat and tore against one another. The current twisted us in the wrong direction, and the oarsmen strained and pulled us back on the right course again. The raid . . . boiled down to a piece of rubber between me and eternity."

As they passed through the south lagoon entrance into the ocean, Carlson hoping against hope that the subs were there, ordered Craven to flash his light. A sudden white stream of light came back at them from the *Nautilus* a dozen yards away.

The Raiders dug their raft forward, tore at the lines coming from the *Nautilus,* clambered aboard shouting, crying, yelling triumphantly. Forty hours had passed since they had left.

Commander Haines grabbed Carlson and yelled, "Squeegie saved the day anyway."

Carlson didn't argue with him.

Below the little wardroom was cleared so that Doctor MacCracken could start operating on Lenz and Hawkins and Daniels and Le Francois. The sub's officers moved in with the crew and turned over their staterooms to the wounded. And for twenty-four hours, no one ate in the wardroom.

Carlson had come to the last section of the report, RECOMMEN-DATIONS. He wrote:

Perhaps the most important result of the raid was the experience gained . . . Some of the errors made have been noted. I would like to list the following with recommendations for their correction.

He suggested that a better radio be authorized; that there be no time limit set for withdrawal but that it should be determined by the commander ashore in accordance with the dictates of the situation there.

The present type of gasoline operated outboard motor is entirely inadequate. The possibilities of getting another motor must be explored immediately.

He wrote that he was more convinced than ever of the value of raids in the Pacific war. It was clear that the Japanese command had been confused. It did not know how the Americans got ashore, whether the attack was merely a raid or the spearhead of a large-scale invasion of the Gilberts.

Even as he wrote, a message came from Admiral Nimitz's headquarters informing him that a large Japanese Makin Relief Expedition, consisting of over a thousand troops from the Marshalls landed on Makin the day after the Raiders had left.

How did Nimitz know this? Nimitz had the Japanese code. He knew everything the Japs planned to do, including the plans for the Battle of Midway.

The Makin Relief Expedition might have been a Guadalcanal Relief Expedition had the raid not been made. Our precarious fingerhold there might have been cut away. Carlson's attack "may have diverted considerable Japanese naval strength from the Guadalcanal area," Captain Garrett Graham stated in the *Marine Corps Gazette* of February 1943.

Finally, I would invite the attention of all military leaders to the illustration provided by our situation on the night of August 17th which emphasized a truth that is as old as the military profession: no matter how bad your own situation may appear to be, there is always the possibility that the situation of the enemy is much worse.

He closed the report with high praise for the men of the submarines and their officers.

A harmony of spirit and self-sacrifice reigned throughout the expedition. This unity of mind and effort brought success.

He gave special credit to Dr. W. B. MacCracken and Dr. Stephen L. Stigler and to Lieutenant Peatross and his "lost" men who in harassing the enemy's rear displayed *"presence of mind, judgment, skill, courage and devotion to duty while under fire for the first time."*

And now he was finished. Pearl Harbor was several hours away. He folded the papers and put them in a battered yellow manila envelope.

The smoking lamp was lit. He sucked hungrily at his pipe and blew smoke up around his head.

Seven faces passed in front of him.

His casualties were thirty; eighteen men killed by the Japs, five men dead by the love of their comrades, and seven men drowned in the surf because the right motors had not been made available.

Seven faces slowly moved in his mind.

He was angry with a deep, scarring anger.

Somehow he felt responsible, and a failure.

14

At school the day before Thanksgiving

They were all in the sun on the deck of the *Nautilus*.

"Quite a crowd down at the sub base," Brockman said, looking through his glasses.

"Looks like they're boarding a transport," Carlson added.

"Guadalcanal, probably," Dr. MacCracken said.

The sub moved in closer to its mooring.

"I don't see a transport," MacCracken said.

From the shore came the sounds of a band playing the Marine Hymn.

"My God, a reception!" Haines said.

Lined up was a battalion of Marines, and in front of them at attention were Admiral Nimitz and Admiral Spruance, Marine General Pickett and Army General Emmons.

"More brass than in a foundry," Brockman said.

The band played another chorus.

The sub threw a line, and as it touched the pier, a great cheer sounded.

Carlson felt excited and frowned. He didn't want a fuss made. Yet being human he couldn't help but like it.

The Admirals and Generals boarded the sub. The congratulations were deeply felt.

There were reporters and cameramen. They wanted an interview.

"There isn't much to say," Carlson said. He felt tired.

Then someone remembered the sword which Carlson had taken from the dead hand of the Japanese commander of Makin, and gave it to Carlson who, as protocol required, handed it to Haines, the commander of the little task force.

"Admiral Nimitz," Haines said, "here's a trophy from Makin on behalf of Colonel Carlson and his Raiders."

Nimitz grinned like a boy on Christmas morning and showed the sword around to everyone. "First souvenir of the war," he said. "Damned good. Going to send it to the Academy museum."

Reporters wanted to talk to Carlson.

"Tomorrow," Nimitz said. "Let the man catch his breath."

"Admiral, could I skip interviews — even tomorrow?" Carlson asked.

Nimitz shook his head emphatically. "They're waiting to hear from you back in the States. Makin has made you and your Raiders famous."

Carlson protested.

"I thought you wanted to let people know about Gung Ho," the Admiral said with a grin. "You kept bending my ear with it."

Carlson stopped frowning. He hated publicity and ballyhoo, but he believed in taking advantage of every opportunity to get his message to people. He turned to the reporters. "Okay, boys."

The next day, Carlson called his battalion together. It was a fine clear day, and the men were glad to be alive, but more tired than they'd ever been at Makin or even on the way back.

Carlson told them that he wanted this get-together so soon after their return because otherwise they might forget where they had made mistakes. And the purpose of the meeting was to see where they had made mistakes.

The men were not bashful.

Why did they have to get off the island that night, they asked.

Why did the rubber boats and outboard motors fail them? (This was asked with passion — and answered without equivocation.)

Why didn't Carlson decide the time to leave the island instead of having it decided before the landing? He was the one who knew the situation best.

And the gripes and criticisms were spoken out, and Carlson noted them down, though he, himself, had said much the same in his battle report.

Could the battalion be improved, he asked.

Sure. They needed more corpsmen, perhaps more light machine guns, more signal equipment, more knives . . .

When the meeting was about over, he said that he would call them together again in a few days.

"I think we ought to have a memorial meeting for those we left on Makin," he said.

The men agreed.

The day of the memorial meeting matched the spirit. It was a good day, warm and promising, almost like spring at home. The boys had fixed up a platform and decorations in an open field where they had always held their Gung Ho meetings. Carlson invited

Nimitz and all the other ranking officers of the base, Army, Navy and Marine. Civilians were invited. A chaplain. There would be a small orchestra for hymns.

Carlson had worked on his eulogy. He wanted it simple, out of his truest feelings, meaningful not only to the comrades of the dead, but to those others who had never known them. Above all, he hoped to be able to give to his own men a sense of what their sacrifices must create in the world in which they died and lived.

The guests arrived; the band played, and the battalion sang a hymn. The chaplain gave a benediction. Carlson went to the microphone. He glanced down at a sheet of paper in his hand.

"We are gathered here today to honor the memory of our comrades who remain at Makin." He paused and looked up directly at the men. "We miss them. Each had his special place among us, and that place is imperishably his. Being human, we mourn the loss of each. But I believe that these gallant men who so eagerly, so willingly went forth to meet the enemy would not have us weep and bemoan their passing. They loved life, those comrades of ours. They were vital, eager, thoughtful and realistic. They had convictions and they lived those convictions even to the point of sacrificing their lives."

His voice was clear now and calm. The wind from the sea whipped back the loose khaki shirt and trousers and as he stood there, he seemed grayer and gaunter than ever before, yet somehow stronger, more lithe, even more youthful. His strong nose jutted out triumphantly. The deep-set unwavering blue eyes moved slowly over the ranks. To his men, he seemed, as he talked, like something out of all their pasts, their fathers, their teachers, their boyhood heroes, the Deerslayer and Abe Lincoln and Robert E. Lee. With the words and the tones of his voice he brought special remembrances; grace before meals, the prayer at school the day before Thanksgiving, gentleness and fervor, an encompassing warmth and love and sadness.

His men loved him then with all the love they had ever known: Jimmy Roosevelt, feeling a high pride, Maghakian, the Armenian, Miller, Nelson, Drake, Al Flores who remembered his Mexican father in the words, Angel, Plumley, Gurman, Peatross, Big Smitty, and the guy from Chicago who talked about how tough he was, and Jessie Hawkins from South Gate who lived to get to the sub and whom they found walking after his operation. "I felt if I just walked, I would live," he had said.

"They are still with us in spirit," he went on. "Allard with his boyish smile, Johnson with his strange scowl, Jerry Holtom with his lumbering stride and eager, half-embarrassed manner, and the others. You know the characteristics of each as well as I. Who will say that the spirit of all these men we knew so intimately does not remain with us?

"It was not possible to render honors to these fallen comrades on the field of battle. I did what I could. I went to each as he lay with his face toward the enemy. I placed each on his back that he might rest more easily, and I said a silent prayer over each. With the native Gilbertese I arranged for each to be given a Christian burial. And so they lie there today, in the soil of that delightful South Pacific isle, beneath the palms under which they won their victory."

He made a simple gesture with his hands, spreading the paper between his fingers, glanced down at it, then rested his eyes again on the faces in front of him.

"It behooves us who remain to rededicate ourselves to the task that lies ahead. The convictions of these comrades are our convictions. With the memory of their sacrifice in mind, let us here dedicate ourselves to the task of bringing into reality the ideals for which they died; that their sacrifice will not have been in vain.

"We salute you, comrades. We salute you as Raiders, as Marines, as Americans, as men! God bless you!"

He stood there a moment at attention; then saluted his battalion, wheeled around and took his place with the staff.

The Sergeant Major gave a command, and the battalion was dismissed.

The men said very little, but returned to their tents and lay down on their sacks and were silent, most of them. They felt sad, and yet withal, angry. Their anger was resolve and decision. Allard and

Holtom and Earles and Thomason and Maciejewski must not have died in vain. That is what they thought.

15

Who is this man?

On Guadalcanal, months later. Admiral Nimitz was there; Major General Vandegrift of the Marine First Division had a citation in his hand. He looked up solemnly at Carlson, and read:

"The President of the United States takes pleasure in presenting the Navy Cross Star, to be worn with the Navy Cross awarded October 1, 1931, to Lieutenant Colonel Evans F. Carlson, United States Marine Corps Reserve, for service as set forth in the following citation:

"For extraordinary heroism and distinguished service as Commanding Officer of the Second Marine Raider Battalion against enemy Japanese forces on Makin Island. In the first operation of this type ever conducted by United States forces, Lieutenant Colonel Carlson personally directed his forces in the face of intense fire of enemy ground troops and aerial bombing barrage, inflicting great personnel and material damage on the enemy. In the withdrawal of his forces under adverse sea conditions . . ."

Seven faces . . .

" . . . he displayed outstanding resourcefulness, initiative and resolute purpose in evacuating all wounded and disabled men."

Lenz with the bullet in the brain lived; Hawkins and Le Francois and Daniels and Lamb lived.

"His high courage and excellent leadership throughout the engagement were in keeping with the finest traditions of the United States Naval Service.

"For the President, Frank Knox, Secretary of the Navy."

General Vandegrift handed Carlson the citation, and Nimitz pinned on him the Navy Cross and said, "Carlson, I hope I have the chance to pin many more of these on you."

"Thank you, Admiral," Carlson said. "On behalf of . . ."

On behalf of them all, of all the dead and wounded and terrorized, on behalf of the sacrifice, on behalf of the years lost in those forty hours, the longing, the loneliness, the fear.

On behalf of seven men, and on behalf of the five who gave their lives in the greater glory.

On behalf of the answer to the question: "God in Heaven, what am I doing here?"

Others were decorated, many others.

And we may well ask what were these men. Out of what sources of America did they come?

Out of what did this one man come? Where is the connection between Norway, the California Sierras, Vermont, and Nicaragua, North China and the Makin atoll?

Trace back the strain and the blood, the single scrawl of a life in the midst of infinite scrawls, the curves of learning and error and heartbreak and heartsease.

"His men followed him into this dangerous mission because they believed in him," wrote one who followed him.

Out of what did he come?

Part Two

1

The born of God

Evans Carlson was born in Sidney, New York on February 26, 1896, but he grew up in three New England towns: Shoreham, Vermont; Dracut, Massachusetts; and Peacham, Vermont.

He was fourteen when he left New England, but fourteen years are long enough to make a Yankee.

Twice he ran away from home. Once, when he was eleven, he came back. The second time was for good.

For as long as he could remember, he had a hunger for adventure, for being on his own, for making his way in the world by himself.

There were stories of adventure in his own home: the Carlson who had left Norway not so many years ago; the Carlson — his grandfather — who had panned gold and silver in the High Sierras and who had died in 1901 in Dawson City, and his Uncle Matt Carlson who was a United States Marshal in Fairbanks. . . . And his mother's family — the Evanses, who claimed, like all Welshmen, to be descendants of the forever ennobled Welsh Kings.

The villages he lived in poured out adventure. Shoreham, Vermont, was Ethan Allen and Benedict Arnold and the French and Indian War country. . . . Peacham, Vermont, was the country of Rogers's Rangers and where Thaddeus Stevens, who adventured with heart and tongue, lived as a boy.

The stream flowed unending from the books he read: Mark Twain and G. A. Henty and Horatio Alger and Fenimore Cooper.

And as if this were not enough, he heard people talking of Admiral Peary and the North Pole, Teddy Roosevelt and Darkest Africa.

Evans Carlson ran away from home twice but he never truly left his home.

A man's home and his people are shadows that walk out with him wherever he goes.

As a boy, Evans Carlson knew the adventures of his father's life. He knew that Thomas Carlson, the son of a Norwegian forty-niner, was born in 1865 in a community of mining shacks in a cleft of the High Sierras. The silver miners shared their legends with the boy, and christened him Tommy, though his real name was Thorstein. They made much of the fact that his middle name was Alpine, after Alpine County, California. They delighted in the knowledge that little Tommy had been the first white child born in that County.

Tom Carlson liked to tell his children about the trip which his family took in 1875 from Silver Mountain, California to southern Wisconsin. There were tales of Indians and armies of locusts and buffalo herds.

The Carlson children, Evans and Karen, his sister, and Dana and Tom, Jr. (when he was old enough to understand) would listen enviously as their father told them his stories in the big warm winter kitchen at Shoreham, or at Peacham, or perhaps while they walked together on a June Saturday afternoon to Larabee's Point on Lake Champlain, or maybe while he poured the fresh maple sugar on the snow for their beloved "sugar-on-snow." They listened and they looked at him, and though they believed every word he said, as if it were revelation, yet they did not easily connect this tall, thin, quiet, humble man with all those young days when he had seen war-painted Indians dance.

Evans, of course, was convinced that such excitement and peril were not dead forever. He would have them some place, some kind, perhaps even more thrilling. But he would have them! On this score, at least, he could equal his father.

On a warm June day in 1944, at Sherman, Connecticut, to a meeting of clergymen, Thomas Carlson recited the story of the fifty years of his ministry and the struggle for spiritual clarity. His speech lasted fully an hour, and it was characteristic of his humility and modesty that he could tell the story of his life without once using "I" or "me" or "mine."

(How like Gung Ho this is! How the patterns repeat!)

"It was not a notable ministry," Thomas Carlson remarked at Sherman. "This is said without compunction or regret."

Nothing but a small parish house . . . the white church . . . the bitter bounty of congregations that were not always generous, and frequently so impoverished that Carlson had to support a family of five on $30 a month. . . . Nothing but the weekly sermon in which, at inspired moments, he spoke out the love of his heart, and at tired moments heard himself, as if in an empty room, repeat old words.

Thomas Carlson first heard the horn of God when he was still a child in Silver Mountain. His mother was deeply religious and a strict disciplinarian. The Old Testament Jehovah was the rod in her strong right hand. Later when his family moved to a Norwegian community in southern Wisconsin, Tom Carlson's grandmother taught him his Lutheran prayers in the ancestral *Norsk*. Here he was formally christened, and he still remembers Pastor Gjertson, robed in black, with the ruffled, white *preste krage* around his neck.

Back in Oakland, California a few years later, Thomas Carlson devotedly attended the Moody and Sankey missions, and at the Oakland High School organized the first Christian Endeavor Society on the Pacific Coast. He wanted to become a preacher, but he wanted first to get a general education. He hoped to go to the University of California, but there wasn't enough money to send him. Instead he took a job as a bookkeeper in a small store in the little town of Port Orford, Oregon.

In 1890, when he was 25, he managed to enter the San Francisco
Theological Seminary. Later he transferred to the Seminary in
Auburn, New York, where "the black tincture of a severe theology"
was somewhat diluted. When he took his first parish at Sidney,
New York, he was determined to reform his parishioners as quickly
as possible. Unfortunately his parishioners were not quite as eager
to be reformed, and so he soon moved to another church, this time
near Middlebury, Vermont. It was a good move for him, for here
he could satisfy his old dream of going to college. His sermons also
by this time had become more understanding.

After Middlebury he moved to a church at Shoreham, Vermont,
near Lake Champlain. Here he came face to face with the greatest
crisis of his spiritual life.

Everywhere eminent ministers, stimulated by the works of
Darwin, Renan and William James, began to question the story of
the miraculous birth of Christ. It was becoming clear to many devout
Christians that the Bible had not been recorded, as John Donne put
it, by "the secretaries of the Holy Ghost."

Thomas Carlson's peace of mind was shattered by this "higher
criticism."

His peace was broken constantly by questions. What was the
Bible? What was the source of its inspiration? How many "jots and
tittles" could be changed without utterly destroying it? Was William
James right when he suggested that the test of the faith in God was
how much practical value it had? Was Christ divine? Was the
Bible pure revelation; to be taken literally as the Fundamentalists
did?

There were times when the world seemed to be slipping away
from him; when there seemed to be no authority anywhere; when
he could not understand even his simplest motives. His Sunday
sermons were becoming shorter and shorter.

He fought his fight in solitude and under great difficulties. For
several months he was sick with typhoid; his wife, Joetta, was re-
peatedly ill; and four children had to be taken care of.

Finally, help began to come his way. Dr. George A. Gordon, the
minister of the New Old South Church in Boston had written a

book, *The Ultimate Conceptions of Faith,* which matched Carlson's conflict with his own. Henry Churchill King's *Rational Living* and Coe's *Religion of a Mature Mind* dispelled more of the darkness. He met and heard Edward Everett Hale who "saw God in the new gaslights" and who could redeem the new learning by seeing it in perspective.

Bit by bit, he shaped together a rational basis for his thinking and living.

"The outcome of it all," he told his fellow clergymen that June day in Sherman, "was the great discovery that, like the Lord and Master, the Book is both human and divine, and that the divine must be followed through its human ramifications."

Thomas Carlson's battle was won. He knew now what to believe and what to preach and how to live. His days, from thence onward, would be simple, day by day fulfillment of the ministry of souls. As the years passed he would go from Shoreham parish to Peacham, and from Peacham to Plymouth, Connecticut; he would see his son, Dana, die, and his wife die; his son, Evans, leave home and make his own way in the world by himself, neither as minister nor doctor nor lawyer, but as a soldier. He would tend his congregations and give them the strength of his words and his acts, and when the time came for him to retire, as it did in 1944, he would say that his life could perhaps be best summed up in the words of the servant of Abraham who set out blindly to find a wife for his master's son. Returning successful, he said reverently, "I, being in the way, the Lord led me."

To say then, in examining the sources of Evans Carlson's life, that he was the son of an impoverished Congregationalist minister would not be enough. To say that his home was strict, that he was brought up with hymns and grace before meals and Bible readings and Sunday School and sermons and lectures on the Holy Land with stereopticon views thrown on a screen by a carbide lamp projector which made the Holy Land seem even more forbidding than it is — is only part of the truth. To say that he had to be a model boy as the son of the town minister, and that he hated it, would still not give us the answer.

No, his father was no routine Christian. He had a deeply in-grained Christly love of men. He was — as his son remembers in after years — the only truly practicing Christian he had ever known.

But it is hard to be the son of a practicing Christian. Evans felt that he could never be his father's equal, that even at his best he would fall far below his father's hopes for him. It was better then to be on his own, to make his own way.

2

"Good marks for lightning"

What then of Evans's mother, Joetta?

"She was, in Scripture language," her husband said, "well-favored, of singular poise and self-possession; her eyes blue and expressive, her hair, naturally dark, was gray at an early age and I never knew it otherwise. She was of medium height and well-proportioned. Her complexion was fresh and transparent, and even in her later years she was known as a woman of singular attractiveness and charm. This arose in some measure, no doubt, from her watchful considera-tion for others. She was the oldest child in her family; and upon the death of her mother, when Joetta was twenty-three, she mothered the household."

Evans was close to his father, and his mother suffered for it. They were always misunderstanding each other. He was self-conscious about being the grandchild of Norwegian immigrants on his father's side. And she was always reminding him that her family had come to this country long before the Revolution. There were the McNabs, the Schraders and the Fordyces. And, of course, the Evanses. He saw the even more painful contrast between his father's constant struggle to keep the family fed and clothed and the ease of some of the relatively well-to-do members of the Evanses. The only one of his mother's family he genuinely admired as a boy was his mother's brother, a United States Treasury man in San Francisco. Uncle Charlie was a real Colonel in the California National Guard and not an "Honorary Colonel" like so many Evanses who were given ratings by their native Virginia.

The boy bridled every time his mother corrected his table manners with "Evans, that isn't the way it's done in the best families." Dutifully he would say, "Yes, ma'am," but he hated her Evans superiority and wondered angrily why the Carlsons, in this rectory kitchen, were not as good as the "best families."

Joetta Carlson had a real taste for painting fragile and sensitive water colors. She loved flowers and put them in her garden even before she got around to vegetables. She played the piano well, and had the patience to teach her children. But even these virtues the boy did not take to kindly. Her very delicacy underscored, in his eyes, her family pride.

It is no wonder, therefore, that young Evans took the opposite side from his mother in every issue. She and her family were great detesters of Theodore Roosevelt and called him "That Man!" And so Teddy became the great hero of his youth. And who else but Jack London, then, would be the boy's favorite author? And what other novel of his but *Martin Eden*? Didn't Martin scorn the snobs in San Francisco (where many of the Evanses lived)? Didn't he prove himself better than the wealthy and respectable?

Evans, at eleven, had read many of his father's books — Scott and Thackeray and Cooper — but not one compared with *Martin Eden*.

"The burden of ministry," Joetta's husband said, "was freely shared by a helpmate whom only the grace of God could have provided. A beautiful woman with a contralto voice that was like velvet; an accomplished pianist; an artist of no mean calibre; an experienced housekeeper and homemaker, and long a devoted church worker. . . . She proved to be an unusual organizer and leader. . . . There is a saying that you cannot draw blood from a turnip. She drew blood from many turnips in the course of this ministry, from church societies that were marking time or were meagerly fruitful. Like the rock that Moses smote, they all became joyous producers of abundance. Unfortunately, like church steeples, the women of the parsonage are good marks for lightning. Those who dare it, some time or other, receive the stroke. In the smaller churches which are many, they bear the stress of household management with slender means. They are the real heroes of the ministry."

Evans didn't know all this then. He didn't know, for example, that his mother had lost the uncertain friendship of some of the parishioners because she would not join the Daughters of the American Revolution. "I don't believe in that kind of pride," she said.

Even if he had known, he wouldn't have understood, for didn't his mother speak with "that kind of pride" about her ancestor, Captain Jack Evans, who had fought the Great Revolution on General Washington's staff?

As a boy, Evans Carlson wanted to make the Carlson in him better than the Evans.

3

All of his best friends . . .

In 1908 Thomas Carlson had the Dracut, Massachusetts, Congregational Church at the corner of Bridge and Arlington Streets. It was an odd-looking, clapboard building with an open belfry.

They had moved from Shoreham to Dracut, a suburb of Lowell, because Joetta wasn't well and needed better medical care, and because Thomas thought his children could go to better schools. For the first time, they lived in a house that had electricity and an inside toilet. For the first time, they lived in a city with paved streets and stores and horsecars. There was a huge textile mill only a few blocks away. Evans was sent to the Parker Avenue Grammar School.

Dracut was no success for any of the family. His mother grew worse; the kids picked up the measles, and Evans, after the measles, came down with rheumatic fever. But for Evans, being ill was nothing compared with his unhappiness at having left Shoreham. There he could move around, feel part of the open country, take a deep breath, picnic and hike, swim in the ponds or over at Larabee's Point on Lake Champlain. There was a different smell to Shoreham, and a different sound. He felt less independent in a city.

But more than any of this, at Dracut he became aware of his family's poverty. It often came down to the question of not having enough to eat — or at least that is how the boy understood it. He was conscious even at that time that he was another mouth to feed, and being the oldest he felt that the time must come soon when he would have to relieve his father of some of his burden.

Tom Carlson had a sense of what was, in part, troubling his son. He found an opportunity one week to take a trip with him. They rented bikes and rode to Boston.

This was an important experience for Evans. Here, with his father, in Boston he saw with his own eyes the stuff of which his school books had been made. It was always what he had needed — to see with his own eyes, to feel history on his skin like rain or heat or cold. Boston was history, even more so than the Green Mountain Boys country of Shoreham, for the Green Mountain Boys were dead and so also was Benedict Arnold, and Fort Ticonderoga was silent and its guns breechless. And more than that, he took his backyard history for granted. But Boston! Even the spreading chestnut tree still grew. The church where Paul Revere had hung his lanterns was still worshipped in. There was something about the Old South Church and Faneuil Hall that was still alive and sounding. To him Boston was Emerson, his father's favorite writer.

He was shown the Boston Tea Party tablet on Atlantic Avenue near Griffin's Wharf, and the Common, where there was quite a crowd listening to the speakers. Bill Heywood's name was flung about like a challenge — he who had been accused of the assassination of Governor Steurenberg of Idaho. The crowd jeered the name of the police spy, McParland; and everyone cheered at the names of Eugene V. Debs and Clarence Darrow. . . . There were other speakers who warned of a depression to come, and who blamed it on the trusts.

It was exciting to hear all the talk, the charges and denunciations and the flinging of names.

And, finally, the two of them, father and son, stood in front of William Lloyd Garrison's statue. The boy, big for his age, but only half the height of his broad-shouldered father, read aloud in uncertain, schoolboyish syllables: "I am in earnest. I will not e-quiv-o-cate. I will not excuse. I will not retreat a single inch. And I will be heard."

"Garrison," his father explained, "hated slavery. Like Abraham Lincoln. They thought it was evil. It was . . ." He paused. "And is."

The boy was not to know until later, in China, how much he had read into those few days in Boston; he was not to know that somehow he had seen beneath the surface and had felt the life of Democracy. He was a New England boy, and Boston was New England's heart. Without knowing it, he would be seeking to find Boston again, and New England, and America for as long as he lived. He would not know he was seeking it, but something in Nicaragua, something on the face of Mao Tse-tung or in the slow smile of Chu Teh or in the songs he would hear from ten thousand Chinese throats, would bring it back to him. He would remember Faneuil Hall in Managua; he would close his eyes momentarily against the dust of Yenan, and remember the Court House and the Meeting House and the Adamses' place on Mount Vernon Street and William Lloyd Garrison's statue.

Before they left Boston for home, they looked in at Harvard.

"We'd like to send you here some day," Thomas Carlson said. "Here or Middlebury. Your mother and I would like you to get a college education. It's very important to have. A man with a college degree can become a doctor or lawyer or a great author."

Evans wondered whether Jack London had ever gone to college. But whether or not, the boy was thoroughly impressed by his father's words. Someday, he promised himself, he would go to college — but only after he had made his own way in the world. How else? Certainly his father didn't have the money to send him.

His family's poverty and his own yearning for an education are reflected in a little invention he wrote at the Parker Avenue Grammar School when he was twelve. It is titled "What I Would Do With a Million Dollars."

> When my grandfather died he left me a fortune of a million dollars. Mother and I had been living alone with barely enough to eat. I had been obligued to leave school and go to work to keep up the expences, while mother had nearly ruined her eyes by sewing by lamplight.
>
> After this fortune came upon us so suddenly I decided to take a college course as I had been perparing to do so when I left school and finally persuaded mother to take a house uptown. After a conversation with mother I decided to go to Harvard college for two years.
>
> After completing my work at Harvard I decided to study abroad as I expected to be a professor of Liturature. After two years of studying in foreign countries I returned and excepted the position of Professor of Liturature in Yale College.

This typically American, Horatio Alger dream of an education stayed with Evans Carlson, in one form or another, during the years to come. But despite his will for it he would never be quite able to make it come true. The dream, however, illumined the whole of his life.

The trip to Boston did not halt Evans's restlessness. In February he ran away from Dracut. He left the day before his twelfth birthday, for he didn't want to wait until he received his presents. His conscience told him it wouldn't have been fair.

He had $2.34 with him when he left Dracut, money he had put aside from chores and doing the neighbors' lawns. The fare to

Boston was thirty-five cents. He didn't tarry there. Boston had become too close to him, too close to home since he had seen so much
there with his father. No — not Boston would be the world, but
Portland, Maine.

Boat from Boston to Portland — one dollar. One piece of pie on
the boat — five cents. Total left: ninety-four cents. You couldn't go
very far in the world on ninety-four cents, and Evans decided not to
spend any more until he had earned something.

It was a cold day when he arrived in Portland and he tried finding a job, but unemployment had hit the Maine city, and there
were not many jobs for a boy when men were starving. That night
he moved along the docks looking for a hideaway. He was cold and
hungry. Most of all, he was sleepy.

He found a wharf where they had been loading coal. A pile of
empty coal sacks made a dirty bed — but a bed. They also made a
blanket.

He was awakened in the morning by a little boy who persuaded
him to come to his house to get warm and eat some breakfast. The
boy's mother — a Mrs. Goldstein who was a widow with five children — welcomed him kindly. When the oldest boy said the grace
in Hebrew, Evans said he had heard his father read that language
from books. Mrs. Goldstein asked him if he were Jewish.

"I'm a Congregationalist," Evans replied.

"We're Jewish," the woman said.

Evans was puzzled. He had never known a real Jew. "I thought
all the Jews were in the Bible," he said.

The kids laughed, but Mrs. Goldstein said slowly, "No, some of
us are still around."

After breakfast, the woman tried to get Evans to tell her who
he was and where he came from, but he was too smart for her. He
knew she'd get in touch with his father, and he kept his secrets. She
pleaded with him to go back home — and if he didn't, she invited
him to come back to her house whenever he was hungry.

Evans left the Goldsteins with a deep gratitude which, like the
experience with his father in Boston, would rise to the surface of his
actions in later years. Even had he not been brought up in a genu-

inely Christian home with all that means in toleration and understanding of other people and creeds, these people alone, the first
Jews he had ever seen, with their warmth and generosity to a run-
away boy who, admittedly or not, was a little scared and even more
homesick, would have sown in him a hatred of anti-Semitism. In
later years, it wasn't that some of his best friends were Jews; it was
that all of his best friends were people.

He got a job that day at the Portland Star Match Factory,
running a block of wood through a series of saws that notched it
into match-heads. His pay was six dollars a week for a twelve-hour
day six days a week.

Mrs. Goldstein's words about his father and mother bothered him.
He did not like the thought that he was worrying them, causing
them grief and hurt. This was going too far. He decided that as soon
as he made a little money — something to show for himself — he
would go back. Unfortunately, the Portland Star Match Company
— even in a depression — was having trouble keeping workers at
low wages, and he had to work three weeks before the first pay
day. He had ninety-four cents for twenty-one days.

His partner at the machine — a quiet old man who taught him
how to work it — became Evans's confidant. The old man, who lived
alone in an attic room, told Evans he could sleep on the floor, and
that he would be glad to lend him a dollar when needed.

During the three weeks, Evans's pride fought with his stomach —
and won. He sustained himself on five cents' worth of pastries a
day — pastries because they looked and tasted rich and seemed to
fill him up. He did not borrow from the old man, nor did he return
to the Goldsteins. If he was to make his own way, he decided that's
what he ought to do, not borrow or take charity or even be helped
by kindliness.

But, finally, his stomach got the better of his farm-boy, outdoor
constitution — and at the end of the three weeks he was sick. He
couldn't even keep the pastries down. The old man wanted to send
him to a hospital. But with an enormous stubbornness — "I am in
earnest. I will not e-quiv-o-cate!" — he bought a new shirt and a

new pair of pants — and a ticket for Dracut. He had made up his
mind to go home — and he would go. The new clothes might help
hide the fact that his adventure had not been a success.

The three weeks had been a severe ordeal for the Carlson family,
but most of all for Joetta. She and Thomas had tried to find him;
they had gone as far as Boston; they had enlisted the police and the
State agencies. For awhile they thought he might be dead, though
Thomas believed in Evans's ability to take care of himself and he
tried to console his wife. But she was beyond his words. Somehow
she felt responsible. If Evans had not been happy at home, it was
her fault. If he had been more restless than most boys his age, it
was her fault. She had not understood him and helped him. If he
had wanted adventure so much, she should have been able to divert
his dreams and energy to something at home. She was sick at the
loss; bone-sick at what she thought was her failure. She did not
forgive Evans, it is true; but mostly she did not forgive herself.
Her nights were without sleep and though she tried hard to keep
it from the children, they heard her weep. There was no solace for
her, not even her husband whom she loved. Evans had hurt her
beyond repair, she said. Evans was willful and capricious.
    She was right.
    Joetta sat upon her bed that Sabbath morning, life beyond the
window as aloof as the life she seemed no longer to feel within her.
The house was empty. Her husband and children had gone to
church. They had told people Evans was off visiting somewhere.
Then as if the world of sounds had combined into a footstep, she
heard her oldest son at the door.
    "Evans is here! Evans is home!" she cried as if everybody was
there to hear her.
    Evans did not get a whipping. He had gotten a few in the past,
but now he was too grownup. He was punished enough by seeing
how much he had hurt his mother and father. His father said, when
all the talking and explaining was over, that Evans had committed
a sin. "Anything that hurts others is a sin," his father said.
    The boy went outside into the cold, snow-covered night, walked
down to his father's church on Arlington Street, not knowing where

he was walking, and leaning against the yellow clapboard wept in shame for the first time in his life. And for the last time.

4

His foot in his hand

In 1910 his family moved from Dracut out into the country to Peacham, Vermont, near St. Johnsbury and the Connecticut River. But the boy still rebelled, still longed for adventure, still got into school scrapes and home scrapes, but he was old enough to make a decision, to keep it, and yet not to hurt the people he loved.

Peacham could not keep the boy. It was too serene, too rustic and languorous. Only, in later years, would he remember with longing the rich-smelling meadows, the slow-moving and cool Connecticut River, the green peaks of the mountains, the old mills and granaries, the cool and clean ponds set deep in the hills, the wonderful peace in the gleaming white Congregational Church that had been built in the 1790's.

Peacham couldn't hold the boy. It was no longer an impulse that drove him out, but a considered judgment. He knew it — and his mother and father knew it. It was simply a question of time before the tide of wanting to be on his own would flood through him again.

The time at Peacham was preparation.

He read more than ever before.

"Man is his own star . . . Our acts our angels are . . ." This from the Beaumont and Fletcher quote at the head of Emerson's essay on "Self-Reliance." . . . And from the essay itself:

> A sturdy lad from New Hampshire or Vermont [who else could that be?] who in turn tries all the professions, who teams it, farms it, peddles, keeps a school, preaches, edits a newspaper,

goes to Congress, buys a township, and so forth, in successive years, and always like a cat falls on his feet, is worth a hundred of these city dolls.

How well Emerson knew! Always to fall on one's feet . . . But always to try . . .

Trust thyself: every heart vibrates to that iron string. Accept the place the divine providence has found for you, the society of your contemporaries, the connection of events.

Traveling is a fool's paradise . . .

No, on this, Evans disagreed with Emerson. The old boy couldn't be right all the time. On this score, Emerson was not as wise as Mark Twain and Jack London, Evans concluded.

There was another kind of book he read — biography and autobiography. It didn't matter who the subject was — Jefferson or Lincoln — divine or politician — swindler or explorer. He read to find the answer to one question: What was the first step these men took which decided the failure or success of their lives? Was it when they left home, or when they took their first job or when they left their first job for another? Or was it something they had learned from an older man or from some book they had read? In everyone's life there was some one step, the boy thought, which was *the* step. If he could learn from others, he would know when the moment had arrived for himself. His father preached many sermons on successful living, scolding those who "gave in" to worldly temptation in order to grow wealthy and powerful and famous. His father preached *selflessness*.

Yes. But it was hard to be selfless.

The time for Evans's departure from home was set not so much by himself as by the Peacham Academy [1] school board. The school's bell rope had been cut. And not for the first time.

It would be reasonable to assume, after all these years, that the

[1] Less pretentiously known as the Caledonia County Grammar School.

principal immediately suspected the son of the Reverend Mr. Carlson. But it is equally reasonable to assume that if he did suspect him, he could not easily make a point of it. Thus, every possible suspect but Evans was gravely cross-examined. Evans knew all this because he listened in on the principal's office from another room via an open heating vent.

There is no record of what exactly made up his mind to confess that he was the chief culprit. It may have been that he feared someone was going to snitch on him anyway, or that someone else was getting all the blame. At any rate, young Carlson made a decision, walked into the principal's office and, with perhaps just a touch of bravado, confessed.

It was the considered and by no means unexpected judgment of the board that the son of a preacher should be made to suffer more than a layman's son. How else did children learn — except by the example of others? The Reverend Carlson's son had to be that example. He was, therefore, suspended from attending Peacham Academy for one year!

Evans was relieved.

But his father fought the decision of the board. He thought it was excessive and therefore unjust.

There was something else in it — something that struck cruelly at the Carlson home and at his son's future. The school board couldn't know, of course, that when it prohibited Evans from attending school for a year, it was cutting away the last excuse for keeping him home. But the father knew that well. He had seen his son's restlessness.

"We can't keep Evans home now," he said to Joetta. "He's going to leave us again."

His wife was silent.

"It's not your fault, Joetta," he said. "It's no one's fault. Evans is a good boy. But his spirit is restless. He broke away from us once before and found that he could take care of himself. There won't be peace for him or for us until he breaks away again."

She listened quietly and agreed. But it was not a happy thing to have a son leave so early, so soon, so young. Of course, there were

the other children, Dana and Karen and Tom, Jr. But Evans was
her first-born. It may have been sinful to think, but there was a
special love she bore for this son, and now there was a special pain.

Thomas and Joetta agreed that they would not say anything to
Evans. They would neither encourage nor discourage him to leave.
But they would let him know, to the best of their ability, that they
had confidence in him whatever he did.

"Let him work out his own salvation," Thomas said. "He'll know
what we've done — and he'll appreciate it."

The picnic that Saturday afternoon was at Martin's Pond. The day
was June and good and warm. The kids wanted to go swimming but
Evans said he didn't feel like it. At about four o'clock Evans went
over to his father and mother, and told them he was going home.

"I've got some chores to do," he said.

His mother was wearing a blue dress with small white polka dots.
His father was in shirt sleeves, his collar was open.

They said they'd see him later, and he went off slowly past the
pond. Tom, Jr., was digging in the mud.

"Find anything?" Evans asked.

"I'm workin' on it," Tom said. "Got three worms now."

He left the pond and walked up the hill toward a stand of maples.
Dana and Karen were racing among the trees. He could hear
Karen's lusty, boyish yells, and Dana's heavy breathing.

Evans yelled to them that he'd see them later.

Up the hill to the road home. The top ridges of the White Mountains across the near-by border never seemed sharper. He felt he
could almost cut a loaf of bread on the edges. He turned back again
to look down at the pond and the maples and his father and mother.

He thought that he ought to tell them that he was going, but he
was afraid. He was afraid that he'd have to explain all the reasons
why — and they were too many and too difficult. And besides, he
couldn't even understand all his reasons himself. He'd better just
go away without explaining. He wished it could have been otherwise.

*   *   *

"He took his foot in his hand," as the old Vermonters have it, and started off for Vergennes across the state, seventy miles away. The first night, at a farmhouse near Marshfield in the quarry country, he borrowed a pencil and a sheet of ruled paper, and wrote a letter to his mother. He told her not to worry, and that he would let her know, as often as he could, just where he was, what he was doing and how he felt. He said he would not be home again for at least seven years. He picked the number because it sounded like something he had read in a book.

He would not be home again to stay — for thirty years.

5

Winding through corridors

"Trust the instinct to the end," Emerson wrote, "though you can render no reason."

For the next twenty years of his life, Evans Carlson trusted his instinct.

"Nothing can bring you peace but yourself," the Concord wise man told the young boy. "Nothing can bring you peace but the triumph of principles."

His instinct sought out the principles by which he wanted to live. The New England within him bred in his bones the conviction that life was not just an intermission of existence but a passage of achievement.

He tried many things.

It was as if he had been placed in a gigantic maze, and his years were spent winding through corridors, butting up against dead ends, moving ahead, backtracking, always trying to find a way out to the reward box. And even while he moved in a trial and error way, the maze was teaching him how to live — and the reward box

was being filled, without his knowing it, with additional goals he
had not dreamed of either wanting or achieving.

If at the commencement of these years he sought an adventurous
life, at their end he was to begin his search for a useful one.

When he first left Peacham, he had his independence — but he
didn't know what to do with it. He figured, first, he ought to
finish up high school. He wanted to show his folks that his running
away did not mean that he was entering a wilderness of "doin' as
he darn well pleased." Going to school, on his own, would prove
that he was capable of self-discipline.

For two years he went to the Vergennes High School, earning
his own way by working for a farmer named Clark who knew
the Carlsons. At other times he worked as a baggage-smasher for
the Rutland Railroad at New Haven Junction. Here he learned to
be a railroad telegrapher, for who could tell — maybe that's what
he would become.

Once, his father saw him at New Haven Junction. Evans was
piling mail sacks into a train. He didn't see his father watching
him.

How grown-up he looks! Thomas Carlson thought. How strong
and capable! How good it would be to take him home again. . . .
At least, to talk to him. Joetta would like him to do that. She
would expect him to do that. And it would be good for her. . . .

The father wrestled with himself. Would it be good for the boy?
Might he not think he was being spied upon? He would be wrong
— but might he not feel that his independence was being threatened? How to speak to him without bringing up old, baseless, yet
confirmed resentments? He could tell him that he had stopped
there by accident. But was it really by accident? He had known
where Evans was working. The boy himself had written home
telling them. No, it was not by chance that he was there. He had
turned his horse down the Junction road, pretending to stop in to
see the Barrowses nearby, knowing in his heart the Barrowses
would not be home.

The father decided not to indulge himself. Let Evans not know he had seen him. Maybe in later years, when they could sit around with the past under their feet, he would tell him.

Thomas Carlson climbed into his buggy and rode away.

1912. Two years of high school were over. He wanted no more of it.[2] What now? Baggage-smashing? Telegraphy? Farming? A writer on a newspaper?

He had thought once before about becoming a writer. It was after he had read *Martin Eden*. He wrote a novel, a long one, too. It turned out to be almost exactly like *Martin Eden*. He decided then that he'd better wait until he had his own experiences before writing again. And besides, his father had told him that a man had to be a college graduate to become a writer.

Where to now? There was always "Uncle" Orville Kellogg.

Orville and Beth Kellogg lived in Newark, New Jersey. They were not related to the Carlsons. Beth Kellogg, however, was Joetta's oldest friend, and they had exchanged visits during the years. Orville was a civil engineer with the Lackawanna Railroad.

Why not be a civil engineer? the boy asked himself. He could go all around the world engineering, in the open, not in the cities.

Or, if not an engineer, what about going to Annapolis? Join the Navy and see the world. He was still a mite too young, they told him at the Vergennes Post Office.

So be it: it was civil engineering.

Orville Kellogg got him a job as a chainman on a Lackawanna surveying gang, and registered him at a Newark night school. Evans learned surveying, but he stopped going to the school after the first month. With the men on the job, he tried to be as good a man as they were. It worked while they were running transit and line. But once when he bellied up to a bar in West Stroudsburg and tried to prove his manliness by ordering whisky straight, he passed beyond all pretense with the first swallow and found himself walking to East Stroudsburg with a large chunk of ice held to his head by a Lackawanna conductor, and his arm firmly supported by a Pennsy fireman.

[2] This was the extent of Carlson's formal education.

He was sixteen now. He didn't want to be a civil engineer any more, and his thoughts went back to the Navy.

All the military men in his family were on his mother's side. Maybe if he joined the Navy, he might work up to be an Admiral, outranking any Colonel there was, including an Evans Colonel!

He told Orville Kellogg his plan, and Kellogg, who was very persuasive, got the impression that he had talked the idea out of Evans's head.

November 6, 1912. Election Day. Teddy Roosevelt versus Woodrow Wilson versus William Howard Taft.

Evans had never been taken by politics. In New England, politics was a struggle between the Republicans — and the devil. Opinion was too one-sided to be interesting to a boy. But this year, now that he was away from home and with his old hero Teddy Roosevelt running, he followed the campaign in the newspapers and listened to the speakers at the street corners, and now and then wore a T.R. button.

The afternoon of the 6th, he left Newark to go over to New York to stand around Park Row and watch the election returns come in. But all the way in, he kept thinking, today would be a good day to join the Navy.

Near the Hoboken Ferry, he stopped to look into the window of an Army recruiting office. The Army? He hadn't thought much about the Army. The Navy, yes. Annapolis, of course. But not the Army. And yet, why not?

There suddenly came to him a very good reason why the Army, and not the Navy. He knew from his earlier talk with Orville Kellogg that the Kellogg family was opposed to any career but civil engineering. Thus, if he joined the Navy the old boy would know instantly where to look for him. But if he joined the Army?

He studied the recruiting posters in the window: dusty colored pictures of the Philippines, of China, of battalions on parade, of cavalry charges. . . . The cavalry would be bully! Lots of excitement, charging on a great horse with sharp sabre flashing. The cavalry for him!

He entered the office and stepped up to the sergeant at the desk, a huge 250-pounder with an enormous peacetime Army belly.

"I'd like to join up," Evans said. He felt no nervousness. Once he made up his mind, he was confident of himself.

The sergeant smiled. "How old are you, son?"

Evans was prepared for this question, and prepared to tell a white lie, not quite a sin. He was sixteen and a half, and twenty-one was the legal age of enlistment.

"Twenty-two," Evans said. To add a year to the legal requirement would allay suspicion, he thought.

The sergeant looked at him closely. Evans was quite tall for his age — almost six feet. He weighed 150 pounds. If you didn't look too close, you could be brought to believe that he was nineteen or twenty.

"Well, you're of age all right," the sergeant said hurriedly. "What branch do you want to join? Field artillery?" The sergeant was an artilleryman himself, and recruiting in the artillery had been slow.

"Cavalry," Evans said.

The sergeant showed his disgust.

"Cavalry," Evans repeated, a little less affirmatively.

"You're too big and heavy for the cavalry," the sergeant said. "Besides, who wants to be nursemaid for a bunch of moth-eaten ponies? Take a clean job with a future. The field artillery."

"What does the artillery do?"

Out of the desk drawer came a reproduction of a painting. Prancing, shiny, fire-breathing horses pulled a caisson. Evans could almost hear the thunder of the hooves and the rumble of the iron wheels. It was a much better picture than the cavalry charge in the window.

At Fort Slocum up the East River off New Rochelle a young artilleryman went to sleep that night a little sad that Teddy Roosevelt hadn't won, nor Taft. They wouldn't be pleased up in Vermont.

Vermont . . . What were the folks doing tonight? Father would

be through with the chores by this time, and was probably reading
to Mother. Karen and Dana and Tom, Jr., were probably wondering where he was. . . . It would be cold up there now, the ground
brittle with frost, the cows in the barn up the hill behind the house
would be restless, trying to keep warm. And like here, the moon
would be high and bright, and a fellow could almost make out the
Presidential Range by its light, but that was only because he would
know exactly where the mountains lay, and would be able to see
them with his eyes shut.

When Evans didn't return that night, Kellogg, having a sixth
sense about such things as adventurous lads, made a call at the
nearest recruiting office. It happened to be the Army office near
the ferry. Soon after he sent a wire to Tom Carlson up in Peacham.

EVANS ENLISTED U. S. ARMY. UNDERAGE. CAN CANCEL ENLISTMENT. ADVISE.

Orville Kellogg was outraged. To nearly all Americans, in the
years of our peace, the Army was the last refuge of failures and
semi-criminals. If they had known it, they would have agreed with
the Chinese proverb: "As you would not use good iron to make a
nail, so you would not use a good man to make a soldier." Too
many young men who had gotten into trouble in their home towns
were given the choice of six months in jail — or the Army. West
Pointers might be all right, but as for the rest, they were a slag
heap of the back alleys, the bad boys, the misfits.

In Peacham, Joetta Carlson wanted her son home again. It wasn't
a question whether the Army was respectable or not. She wanted
him home again.

But her husband, fighting the dearest wish of his own heart, reminded her that they had agreed to give Evans his head. He
pleaded with her softly, lovingly.

Joetta was silent for a long while.

"What do you want me to say to Orville?" he asked finally.

How to know what to tell Orville? What is right or good?

"Tell Orville we love Evans and believe in him. But tell him to let Evans alone," Joetta said, at last. "The boy has to learn from his mistakes."

6

"I've neglected you"

And so Evans Carlson was a soldier, an artilleryman. Following Emerson's advice he had not postponed life; he was living it. He had made a choice. True, only for the years of his enlistment term. But for those years he would see what there was to see. He was young enough. Let the years and adventures fall where they might. . . .

Adventure, of a sort, fell just two months after his enlistment.

He had said he was twenty-two, and he had to act his age. It was like when he was working as a chainman. His fellow artillery-men were hard-drinking, hot-time-in-the-old-town-tonight boys, and he had to be as good as they were   or at least say so. It was easy enough to talk about mythical hell-raising but the day came when he had to put up or shut up. Frenchie, a Paul Bunyanesque loose liver from Canada, decided to buddy up with Evans on their first leave.

"What do you drink, Carlson?" Frenchie asked when they had made their choice of a saloon.

The boy hesitated. "What're you going to drink, Frenchie?" He'd have to watch his step. Learn what the others did.

"I always drink Irish," Frenchie said.

"Me, too," Evans said.

"Two Irish," Frenchie ordered.

"Straight or with water chaser?" the bartender asked.

"How do you like it, Frenchie?" Evans inquired cautiously.

"Straight. Until I warm up."

"Me, too."

Even before he lifted the glass, Evans's head throbbed uncomfortably in memory of the awful night in West Stroudsburg when one gulp threw him into the sea.

He woke up with a gear-stripped head, a sawmill stomach and boneless legs in a cheap Bowery hotel room, a day over leave!

Overleave! Ruined! Disgraced!

Life fell away from him like swirling top snow before a Vermont twister. . . . He could see the posters: WANTED! Evans Fordyce Carlson, private, U. S. Army, DESERTER . . . The Post Office at Peacham . . . Mother and Dad and the kids ashamed of him . . . The teachers at Peacham Academy saying "I told you so" with the smugness of fed cats.

"Run away," he heard something inside him say. "Face the music," something else said. . . . What would his father want him to do? What would Mother say?

That made his decision easy. He went back and was given a summary court-martial. Verdict: guilty. Sentence: to be fined five dollars.

This was his first and last violation of service regulations. He was through pretending he was more of a man than he was.

The court-martial made a "Christian" of Carlson. He began to look around, to observe, to draw conclusions, to figure the way of making a success of the Army. He noticed, for example, that most of the men in his barracks and battery drank a lot and swore and went whoring and overleave and had piled up lots of guardhouse time . . . They "soldiered" on the job. They had reputations for being unreliable.

Evans made a simple deduction: if he didn't swear or drink or whore or stay overleave or "soldier," soon, without his half trying, they'd say, "Carlson? A good man. A reliable man."

And so he kept his mouth shut, his ears and his eyes open, his record clean. He never spoke to an NCO without being spoken to, and soon old Bob Evans, his First Sergeant, came to think of him as his number one disciple and support.

Now, he became the go-getter, the smart, jump-to-your-feet,

prompt, efficient, think-ahead young man. The Army would be his career. Like banking. He was the keen assistant cashier who would beat off the bank robbers singlehanded, save the gold, get a promotion, marry the boss's daughter — and live happily ever after.

In February 1913 Carlson was ordered to Camp Stotsenberg in the Philippines, and for the next three years he served there and on Corregidor and at Schofield Barracks in Hawaii. During his tour of duty in the Philippines came the scare of war between the United States and Japan over California's anti-alien landownership law. The young fire-eating artillery man eagerly awaited his first combat. But the war scare died away as quickly as it emerged, much to his disappointment.

Carlson had a chance to see Japan and the Japanese for himself when he was transferred from the Philippines to Hawaii. His ship had to go roundabout to Nagasaki for coaling purposes. He spent two days in the city, and although he thought it was quite beautiful, he was shocked by its many streets of whorehouses and by the sight of a human chain of young girls and young mothers, with infants strapped to them, passing heavy baskets of coal from hand to hand from barges below to the open hold of ships above. His seventeen-year-old romanticism made him rebel at this cruel exploitation of women.

At Schofield Barracks his "plan for reliability" worked. He was promoted rapidly from Private to Assistant Sergeant Major — a jump that was rare in a first enlistment in the old regular Army. Captain "Happy" Glassford who was to become a Brigadier General was much impressed with Carlson and wanted to recommend him for a commission. But the "sin" of lying about his age when he enlisted came back to Carlson. Officially he was twenty-five, actually he was only nineteen, and too young to accept a commission. Although he knew the additional money would be helpful back in Peacham, he decided he could not continue to live with the falsehood. A man could enlist with a lie but he could not remain a liar and become a gentleman by an Act of Congress. Carlson confessed to Glassford, and Glassford, acting by the same mores of the military, understood. There would be no question, of course, of re-vealing that Sergeant Carlson had enlisted fraudulently; but then again there would be no question either of the commission. Carlson would have to wait.

Another friend of these days was Jimmy Ulio who was to be-come Adjutant General under George C. Marshall in World War II. Ulio remembers Carlson from those days as a man "of ex-traordinary ability and always a gentleman."

If he had known that then, Carlson would have considered Ulio's opinion about his being a gentleman the highest possible recom-mendation. It would have meant to him then that he was on the way to proving that a Carlson could be as good as an Evans.

While in Hawaii, Carlson's ambition to improve himself made him a very conscientious student. He mastered touch typing and shorthand; he took army correspondence courses in handwriting, administration and tactics. He signed up with the International Correspondence Schools for a course in surveying. Every mail from the mainland brought him college catalogues.

In his letters describing all he was doing, he tried to keep from his father the fact that he was very homesick.

"How is Peacham?" he would ask. "It won't be long before you'll all be wallowing in snow. . . . Tom must be a big boy by now. . . . I've tried to imagine what Karen and Dana look like now, but my imagination has failed me. . . . By the time I get back home, all the fellows that I went to school with will be married and have children. It makes me feel old."

Whenever he thought of Peacham it was as if someone was hit-ting the flesh over his heart, making it black and blue.

"I know that I've neglected you," he wrote his father. "You and the entire family. Still, I am proud of all of you. The whole amount of it is that I have put other people ahead of you, thinking that all of you could wait, while other people would get restless. I am going to be different now and see if I can make up for lost time."

Using the mask of the words "other people," he hoped that his father would see that he really meant himself.

From the admission, he went on, in natural succession, to won-der where he stood with God.

In November 1913, he wrote again to his father. "I am not much of a hand on religion, but you know, Dad, that my views are the same as yours, though I don't get much of a chance to live up to them here. There is a small chapel here but I don't go often."

With his father he was irrevocably honest. Nothing bound them together so tightly as the truth. Carlson, even as a boy, knew that.

"Dad, I think that I am in a position to say that I can now join the church with clear conscience," he wrote in 1915. "You know I always believed in the principles of the church, but somehow I never could bring myself to say truthfully that I could join and practice its teachings. I have been doing a lot of serious thinking in the last year or so and have done my best to live a right life. I have confidence in the future."

The opening of the Panama Canal caused more ripples in the Hawaiian Department than the declaration of war between the Entente and the Allies. The Panama Canal, at least, meant the possibility that the Eastern boys, Evans Carlson included, might be sent directly to an East Coast port when their orders came to return home.

There *was* a kind of a war 10,000 miles away, and some hotheads in the barracks argued one way or another about it, and some wished that we'd get in it quickly, before the glory was faded. But most of the heat in the barracks was expended on protesting, even at a distance, the closing of saloons in Chicago on Sundays. . . .

He did not have the world by the hair when he landed in San Francisco at the end of 1915 to be a civilian again. He had merely eighty dollars, all that he had saved. He was nineteen years old — and only somewhat wiser than when he left home. The Army had neither made nor broken him; it had merely confirmed and deepened what was already in him.

He was sick for Peacham. But he wasn't ready to go back yet. He had nothing to show. He had proved nothing. He would not go back until he had some achievement. Then he would "make up for lost time."

He hadn't the slightest idea of what he was going to achieve.

After a few days in San Francisco he moved down to Los Angeles to get warm. He rented a room near the old Biograph Studios, looked for a job, and had a beer with ex-First Sergeant Bob Evans, who was now a Los Angeles policeman. After a few weeks, his eighty dollars were only ten dollars. It was time to act!

He distrusted big cities, where failure was a cardinal sin and people might not understand a young man just out of the Army who didn't have his mind set on a specific career.

He went into a secondhand book store on Sixth Street, found a map of California, twirled it around a few times with his eyes closed, put his finger on a spot — and looked. Perris. Outside San Bernardino. Population: three hundred people.

Carlson had come to count on luck. Perris had his number on it, else why had his finger picked it out on the map? And Perris was small-town country, out in the open where a fellow might pretend, if he weren't too persnickety, that he was back in Peacham or Shoreham.

Perris, not Peacham, it was. Perris, where awaited him the unexpected and unplanned-for harvest — a job, a wife, and a son.

7

On the map of California

When he was eighteen, Carlson wrote his mother a letter from Hawaii, the substance of which he was to contradict a year and a half later. In matters romantic, this was to be a decided pattern of the future.

It makes me feel old to hear about all those young people at home getting married. Who will be next? I can't see how anyone can get married until they have their future clinched and know where everything is coming from. A man is foolish, anyway, to marry before twenty-five. Of course, some are different, and *circumstances* alter cases.

Carlson himself underlined "circumstances."

The circumstances were these. Perris was a lovely and romantic spot, in a new valley, with a semi-tropical richness and fertility. The San Gabriel Mountains beyond with their white crests of snow brought evenings as cool and as clear as Vermont.

As luck would have it, [he wrote home] my landlord — a Mister Seccombe, is a Christian. This morning he asked me if I'd like to take a ride to a place about five miles from here where he assists at a little Sunday School. Of course I went and I certainly enjoyed it. There were just a handful gathered in the schoolhouse, and they were so in earnest that I was very much impressed. . . . I like this place and I hope that I can locate here and grow up with the country.

But the beauty of the place and the piety of the landlord, though pleasant enough circumstances, were merely the background to his meeting with Mr. Seccombe's daughter, Dorothy. She was not in Perris when he arrived, but in Los Angeles where she was studying singing. She came home at Christmas time. He saw that she was as young as he was, beautiful, clever and resourceful. "And practical, too," he thoughtfully wrote to his mother.

These were all the circumstances of which he was aware. But there were others of which he was not aware.

He had been away from girls like Dorothy Seccombe since leaving home four years before. And during that time he had grown to manhood. In addition, his life had been a kind of wandering, and he had idealized the peace of a home of his own.

"You don't know how much I have longed for a home of my own, mother dear," he wrote after meeting Dorothy. "And children. I guess I am realizing how much home life and affection I have missed by running around, for I simply crave it now."

The craving for affection plus absence from girls plus a youthfully verdant romanticism in which a kiss on the cheek of a respectable young woman meant a commitment for life were the unconscious *circumstances* which brought the summer lightning of young love.

But there was a part of that early letter to his mother — his conviction that a man ought to know "where everything is coming from" — which he tried hard not to contravene. He had no money for marriage, but he worked ceaselessly and frantically to get some. He found a job running a pumping plant for the Hyde Construction Company at Elsinore, California. He started by working on both the day and night shift, training himself to go without sleep except for two half-hour periods between shifts. His pay was thirty cents an hour.

"I've got to get some money ahead," he told Dorothy.

But he couldn't continue. The lack of sleep wore into his flesh like acid. He lost weight and he lost wakefulness. One night the open gears of the pumping machine caught his knee and crushed the bone. But, even while being cared for, he worked thirteen hours a day, and when he felt a little stronger he put in twenty and twenty-two hours. Always, he was driven by "getting a little ahead." A man had to have money to get married. But the days vanished and the hunger of love seemed more debilitating than sleeplessness.

He and Dorothy talked the matter over. All the old rationalization came to their aid: two could accomplish more together than separated. He could go on with his studies to be a civil engineer while she continued with her music. It's foolhardy to marry on little or nothing, but in our case it's different.

They planned to get married in July. Trouble rising over the Mexican Border threatened to change their plans. Pancho Villa and his men, haters of *Yanqui Imperialismo,* came riding like the wind into the town of Columbus, New Mexico, and killed nine civilians and eight troopers of the Thirteenth United States Cavalry. They were chased back with more loss of life on both sides. President Carranza apologized and promised to find Villa and punish him. But this wasn't enough. Brigadier General John J. Pershing and 6000 men crossed into Mexico to punish him themselves.

This was war! The Army Reserve, Carlson figured, might be called up to fight Mexico. The other war? In Europe, now only 6000 miles away? It wasn't likely that *that* war would affect the Reserves?

But *that* war did affect the Reserves, and he got word that he'd be called back to active duty that summer. The excuse was Mexico, but the reason was President Wilson's ultimatum of April 18, 1916 to Germany threatening to sever diplomatic relations unless Germany abandoned her methods of submarine warfare.

Evans Carlson and Dorothy Seccombe were married in May instead of July.

They had not been too quick. On July 15th, Evans Carlson wrote his folks a card from Riverside, California. "I report for duty tomorrow at San Diego. Will let you know address as soon as I get my orders. Dorothy will be at Hotel Harvard here. Love, Evans."

Between his marriage day and July 15th he had to earn a living. He took up his old line of surveying, and laid out parts of Highway 395, from Perris to the San Diego county line.

He loved surveying. Laying out the lines between the hills and over the grades, breaking boundaries, figuring the rise and fall of the land gave him a sense of pioneering. Here would flow a road where none had been before. Here would be towns and villages and churches and schools, woven together by him, his road. And he loved the open country life. He had an eye for its beauties. . . . The Temecula Valley where once the wheat fields of Mission San Luis Rey swung gently in the breezes and flourished under the warm winter sun. And Rainbow, on an upland valley where the road moves upward even higher to Red Mountain and thick, rugged chaparral. Fallbrook, Bonsal, Vista, where the vineyards suck the sun. San Marcos, and Escondido, whose loveliness delighted him and where he swore he would live some day — and did. Escondido, where he would return twenty-seven years later with the wounds of Saipan in him, with the decent wisdom of a life that lay behind and ahead of him like the road he had marked on the map of California.

*   *   *

He was unhappy about going back to the Army. Marriage had brought him contentment, peace for the hungers of his body, and the hopes of a home. But as long as he had to go back, perhaps something might turn up in the Army that would be what he wanted, something that would make him say: Yes, this is it! This is what I am going to do with my life!

"Happy" Glassford, his old friend and now a Regimental Adjutant, did a little talking about a commissioned rank for Sergeant Carlson, but they weren't commissioning married men those days. The Army, for a moment, looked more like a trap than a career.

He was sent to Camp Fort Bliss in El Paso, where he became an instructor to National Guard Artillery outfits, on which he looked with considered disdain, for he was a first-class snob from the regulars.

But he was a good instructor. Anyone could see that. His batteries were shaped up a bit faster than others. Of course, they didn't have the savvy of his old A Battery of the Fifth, but what could he expect of a bunch of militiamen? They were as good as he could make them. And yet . . . yet . . . Why weren't they better? What was the sand in the gears? Was it his fault? No! When it came to his job, he had no quibble or self-doubt. He knew what he knew!

He knew this much: he could get better results from his battery when they knew what they were doing — and why, and what the other fellow was doing — and why. And that all this somehow depended on whether he could get them to work together. But how could he get them to really work together? It was hard. He realized that each man had a kind of sovereignty that he held with stubborn strength — even at the cost of the battery's welfare. Maybe he couldn't make it work. Maybe it was just human nature.

He didn't question further, for in those days he didn't have as much confidence in his ability to handle *ideas* as he had in his ability to handle *things*.

In this intellectual self-doubt Carlson's uncertainty came, in part, from a gigantically inflated conviction that a formal college education kept him from having ideas of worth.

"It is curious," he wrote home at this time, "that during these last months with the militia, I have constantly come in contact with college men from all over the country, and always I have been received as one of them and have held my own. Unless I told them otherwise, they have taken it for granted that I was a college man. . . . It has been a great step towards broadening me."

In the meantime, the war was crossing oceans and moving up on those training camps.

On January 22, 1917, President Wilson made a speech to the Senate calling on the warring powers to make a peace without victory — an offer rejected as vehemently by the Allies as by the Central Powers. On the thirty-first, Germany informed us that she was returning to unrestricted submarine warfare. Three days later, we broke off diplomatic relations. And on March 12 Congress authorized arms to the first American merchant ship.

On the twenty-seventh of March, Evans wrote to his father that the time had come for war. "Our dignity and honor must be preserved. . . . We are better prepared than our enemies think, although the deaths of Admiral Dewey and General Funston will be severely felt." And then, as if the suck of war was already pulling him forever from his home, he added: "If I could only get a glimpse of Vermont again, I would be satisfied . . ." But the soldier in him returned. "What is the feeling in Peacham? Will a company of volunteers be raised in that vicinity?"

Before he received his father's reply, we were at war.

War, to a citizen who becomes a soldier for the duration, means that his life stops. Everything he had prepared for — work, farming, teaching, law, marriage, a family — has to go by the board. But to a Regular Army man, war means that life begins. For what else has he prepared for — but war! For years he has been building houses out of straw. But now the game is over. A real house is to be built — out of combat. With war, he begins to feel he has a function in life.

It was time for orders, for commands, for getting things done.

Line up! 'Bout face! Six-inch guns, rifles, mess, K.P., right shoulder arms. Who cares what you did before, soldier? Who cares what you can do now? You're in the Army, son! Forward 'arch!

To the brass hats of 1917, as to the brass hats of 1941, as to the brass hats of all times and everywhere, a citizen army meant that while citizens composed the Army, the Army was not composed of citizens. All civic interests, responsibilities and duties were packed up and sent home with a man's bundle of civvies.

In June 1917, Carlson became a Second Lieutenant in the Regular Army, assigned as Battalion Adjutant in the 13th Field Artillery. What a difference now! Good chow! Good company! College men! Retirement, if he were disabled, on three-quarter pay. His life had not been wasted, after all.

On September 20, the President made him a First Lieutenant, and ten days later Dorothy made him a father. "Evans Junior. Born at 5:30 A.M. With ten fingers and ten toes, a full crop of hair, and the strength to hold onto his father's finger with the grip of a python," he wrote home.

Up in Peacham they all read the news, or rather Thomas Carlson read it aloud to make the pleasure fuller, if possible. "He has my lower lip and my head. . . . He sure has *my* feet. Big feet!"

Five months later, at Camp Pike, Arkansas, he received his captaincy. . . . "Everything I received I earned," he told Peacham.

The Staff officers had noticed this lanky lad. He was given jobs of responsibility, jobs that made demands on his ability to get on with men. He was, in short, being tested for leadership. And there was no doubt that he passed, for he had the skill of leadership, a skill that is indigenous and cannot be acquired, and comes to a man like an ear for music or an eye for color. He had what the military technicians call "the command presence." This meant that Carlson could give orders clearly, emphatically and resonantly. It meant that his commands had the seed of obedience in them, that when he gave an order he conveyed the impression, at the same time, that he himself was capable of fulfilling it, that the men who obeyed him could do so without feeling humiliated. It meant, ultimately, that he created confidence. It did not mean necessarily he had the love of

his followers. That precious element of leadership unfortunately
was not required in the "command presence."

He began to articulate certain principles of leadership that had
come to him through three years as an enlisted man and a year as
an officer.

He wrote them down in a letter to his father.

> I love my men but I must keep them working. When the
> work is over, I must see that they have some recreation. I must
> always see that they have sufficient food and shelter wherever
> it is possible. I will lead a man, if he will be led. But I'll get
> him where he's got to go, even if I have to drive him. I never
> ask a man to do something I won't do myself. This applies to
> everything from dismounting a gun to riding a bad horse. This
> inspires the confidence of the men. . . . But I must never be-
> come too intimate with the men. That is the downfall of many
> officers. An officer who can mix with his men and show them
> that he does not feel himself above them, but still keeps a cer-
> tain reserve, always holds their respect and loyalty. It is the
> great secret of leadership and requires a great amount of diplo-
> macy. . . . Oh, it's a great game. I would be in no other.

In 1917 Carlson was dealing in the common coin of the American Army, paradoxically modeled in part after the Prussian system.

He was proud, somewhat arrogant, formal, straight-backed, con-
descending to the militia and National Guard and standoffish to the
enlisted men.

Now that the 334th Field Artillery was at Camp Dix en route to
France, he was going home on leave. This was the first time in
seven years. He had left when he was fourteen. He was now a man
of twenty-one, married, with a son. He was a captain in the Regular
Army. He was the prodigal son with the double silver bars.

Unhappily, he would not be returning with Dorothy and Evans,
Jr., to show them off. They had gone back to California.

His father was harder-worked and thinner. His mother, sick —
grayer in her face, small brown mottlings on the back of her hands

he had never noticed before, or had forgotten. And Tommie, last seen scratching worms out of the mud, now in high school, now studious and solid. No one had to worry about Tommie. *He'd* plant his feet in the world soon; he'd know what he wanted. And Karen, beautiful in a way that made him gasp. Tall as he was, looking like him in a way, except that all the masculine boniness of his face was gentle and rounded in hers. But the same eyes, the same laugh — like Dad's. And Dana, eighteen, eager, ambitious, straight as a spruce, a sophomore at Middlebury.

His father gave a special sermon that Sunday at the clean white Congregational Church, standing lean and gentle, looking at his son when he announced the text with a touch of a smile. "In quietness and in confidence shall be your strength." It was his father's favorite. It gave him a chance to speak of neighborliness and mutual respect. "Christianity has not failed; it has never been tried." It was a quote from Henry Ward Beecher, but it wasn't the source that mattered, it was the way his father said the words.

When Evans Carlson said good-by to his mother he asked if she had forgiven him for running away.

"It's all past now, Evans. There's nothing to forgive," she said.

Tom Carlson, tall as his son, with a Viking's laugh that matched his, put his arm around Evans and went down to the depot with him.

Going home was high noon.

8

"I shall go up!"

When Captain Evans Carlson and the 334th Field Artillery of the 87th Division marched off the Cunarder *Mauretania* onto a Liverpool dock the war was coming to an end.

On the 8th of November they were on French trains nearing the shooting. On the 11th, they were still on the trains. Peace had come, the 87th hadn't fought, and the men were disgusted. What the hell do you tell your kids? I fought the last war on a train.

Carlson felt even a keener disappointment. Soldiering was the only career he had; it was his profession, and now life again was empty. How could he tell he was a good soldier unless he had fought? How could he compete at promotion time with those other Regular officers who *had* fought?

Carlson didn't want to leave Europe. He finagled around General Staff Headquarters at Chaumont until, by means of Lieutenant Colonel Jimmy Ulio's helping hand, he was taken on Pershing's staff. His job was to investigate recommendations for the Congressional Medal of Honor. He traveled through the Rhine cities where units of the occupying Third Army were stationed. He had a car, a chauffeur, chocolate bars — and a good time. When he got back to Chaumont, where world history was refracted in the glass of special interests, he studied French, inveighed against the "bloody Bolshies" and pondered the terms of the Versailles Treaty.

President Wilson's luminous and far-seeing Fourteen Points had been obscured for evil by the old imperialistic gangs whose agents wrote the important sections of the treaty. General Smuts of South Africa protested its short-sightedness and illiberality. Ray Stannard Baker, Wilson's confidant and press secretary, thought the treaty was abominable. "Are we not all disappointed to the souls of us," he wrote in his diary.

But Carlson did not see the betrayal. In a letter of May 9, 1919 to his father, he said:

> The conditions of the peace as handed to the Germans yesterday are great. The instrument was admirably drawn up. Most of the Wilsonian idealistic points that were in evidence in the original draft of the League of Nations have been modified, revised and even amputated by the practical Clemenceau to *where they are better able to serve a progressive and practical world*. [Author's italics.]

Word had come to Carlson in late October that Dana was sick with influenza. Before his letter inquiring for more information reached Peacham he received a cable with news of his brother's death. He was stunned.

Carlson's grief exposed with one stroke his deepest need.

"My father, my mother, my brother, my sister," he wrote in the first letter home. "Let us draw our little circle closer together now. We need each other. Life is too short . . ." And added: "I shall never forgive myself for not spending more time with Dana on my leave last summer. I can't forgive myself for all the time we had been separated . . . Do you remember what I said when I was home? I said that Dana had the makings of a great man; that some day he would be heard from in this country of ours. I believed this. He would have been the greatest of us all."

He tried to reassure his father and mother that their loss might not yet be without a gain, as small as it was. He tried to tell them that with Dana's death Karen and Tommie and he would strive even harder to bring them happiness, and that Karen and Tommie, and even possibly he, would succeed.

Although in the years to come Carlson would see deaths intimately, none would match Dana's. He knew for the first time a grief that was guilt and pity and love. "Draw closer together now. . . ." It is the only way, he tried to tell them in Peacham. No one is free of guilt, but let us be proud of our love and pity. It will some day be all that we have left.

In the late fall of 1919 Carlson was ordered back to his "progressive and practical world" after having received a citation for meritorious work from General Pershing and decorations from the French and Italian governments.

Back in California. December 1919. San Francisco. What next? What should he do now?

Staying in the Army with the rank of Captain had many advantages. If he stayed in for thirty years and minded his own business, he would retire on an income which for a Colonel or a General

Officer — a rank he would inevitably reach — was considerable. Perhaps as much as four to five hundred dollars a month. The Army was security. In addition, the Army was a pretty easy life in peacetime. He would move from post to post with his family and all expenses paid; his living wouldn't be too high; and he would have privileges and standing in the community; and the sport of being among men who shared the same code, who spoke the same language, who did the same things. He would travel, meet dignitaries, even have a chance to study. Yes, the Army in peacetime was a safe place, a "better 'ole." But perhaps for that reason he wondered whether it would be good for him. There was something damning about it, something debilitating. His future would be too secure.

This prospect of being tamed, of not having genuine responsibilities, caught in the craw of his ambition. The Army game meant that you never stuck your neck out or initiated anything of importance on your own. Evans Carlson had always enjoyed using his initiative. The Army, as he had known it, did not encourage the use of that talent.

And so he decided to resign. He would try a different life, the competitive world of business where there were no dead certainties and where inventiveness was a capital gain, not a hazard. Behind his choice was perhaps an even stronger reason. To "make good" is strictly an American idiom, and up to our own times, to "make good" meant commercial success.

From the day he ran away from home he had tried to "make good," to return a completely successful man, perhaps a wealthy man able to give his people the security they deserved, and to show them, if possible, that he had done all this on his own. To succeed while maintaining his independence was the formula of his ambition. The Army had not quite given him what he had sought; perhaps business would.

He resigned and took a job as a salesman with the California Packing Corporation. It was the best he could get in the unstable postwar world of 1919–1920 where call money was at 30 per cent and a panic of deflation was creating unemployment, commercial failures and farm bankruptcies.

But he found selling a gray drudgery. If a man needed something and bought it — that was natural. But when a man had to be sold something, the need for which was an artifice, it seemed to Carlson that the transaction was a violation of basic instinct, and a humiliation for both seller and purchaser. Despite this he worked hard at it in the Oakland area, doing well and priming himself with the thought that this was the way everybody must begin, and that he was learning the methods of business. Like many other American businessmen who were eligible, he joined the American Legion, becoming a charter member of the Oakland Post.

About this time he and his wife Dorothy concluded that it would be best for them to part. There had been difficulties from the beginning. Their work and interests had little in common. The war had not given them a real chance to live together. Perhaps most important was Carlson's immature romanticism which made him ill-prepared for the responsibilities of marriage. He felt rebellious under the burden; the marriage had been a mistake for both.

Their separation was decided jointly "without the heat of anger nor under the sting of any alleged injustice. But with discretion, prudence and deep affection," he wrote reassuringly to his father and mother.

He knew he would miss growing up with his son, and he was saddened. He tried to reason that the parting with Evans, Jr. was a necessary sacrifice for a mistake he had made. The thought helped, but it was New England, not the father, that was reasoning.

For two years he sold the fruits of the California Packing Corporation in little villages throughout Texas and Montana. It was open America and he loved the country. But he was not happy.

At Christmas, 1921, business was so poor he didn't have enough money to send home any presents.

His pride was deeply hurt, and when he took his first vacation at the end of 1921 it was no accident that he spent it in the country that had known his father as a youth. It was as if he were seeking redress for his bruises. He went up to the gaunt ghost country around Silver Mountain, and down to the coast to Port Orford, Oregon. He found the old crossroad store where his father had worked, and even a few people who had known him. He walked among the great dark cedars and tried to visualize his father's youth.

The past brought him a feeling of continuity, of coming forth from something, and of growing into something.

In the middle of April 1922, he was at Marshfield, Oregon, a wild and sparsely settled country over which still lingered the bitter and rugged spirit of the old pioneers. He hunted and fished along the rivers and alone with himself in this untouched wilderness he tried consciously to weigh his life and his future.

He had failed; he had drifted; he hated his work; he was getting old. . . . To a New Englander, to Carlson, to grow old without the satisfaction of work and achievement is to die slowly without having lived, for a man must perforce fill his life with work, whether it is a family or a farm. An empty life is a plague of the soul.

"What shall I do?" he asked.

He tramped the trails near Marshfield and tried to find the answer. He walked along the coast and watched the great waves batter against the continent.

He drew up balance sheets, saying he was not for business, nor business for him; that he wanted to go to school somehow and he wanted time to think and write; that the only possibility for him to get what he wanted, now that he was twenty-six and too old and too economically insecure to go to college, was to join the Army again. He re-examined his old arguments against the peacetime Army life, and in the process of examination necessity mothered reasons. He understated the drawbacks and underlined the advantages, and concluded that if he set himself to it, he could get a fine education in the Army without being stunted by its rigidity.

He was unaware, of course, of the extent of his fear, not only of civilian life in general with its indecisiveness, complexities and failures, but also of the anarchy of business life in particular where a man has to be tough in a special and sometimes degrading way in order to succeed.

But there were other elements which went into his decision — basic and unconscious conflicts. As part of Carlson's psychological need, he had erected a structure of self-reliance. He wanted, above all, to be "master of his own fate." It would appear that he was so unsure of himself that he could not bear the thought of anything less than complete self-possession. But what were the other sides of his needs? Despite his eagerness to be his own master, to be commanded only by himself, he still desired to be socially acceptable, to be as good as an Evans, to prove himself, in short, on a social as well as an educational plane. But the heart of his dilemma, being the son of religious people, was Carlson's consciousness of sin. He knew, for example, that he had hurt his mother by running away. No rationalization lightened this thought. A Yankee and the son of a conscientious preacher, he could not escape it, and must suffer for it.

Military life, for the time being, could work toward resolving these unconscious dilemmas. A soldier was subject to discipline — a discipline which might, in the complex workings of a man's psyche, become a kind of atonement for a sin. Yet, with all its order and rigid code and discipline, military life held opportunities. A man with the capacity of leadership could become an officer (acceptable to the Evanses of our world), and, as an officer, make his own decisions and act on them. Within a circumscribed area, an officer could feel a strong sense of self-reliance, especially in battle. This may not be literally true, but there is something in giving orders and having grave responsibilities which implies being a captain of one's own soul.

Carlson decided to go back into the armed services of his country. It was fitting that the decision made him "so happy I'm almost moved to tears." The military was a good way out for him in many respects. If it did not completely resolve the warring within him, at least it would wipe the taste of failure from his lips. The uniform was a quick way of restoring pride. Like the joining of a religious order, becoming a soldier as an act of free will reveals a man's contempt for the confusion and trickery of the outside world.

But there were complications. Some time before the War Department had informed him that he could rejoin the Army, but as a Second Lieutenant. Now, if he accepted the offer, he would be outranked by those of his colleagues who had remained. He was conscious of rank, and he did not want to work under this burden in addition to his already deep sense of failure. The Navy, of course, was out of the question. He had too much experience as a soldier to throw it all away.

Only the Marine Corps was left. It was not merely a question of the Corps being the last choice; rather it seemed to fit, in all respects, his requirements. The Corps was more active than the Army; it was smaller and constantly alerted. Moreover, in the Marines he would be able to get out to China. He wanted strange places and new opportunities. America was Carlson's home town, and to a man who believes he has failed a home town is an intolerable place to live.

And so on April 28, 1922 he resigned from the California Packing Corporation, though they had just offered him a better job, and three days later a letter came to the Reverend Thomas A. Carlson in West Rutland, Vermont, where he had a new parish. The return address was Private Evans F. Carlson USMC, Headquarters, Marine Barracks, Mare Island, California.

> DEAR DAD:
> Well, I'm back — in the service. And believe me, I'm so happy I'm almost moved to tears. Lord, I've fought off the desire to get back into harness but I'd rather be a buck private in the Marines than a Captain of industry. . . . My heart is in the service — and here I must stay. . . . *I shall go up, of course.* Sit steady in the boat and don't worry. *I'm coming out on top.* . . . Hope to get out to *China* soon. . . .

I shall go up . . . I'm coming out on top. He underlined the words. Let them know at home how he felt; let them see that he was still ambitious and still confident, and that he was not going into the Marines just to be a thirty-year man for retirement pay.

He wanted them to know. He wanted them not to share his failure. They must see that he was looking for something that would make his life meaningful, that would bring him peace.

Part Three

1

The shores of an idea

When on an April day in 1922 the Sergeant at the Marine Corps Recruiting Office in Portland, Oregon asked the tall, thin, twenty-six-year-old, good-looking fellow whether he had had any previous military experience, he almost fell out of his chair when he heard him say: "Yes. The Army. Seven years. Captain in the Field Artillery."

"That doesn't make sense," the Sergeant said, and called in the officer-in-charge, Captain James Schwerin, who was nothing if not pleased at the thought of snagging an Army officer. After all, everyone in the whole wide world knew that a Marine Private was the equal of an Army Captain. He gave Carlson the oath, endorsed his enlistment papers and asked him his choice of duty.[1]

"The legation guard in Peking, or a chance at Officers' School, in the order mentioned," Carlson said.

He was sent to Mare Island, and twenty days after his enlistment he was promoted to corporal. That meant Officers' School, for a non-commissioned rank was a prerequisite. On the same day he shot for record on the range, qualifying as an expert in both rifle and pistol.

> How fortunate I am! [he wrote home]. Now all I have to do is to pass my exams for Officers' School. . . . If I pass, I'll be in Washington in the latter part of June. . . . Next Christmas, I

[1] Twenty years later, almost to the day, James Schwerin, then a Lieutenant Colonel, gave the same oath to the author in the Federal Building, Los Angeles.

may be in Vermont with you. That is, if I'm lucky. I'll play this with an ace in the hole — so that I'll not be disappointed if my plans don't turn out as I expect. . . .

He passed the examination.

This whole business of enlisting in the Marine Corps genuinely excited him. It was a new exploit, an adventure that had all the novelty of the old ones, and there was the added fact that being older and wiser in the ways of the service he could enjoy it more. After all, now he was an ex-Captain with ribbons and decorations, and he had seen the world and the wars. He was back in his milieu, in which men and things could be handled with confidence.

The smoke of failure which had filled his lungs had blown away. He saw a future now. The same security which once had seemed to him hampering and restricting now became a goal. It was a joy to walk down the streets in uniform, Marine Corps especially, and know with satisfaction that people would accept you without having to prove yourself. It was all to the good; a man could feel a man again.

When he arrived in Washington the first thing he did was to call on a friend in the Adjutant General's office to see about correcting his age on the records. If he was going to become an officer and go up in the Corps, the original lie had better be expunged. And so it was — with no trouble. They were accustomed to this kind of thing at Headquarters.

But he did not make Christmas home that year, 1922. He spent it studying. There were so many things he had not known about history, geography, trig.

In all his classes at Officers' School Carlson was high in the list, but in the course on military efficiency he was top man. Efficiency had always appealed to him; it was the way you made things work. Up to this time, military efficiency as far as he understood it meant planning and discipline and promptness in the execution of orders. But he sensed that there might be something even more conducive to efficiency than these.

He was required to write a short essay on military efficiency or any allied subject, and it is indicative of his thinking at this time that he chose to call his essay "An Interpretation of Military Ethics." In ethical practice he thought he had found the answer to making men more efficient. He wrote:

> To the great mass of men in the service, military ethics is nothing more than a meaningless term. It is accepted as one of those arbitrary adjuncts to military phraseology . . . which convey no tangible significance. . . . I cannot emphasize too strongly the necessity for a definite understanding of a term which is of such vast import to our profession. . . .

Military ethics, he said, was the adaptation of general ethics or morality, and morality was the consciousness on the part of men to strive for the welfare of society as a whole. This meant that society had a code of rules, and that the individual must subordinate his interests wherever they came in conflict with the code. . . . In the military life, the same thing applied. Through custom and the experience of tried leaders, rules were set down. These rules, like saluting and the prompt and precise execution of orders, had to obtain over anyone's personal desires in order "to achieve the welfare of the whole and the efficiency of the fighting machine."

Although the twenty-six-year-old officer candidate accepted the tradition and did not push back the dark frontiers of the "code" by even a question, in this essay he brought an old truth into a new situation.

"Are you honest with yourselves at all times?" he asked his fellow officer candidates. "Do you adhere as rigidly to the code when you are alone as when you are under observation? These are moral obligations." It was refreshing to say so, it was refreshing enough for some of the officers to begin thinking of Carlson as a maverick. He tried to show that by accepting these moral obligations, officers "became more competent moral agents." And that, in turn, would increase their own efficiency as well as the efficiency of the men whom they led.

He was still barely touching the shores of an idea. His experience had been too limited to strike out beyond. All he knew was that at Camp Fort Bliss the training of his batteries had suffered somehow by the seeming incapacity of men to genuinely sacrifice their interests to the whole.

He could quote Polonius's advice from reveille to taps, but still it did not help him know how to make men act on the advice.

On December 23, 1922, he was commissioned a second lieutenant, on probation for two years, and ordered to Quantico to join the Fifth Marine Regiment.

The Marine is a very special animal; and he lives in a very special world. In numbers, the Corps is the minority of our armed services, limited by law to 20 per cent of Navy strength. During the pre-Pearl Harbor peace it was never larger than a large Army division — about 18,000 men and officers. Being conscious of its small size and constantly harassed by the Army and Navy, the Marine Corps is guilty of everything ever falsely charged against any minority. In defense of its existence it appears to be boastful, loud, arrogant, proud, energetic, clannish, hyper-sensitive — and sentimental. It knows all the pains of the minority, including the horror of feeling that extinction (by Congress) is just around the corner. For this reason it never forgets its history and waves it endlessly in the faces of its private enemies and public admirers.

It is no accident that so many men and officers in the Corps are from the South. Where else could the grandsons of a people still sensitive to defeat feel more at home than in an organization which by tradition, practice and psychology considers itself the elite soldiers of our nation? No other branch of service is so helpful to a man who, like Carlson, suffered from a sense of inferiority.

A Marine, like a Jew, has to be doubly good to succeed. This makes smarter peacetime soldiers, better wartime fighters, greater casualties in battle than absolutely necessary, and quicker and more decisive victories.

And so when Evans Carlson reported in to Quantico, the heartland of the Corps, he was entering the brotherhood of the elite as well as a community of a military peacetime post.

Life at Quantico in peacetime was life devoted to eating of the lotus. The hours were short, the duties light, week ends long; and polo, hunting, boating and other kingly sports were commonplace. It was, in short, a country club village in uniform.

In this "village" there was no economic competition, for everyone's basic income was fixed by law. It was a community where all differences of opinion were throttled by mutual consent, where people lived and worked by the unspoken code that no officer talked politics, past or present or future, and no officer commented on the ability or lack of ability of his fellow officers. Domestic problems which, in this tight and almost incestuous world, were an open secret were never referred to in public. If Colonel So-and-So's lady was a drunkard, no one mentioned it. If the Colonel himself had to be carried home from every party, his bearers followed the code so rigidly that though they might perform the rites twice a week for a year, they never mentioned it to the Colonel and rarely among themselves.

In this world no officer could do for himself as much as his wife could do for him. It was strictly a woman's job to strive for her husband's career. It was expected of her. At sewing, tea or bridge the millrace of gossip flowed through the room, and it was up to each woman to extract the nuggets which would be most useful to her man. If an officer wanted to get some information to his chief, he transmitted it to him through the parlor magic of a bridge game where wives were free of the burden of being "gentlemen."

Though wives were rivals when it came to fighting for their husbands' careers, an instant unity possessed them whenever one of their circle had her domestic security threatened by another woman. The group moved in, as if by command, to isolate the offender, even punish her by severe ostracism if she was available; and if she was not, they worked on their husbands to see that the erring husband was transferred to some other post out of Delilah's range.

The only meaning this tightly woven, almost matriarchal society had for Carlson was to give him the understanding that if he married again he must find not only a wife with whom he could be in love, but also one whose personality made it possible to live and thrive in this most exacting and unique tribe.

And so, after graduation, he went "society"; he did what was ex-

pected of him, though he went into debt for it. He bought all kinds
and varieties of uniforms, khaki, white, green, blue, dress, undress,
garrison, field, riding. He made his protocol calls, joined the Army
and Navy Club in Washington, attended horse shows and dances,
squired the Colonel's daughters, sent flowers, went fox-hunting in
Virginia, played polo in Chevy Chase and attended church.

Everyone was impressed with Lieutenant Carlson. He was clear-
skinned, handsome and gracious with the ladies. He had a courtier's
manner. His social tasks were fulfilled with cheerfulness and
efficiency. He was a gentleman as well as a fine officer, a perfect
extra man for the girl coming down to visit her aunt and uncle for
the week end.

During the years at Quantico and later in Puerto Rico, in Nicaragua and China — in short, during the fifteen years between 1922
and 1937 — Carlson was "regular." He did his work "by the book,"
and apart from an extraordinary conscientiousness in line of duty,
he was indistinguishable on the surface from other ambitious Marine
officers who tried hard to keep their record clean in order to end
up with a Colonel's eagle or a General's star.

Even the temporary reputation he won as a maverick with his
essay on military ethics was quickly dissipated.

But beneath the surface of this "regularity" he was restlessly searching for something: to make his life meaningful and, without his
being aware of it, as significant as his father's. His pride resisted
acknowledging even to himself that he was unhappy, and his reserve stopped him from confiding in others.

And yet, at times, shapeless impulses would seize him, and he
would look at his life with dissatisfaction as he had done at Port
Orford. After such self-examinations, he usually took some step
which he hoped would change his life and would bring him closer
to what he was seeking.

Such a time came again during the Marine winter maneuvers in
Puerto Rico in 1924.

At a tea dance at the Hotel Miramar, where he went to give the
girls a once-over and to ask the prettiest for a dance, he met his
second wife.

Etelle Sawyer was in Puerto Rico on what was to be known much later as "good neighbor" business. A graduate of the University of Maine and Wellesley, she taught Spanish and Latin in a Massachusetts school and English in the high school at Fajardo, Puerto Rico. In 1923, Mrs. Herbert Hoover asked her to help organize the Puerto Rican girl scouts.

Etelle Sawyer liked Carlson from the start. He had almost an old-fashioned courtliness and a way of listening to her that made her feel that he was deeply concerned with her opinions. His earnestness which was his most outstanding characteristic was lightened frequently by a rich humor. And, of course, he was very handsome, she thought. Tall and erect without being stiffly military; a clear skin and blue eyes. His long nose and long chin of which he was somewhat self-conscious, she thought, gave his face great strength. She knew that he would be very attractive to women — as he was — not only because of his appearance and thoughtfulness but also because of his quiet competence which made her feel that he knew what he wanted out of life and would get it.

"I could tell this about him," she said in later years, "the way I can tell that black is black and white is white. You just had to talk to him five minutes, or look at him, and you saw it."

They danced and had some tea, and he asked if he might see her again. When she hesitated, he told her that he had been commissioned to write some articles for the San Juan *El Tiempo* and would need help with his grammar.

She agreed to help him.

Etelle Sawyer was more to Carlson than a source of grammar. She was charming and very attractive. Tall, with dark-reddish hair, warm and friendly eyes, she carried herself with grace and dignity. He thought of her as not only a woman who would be a fine wife, but someone who could move through the strange waters of the Marine Corps life, understand it, and know how to live by the "code."

He met her in the end of January 1924, and by the middle of February, fleet maneuvers and all, he was able to write home that they were in love with each other and were going to marry.

With Etelle Sawyer, Carlson felt he stood a better chance of making a success of marriage. This was not a summer-lightning romance. They were both mature people, equally admiring and respectful of each other; she of his earnest and humane love of life and adventure, he of her independence, her education, her wit and ease with people. She relieved his sense of inferiority at being self-taught; he brought excitement into a schoolteacher's life.

"I took her over to Headquarters at Culebra Island yesterday," he wrote his mother. "In fifteen minutes every officer, from the General down, was her humble servant. And the beauty of it is that she is entirely unaffected. . . . The date of the wedding will be set when I know what is to become of me this summer. It might be June, and we might spend our honeymoon in Vermont. How would you all like that? . . . Tell Karen that Etelle is a Pi Beta Phi. I am so anxious for you to love her."

For this, his mother was more important than his father, for he knew that she was skeptical of the stability of his emotional life. His divorce from Dorothy had hurt Joetta. It had seemed so unnecessary. But then, too, the marriage had seemed unnecessary. Joetta had a hard time believing that her son had grown up. It was as if she were still sitting on the couch in the parlor of their Dracut house waiting for the footstep.

As the special correspondent to *El Tiempo* Evans Carlson, under his pseudonym "Incognito," had the pleasure of seeing his lengthy analysis of the sham battle given four columns on the front page. His report is interesting in the space he devoted to the use of air power. He showed how the defenders of Culebra Island not only had successfully "bombed" the ships of the attacking fleet, but had also drawn off the protecting Voights from the aircraft carrier *Langley,* leaving the fleet naked of air defense against a flight of Marine planes which attacked from another direction.

In 1924, only a few somewhat unpopular officers spoke their piece out loud about the strategic use of the air. Brigadier General Billy Mitchell was fomenting revolution of a sort in the War Department. The Army and Navy together had but 800 planes, compared to

France's 1250. Our entire air personnel was one-half that of France.

But as a result of what he saw on Culebra Island, Carlson immediately put in for transfer to Pensacola Naval Air Station for training as a Marine flyer.

> My main reason for desiring aviation training [he told his father in a letter of March 1924], is the fact that the day is not far hence when this branch of the service will be the dominating factor of all wars. The man who knows aviation *and* possesses a knowledge of the other branches is the man who is coming into his own. I want that knowledge. Moreover, for the first time in my life I have a mature desire to fly. I have confidence in my ability and I have a "hunch" that it's the time to get the training. My "hunches" are always good ones. I had a "hunch" when I was down in the Port Orford country that it was time for me to get back into the service. And it wasn't a minute too soon. It's the same for aviation. . . .

Carlson returned to Quantico, and Etelle Sawyer reported to Mrs. Hoover in Washington just an hour away. The Richmond, Fredericksburg and Potomac Railroad from Quantico to Washington had a steady customer, or rather a hardy customer, for only love could impel a man to make the trip daily on the dullest, dirtiest, most inefficient trackage in America. Any old Quantico Marine will confirm that.

At a little South Portland church, they were married on April 29, 1924. Joetta Carlson was ailing and neither she nor her husband could make the wedding.

They drove to West Rutland for their honeymoon and stayed with Carlson's parents. On a wave of sentiment, Carlson drove his new wife to Peacham, Shoreham, Vergennes and New Haven Junction to have her see where he had lived and gone to school and worked and played.

Back in Quantico, of course, parties were given for the Carlsons, for in this manner the matriarchate could make up its collective mind about the new member. Etelle Carlson was acceptable. She knew the language, and enjoyed the "code." There was no more that could be asked of her.

Carlson looked around him. His life seemed good. Perhaps he would find himself in the Marine Air Corps.

2

Beyond the seas

He worked hard at Pensacola, and passed the five-hour check, then the twenty-five hour check was down on the books, and he felt fine. The time came for him to make his stunt check on the H-type plane. His check pilot was a Navy man; his instructor had been a Marine. Their methods did not agree. He flunked his test and was busted out.

Furious at what he considered an injustice, he would have protested, but he realized that to do so would embarrass the Marine Corps. It wouldn't be quite "code." Thereupon, he asked the Aviation Board for permission to join a new class and start again from the beginning. The request was denied him on the grounds that it was "contrary to the policy of the Bureau of Aeronautics to re-detail for a course of instruction at Pensacola any officer who has once failed in flying."

"Failure," he wrote his father, "is hard to take gracefully. But perhaps it was my destiny not to fly. Where to now? The wide world is a prospective station."

This was June 1925. The half-year preceding was eventful. Trotsky had been expelled from Soviet power, King Boris of Bulgaria just missed being assassinated, Hindenburg was elected President of the Third Reich, the Kapp putschists and the German industrialists were working to overthrow the Weimar Republic. In China there were continued attacks on foreign imperialists by people who called themselves Nationalists and who were, according to old China hands, connected somehow with the "disreputable" revolutionist, Sun Yat-sen.

Again, Carlson requested the Major General Commandant of the Marine Corps to assign him to duty with the American Lega- tion in Peking. This was the second time he had put in for China. Each request followed a period in which he felt that he had failed. First, when he had joined the Marine Corps, and now when he was busted out of Pensacola.

He had a hunch that perhaps China would give him what he was looking for.

But "destiny" and Headquarters were slow to act. From Pensacola, Carlson was ordered to Hampton Roads, Virginia; and from there on the old transport U.S.S. *Vega* to San Diego to command a rifle company of the Fourth Regiment. It was here he started to read, to educate himself in the world outside of the Marine Corps.

At first he read authors that gave a critical and a rebellious view of America: Upton Sinclair, Theodore Dreiser and Sinclair Lewis. Then he read a biography of Walt Whitman by Cameron Rogers, and turned for the first time in his life to *Leaves of Grass*. What a continent it opened to him! Night after night he would read aloud the long rolling lines of poetry in his house at San Diego.

From Whitman, he went to Carl Sandburg's *Abraham Lincoln*. He moved from the criticism of our life in Dreiser and Lewis to its affirmation in Lincoln and Whitman.

In the fall of 1926 Carlson had a brief tour of duty at Portland, Oregon, in command of a detachment ordered to guard the United States mails. Brigadier General Smedley D. Butler, who commanded the Western Mail Guard, when asked by a reporter of the Portland *Telegram* the reason the Marine Corps was so popular, replied: "It's because we've a lot of officers like Carlson who take care of their men." Butler had always liked Carlson. Once in a letter to him he wrote: —

> You always do the right thing, and it is one of the mis- fortunes of this wretched system of promotion we have that you are only a lieutenant. Only wish I could make you a Major.

Most excellent reports of your detachment continue to come
in here, and I want to congratulate you again and thank you
for your fine work. You are a "hell" of a fine officer.

On January 8, 1927, Carlson was ordered to leave Portland and
to proceed immediately to San Diego for duty with an expeditionary
force being organized there. When he arrived he found that Major
A. A. Vandegrift had been designated by General Butler to organize
a special battalion for service in Nicaragua. Vandegrift selected his
own staff and he had chosen Carlson to be his operations and training officer.

But after a few days Vandegrift's battalion had its orders cancelled.

The men and officers griped like hell. It was all "Nervous Nellie's"
fault. That damned Kellogg! He let the damned pacifists and anti-
imperialist Wobblies, Bolshies and Do-Goodies talk him out of it.

In San Diego the stew boiled among Carlson and his friends and
brother officers in the Regiment, among Vandegrift, Roy Hunt, Jim
Underhill, "Johnnie" Clement, Tommy Watson, Harry Liversedge
and Irv Odgers. They were all about his age, though some had been
in the Corps much longer. As the years went on, they would all go
up together; among them would be Colonels, Generals, and even
a Commandant; they would one day together sweat and fight on
Guadalcanal and Saipan.

On January 31 secret orders arrived. The Fourth Regiment, under
the command of Colonel Charles S. Hill, was to leave for "special
temporary duty beyond the seas" aboard the U.S.S. *Chaumont.*

"We're leaving soon," Carlson said to his wife.

"Nicaragua?"

He smiled and shook his head.

"China?"

"The orders are secret," he said with a smile. "I can't tell you."

"Where else in the world do they send Marines?" she asked. "If
it isn't Nicaragua, it's China."

3

That bloody Shanghai night

According to the Marines, everyone but a few "milky-mouthed
pacifists and radicals" seemed to take for granted that the Marines
belonged in China. The popular barracks ideas went something like
this:

"The Chinks are an ignorant people and they get very violent.
Well, some guy named Sun Yat-sen started a revolution against the
Government. Maybe he started it years ago, maybe he just started
it, but at any rate, these damned revolutionists are the same as the
Russian Reds, and they're trying to kick out of China all the missionaries and the people from the Standard Oil Company who have
been China's best friends. Well, they're Americans! And they're
being threatened and killed and raped. It's just horse sense to send
us in to protect American lives and property. Anyway, we got to
keep the Chinks from turning Red."

Our official policy in those days differed from the conception of
the average American and Marine only in that it was composed in
language that exceeded it in elegance. The State Department, of
course, knew much more than the citizen; it knew with precision
that Sun Yat-sen had started his revolt against the corrupt Manchu
Empire in 1911. It knew that we, in co-operation with the other great
powers, particularly Great Britain, had not only refused Sun Yat-sen
help but had, in 1923, deprived him of any possibility of success by
refusing to turn over to him the customs of the South China ports
which we controlled by treaty with the Manchus. Our government
knew most definitely that Sun Yat-sen, his People's Government
and his Kuomintang or Nationalist Party, isolated for years in
Canton, intrigued against by England, France and the United States
in cahoots with the Manchu war lords, harassed and bullied by the
warships that moved freely up and down the great rivers of China,

had only one great friend in the world — the Soviet Union. The Chinese people, apart from the war lords and their mercenaries, turned to this friend with hosannas. Sun Yat-sen soon had what no one else in the world would give him in his fight against feudalism and corruption — military advisers, arms and money.

These were the facts: our wise men knew them, but instead of sending our official Lafayettes and our von Steubens to help the Chinese Revolution, we sent our Hessians, for by 1927 our own revolutionary spirit had become encrusted with the false complacence of rising prices in Wall Street. We who should have been the first to support Sun Yat-sen and his people's movement, were the most eager to see it fail, for oddly enough, we distrusted the full implications of democracy everywhere, including our own country.

There were, of course, unofficial Lafayettes in China. Theirs, the bravest history of our time, is recorded in Vincent Sheean's *Personal History,* André Malraux's *Man's Fate* and in *China's Millions* by Anna Louise Strong. But in the deaf minds of their own countries they were dishonored prophets whose lives were not eagerly protected by American consuls and whose property, chiefly ideas, were better destroyed than saved.

When Carlson and his fellow officers and men embarked on the *Chaumont* for "duty beyond the seas" they looked forward to a war against a rabble. If they did any reading or studying on China it was along the lines of a memorandum which had been circulated by official permission through the Fleet.[2] It was written by a Lieutenant Stanley A. Jones of the U.S.S. *Cincinnati* as a kind of pioneering effort in political orientation of the Armed Service. It was addressed to the crew.

Lieutenant Jones asked and answered six questions. Between the questions and answers were many pages of official argument, citations of treaties and apologia, the sum of which is this: (1) American citizens were in China to engage in legitimate trade by rights of treaty, and (2) while we would accept the right of the Chinese

---

[2] The full text may be read in *The Dragon Stirs,* by Henry Francis Misselwitz, correspondent of the *New York Times.* Published by Harbinger House, 1931.

to rebel against their government we "should at least protect American citizens . . . representatives of commercial interests . . . against the laws of a country where the loss of a human life is not often recorded." (3) If China thinks our treaties, which give us rights which no foreigner has in our own country, are unequal and unjust, let her remember her barbaric past and her national indebtedness of one billion dollars. (4) All the great powers in Europe and the United States and Japan are determined to see that their foreign settlements in Shanghai which were granted to them by treaty shall remain unmolested against "the war lords, Chiang Kai-shek, etc. . . . (who) are often disloyal and will fight for anyone who is able to pay them." (5) Only Red Russia is aiding the Chinese people in their present stand, "trying to drag China down to her own level." (6) And, finally, "the Chinese are not capable of governing themselves."

Lieutenant Jones's answers were what Carlson and his fellow Marines believed about China in 1927. They had no thought of a people's aspiration toward self-government, nor of a nation's dream of independence from foreign interference. China, to them, was a vast area of mob violence to which the Marines had come by the grace of God to establish law and order.

The U.S.S. *Chaumont* with two battalions of the Fourth Marine Regiment aboard, moved slowly up the Whangpoo off Shanghai on the morning of February 24, 1927. Its captain's orders were to anchor off the Standard Oil docks, and stay there. Marine Colonel Hill and his men who were eager to get down to business "taming the wily Chinese" got the blue word that they were to remain aboard. They felt no less depressed when daily for the following three weeks they disembarked at the Standard Oil docks for close order drill on the Standard Oil golf course and returned to the ship. It looked for a while as if they had sailed seven thousand miles to drill on the clipped greens of an oil company country club.

All around them the Whangpoo was filled with life and excitement. Foreign battleships rode smugly as far as the eye could reach. Transports, destroyers, patrol boats flew the flags of twenty nations. British Tommies, Jap and French Marines were being landed every day. They would be getting all the fun. And fun there was, not merely in the Club of Night on Szechuan Road and at the Trocadero on Range Road which the "old China hands" among the enlisted Marines described in rich and seductive language, but also in the enticing sound of the guns which came like mountain thunder across the greasy water from the battles being fought about twenty miles away between the Cantonese People's Army and the Northern Army of the Mandarin war lords.

The days went by slowly, exasperatingly. China lay off the starboard quarter a hundred yards away, but it could have been a million miles away. When the men of the Third Battalion asked Carlson, their Operations Officer, what the hell it was all about, he could tell them nothing.

Even more frustrated than his men, he spent many hours on the deck of the *Chaumont* gazing inland at China, at the International Settlement, "the political ulcer on the face of China" as John Gunther was to call it. The modern gleaming white buildings, hotels and clubs where none but occidentals could enter rose from the China soil like a mélange of San Francisco, Paris and London. But beyond, in the plains and gorges where the broad Yangtze flowed southward out of the heartland, was a China so vast and alien, so untouched and incomprehensible that, as he had dreamed, it appeared the final valley of adventure for him. He was thirty-one, and there was China . . .

On March 5 the Fourth Regiment was ordered ashore to make a demonstration march through the International Settlement. It was a custom of the Shanghai Defense Force, consisting of the troops of Great Britain, Italy, Holland, Spain, Portugal, Japan and the United States to parade through the streets of Shanghai and the International Settlement in order to impress the Chinese with the strength and efficiency of the foreign forces. On the 5th of March the turn of the Marines had come. In the tugs of the Dollar Line, they landed at the Customs Jetty adjacent to the business district and marched up Nanking Road. Tin hats, rifles and machine guns glistening in the sun, they paraded smartly by the cheering foreign residents and the silent Chinese who, no matter what politics they followed, watched this display of foreign force with clear hate.

The streets reminded Carlson of the Western Front; the sandbags, the machine-gun nests, the barbed-wire entanglements, the faces and uniforms of strange allies; British Sikhs, French Annamites, Italian, Japanese, French, Portuguese Marines, British Tommies.

His first impression of China was people and smell. The streets were crowded with Chinese, moving each on the heels of the other like the senseless, purposeless threshing about of fingerling trout in a breeding pool.

And then the smell! It came from the stagnant creeks and canals whose water lay under a greasy silk of scum. It came from stale, dead and drying fish, the bitter coal smoke from the docks, the sourness of decaying and unburied human flesh. The smell had an impact and a dimension as tangible as the endless crowds of people.

He was a little frightened of China when he first saw her that day. China was too big; there were too many people, all anonymous. How could he ever get to know them, or even get to know one well enough to tell him apart from his brothers? Their language, dress, habits of life stretched in front of him like the Chinese Wall. Could he ever breach the wall?

On the night of March 20, while Carlson looked at the lights of Shanghai from the *Chaumont's* deck, history was happening near by, behind his back; history that would, ten years later, almost to the day, prove that one hunch was at least correct, that China would end his search.

That night a full moon softened the hard lines of the men-of-war astride the Whangpoo, and even brought a softness to the white modern buildings in the International Settlement. Tension among the foreigners relaxed in the waltzes from the Shanghai dance floors and in the Shanghai bars where conversation ran hopefully.

"Hadn't the Reds at Hankow ordered Chiang Kai-shek to steer clear of Shanghai and head for Peking?"

"Whatever else you say of Galen and Borodin, the Bolshies who were doing all the advising for the Kuomintang, they know what side their bread is buttered on. A move into Shanghai would mean a war against Britain and the States. . . . Look at all our ships out there. . . . They'd have to eat out of our hands."

But General Chiang Kai-shek, who had earlier decided that the Revolution was becoming too revolutionary, disregarded the orders from his Nationalist Government to move for Peking, and gave the word instead to advance against Shanghai.

Across the newly green meadow lands shining in the moonlight, the dissident Chiang Kai-shek Kuomintang troops moved against the city, in whose streets, in air that was warm with Spring, detachments of 600,000 striking Shanghai workers were capturing points of resistance held by the defending troops of the Northern war lords. Guerrilla warfare shattered the silent alleys, dark clusters of nervous buildings were fretfully illumined by the flash of rifles. By morning, when Chiang Kai-shek's advance guard entered the city, there were few defenders to bar its way.

"It was the work of laborers that conquered the city," the German, Gustav Amann, wrote in the first documented eye-witness report.[3]

By early Monday morning the people of Shanghai had won their city.

And on that morning a second demonstration Marine Corps march was scheduled. They took off as they did before in a bright and sunny morning, down to the Customs Jetty, up Nanking Road, past more silent Chinese faces and the gaudy posters being carried by some of the 600,000 striking Shanghai workers. They noticed a number of Cantonese blue flags flying over store fronts where once had flown the ensign of the war lords. The streets had a tension like a gigantic wound-up watchspring. At the end of the march, as the regiment started back to the ship, excited rumors went through the ranks as sounds of gunfire from the outskirts of the city came to them. However, the regiment boarded the tugs and

[3] His book, *The Legacy of Sun Yat-sen* (Montreal: Louis Carrier, 1929) incidentally contains an introduction by Karl Haushofer, the famous geopolitician, who saw clearly the intimate connection between the Chinese fight for liberation and the "woes and throes of central Europe."

returned to the *Chaumont*. Fifteen minutes later, orders came to land again and to take up the defense of areas previously assigned by the Shanghai Defense Council. The Cantonese had arrived; the Reds were on the march; the lives and property of American citizens were being threatened.

It is true that the International Settlement was endangered, but not so much by the Kuomintang troops as by the anti-imperialist spirit of its whole Chinese population, who were rebelling against the unjust special rights given to foreigners.

The Marines moved into position in support of the British Durhams at Soochow Creek alongside the Bund and at the northern borders of the International Settlement. Ahead of them, a half mile away, was the North Station where sharp fighting was still going on between the advancing Kuomintang and some White Russians who had commandeered an armored train and were fighting with the despairing fury of men whose hatred of Communists was greater than their love of life. From houses on the other side of the creek, blue rags hung — the color of the Nationalist flag — and vertical banners with Chinese characters painted on them, saying:

A TWELVE-HOUR DAY . . . NO MORE EMPLOYMENT OF CHILDREN UNDER EIGHT . . . RIGHT TO SIT DOWN FOR WOMEN WORKERS . . .

"I spent Monday, Tuesday and Wednesday nights in the lines," he wrote home on the 24th, "and crawled around the outskirts of the Settlement during the day. . . . I want to know what's going on."

On the 24th, word came to Shanghai of the capture of Nanking by the Nationalist troops and the killing of one American and two Britishers. Three United States men-of-war fired on Nanking in reprisal, and everybody in Shanghai was talking of moving up to Nanking to wipe out the "bloody Chinks" in revenge against the "outrage." [4]

---

[4] Compare this "outrage" with the one committed by the Japanese in 1937 when 42,000 Chinese in Nanking were murdered and the U.S.S. *Panay* sunk. We made a verbal and ineffectual protest and continued to ship Japan the war material she needed for her Chinese war.

Suddenly, for days everything became quiet in Shanghai. The Marines and their Allies continued to stare across the open barbed wire at the resentful faces of the Cantonese, but neither Chiang Kai-shek's soldiers nor the Chinese civilians made any attempts to move into the Settlement. Occasionally, Carlson was ordered to lead a detail of men in a raid on Chinese residences in order "to confiscate arms and inflammatory literature." But there wasn't much trouble at all. In fact, the eager Marine bullets were not used, nor were the "nickel-plated bayonets, the flash of which has a decided moral effect on a mob," as Carlson triumphantly described it in a letter. . . . It looked very much as if Carlson was about to miss another war.

> However, we are watching with extreme interest [he wrote on April 9th] the situation in the North. The raiding of the Soviet Consulate at Peking may cause some trouble. England is undoubtedly only looking for a good excuse to declare war on the Moscow Government. Japan would welcome war with the Soviets. And I wouldn't be at all surprised if the Washington government wouldn't grasp the opportunity to wipe the Bolshevists off the map, once for all. Well, we're here for the job.

As he wrote this letter he heard from the streets below Marines sing a parody of the Marine Hymn:

> From the dance halls of old Shanghai
> To the walls of old Nanking,
> We've met all kinds of women
> And we've met all kinds of men.
> If the Tommies and the Fourth Marines
> Ever join in fight again,
> It'll be good-by to old Chiang Kai-shek
> And to hell with Borodin.

The raid on the Soviet Consulate was only one of the signs of what was to come. As is inevitable in all revolutions, the moment of victory is the moment, in Vincent Sheean's words, when those "who wished to change the conditions of life, and not simply the forms or names of governments," come into conflict with "those who took part in the revolution for their own advantage or were prevented by the tenacity of middle-class ideas from wishing to disturb the established arrangement of wealth." [5]

In every revolution there are always betrayers and compromisers: Caesar, Napoleon, Hamilton, Kerensky, Scheidemann and Chiang Kai-shek. Some of these men compromising, not only with the *status quo* but with the revolution as well, as did Hamilton, live on, not in infamy but as founding fathers. Others, like the German Scheidemann and Chiang Kai-shek, remained in power in an atmosphere of disunity where civil war and fratricide were part of the air their country breathed.

And so, at the moment of victory against the militaristic corrupters of China, the Kuomintang split into two sections. The right wing led by Chiang Kai-shek, encouraged by foreign applause at the raid on the Soviet Consulate in Peking, had among its patrons the Shanghai and Nanking bankers who, according to Vincent Sheean, arranged a $30,000,000 loan for Chiang Kai-shek, providing he fought the Reds.

The left wing, with its headquarters in Hankow, was supported by the Communists, trade-unionists, many liberals and Kuomintang soldiers, and by Madame Sun Yat-sen, the widow of the great man of China. She opposed Chiang Kai-shek and his new advisers because they had "turned the maxims of Sun Yat-sen into their opposite; whereby the revolutionary regime had ceased to be revolutionary and had become the organ which, under the banner of the revolution, restored the very order of society which the great innovator Sun Yat-sen had gone forward to change." [6]

It is hardly speculation to say that this split and the subsequent entrenchment of Chiang Kai-shek determined, in large part, the history of the next twenty years not only of China but of the world. The failure of the Chinese Revolution of Sun Yat-sen who made a principle of intimate relations with the U.S.S.R. and collaboration with the Chinese Communists meant that Russia's isolation from the world became intensified. This, in turn, helped increase the

[5] *Personal History*, Doubleday, 1935.
[6] Gustave Amann: *The Legacy of Sun Yat-sen.*

mutual suspicions between the U.S.S.R. and the capitalist West, and
gave rise to the West's support of German Fascism and Japanese
militarism as part of a *cordon sanitaire* against Russia. Out of it
came the Munich appeasement, the Nazi-Soviet non-aggression pact
of 1939, the attack on Pearl Harbor — and the second of the great
world wars.

"Perhaps it is historically true," J. M. Keynes wrote, "that no order
of society ever perishes save by its own hand." To the short-sighted
and self-destructive European and American worlds, Chiang Kai-
shek's "compromise" brought enormous relief.

With Shanghai, $30,000,000 in Chinese currency in his hands, and
a government at Hankow in the process of disowning him, Chiang
Kai-shek began to uproot the forces under his feet who opposed
him by remaining loyal to the National Government. His spies,
police and troops were ordered to destroy all opposition within
Shanghai, the same men and women who had made it possible for
him to take the city.

"The job was done with bloody thoroughness," writes Robert
Berkov, Manager of the Shanghai Bureau of the Associated Press
in his biography of Chiang Kai-shek. "Thousands of workers were
shot, hundreds of intellectuals. Approximately fifteen hundred were
wounded. . . . Victims were beheaded as well as shot. . . . The
drive claimed several times as many victims as Hitler's blood purges
in Berlin and Munich."[7]

During one of the nights of the long knives, Carlson was sitting
in the writing room of the Shanghai Club composing a letter
home. A few streets away, a slim and handsome Chinese, one of the
leaders of the strike of 600,000 Shanghai workers who made possible the victory for Chiang Kai-shek, cautiously opened the door
of his hiding place to find himself confronted by officers of Chiang
Kai-shek's Second Division with a warrant for his arrest. The
Chinese, who knew that he was on Chiang's list for beheading,
looked at the faces of the officers and figured his chances of escape.

[7] Robert Berkov, *Strong Man of China, The Story of Chiang Kai-shek*
(Boston, Houghton, Mifflin, 1938).

He knew one man well. He had had him as a student at the Whampoa Military Academy. Once they had been genuinely fond of each other. Perhaps this old friend and student might help him, although who could tell these days? So he put aside thoughts of a fight and followed his captors.

The name of the Chinese — let it be remembered — was Chou En-lai.

On the same night the Propaganda Commissioner of the Shanghai Kuomintang, which was opposed to Chiang Kai-shek, went into hiding. He was a writer and a brave man, and his mouth would be better stopped up. His name was André Malraux, who would one day write *Man's Fate* and become a leader of the French underground against the Nazis.

Chou En-lai, Malraux and history passed Carlson by, that bloody Shanghai night. It would take years before he caught up.

In his letter home, written dutifully before going to sleep, Carlson, parroting the vicious superior-race imperialistic phrases he had heard, said, "The only effective policy is to teach these Chinese a lesson. Unless we occupy Hankow, Nanking, Tientsin and Shanghai, and severely trounce all who make overt acts, these people will lose their respect for foreigners."

4

Men who are loyal and incorruptible

For the Marines in Shanghai, the dog days of their occupation had come. Nothing was happening. Elsewhere in China, grave events were passing their crises: Chiang Kai-shek was consolidating his power, the Hankow Government was dissolved, the Russian advisers went back where they came from and an Army soon to become the Red Army under Chu Teh, Mao Tse-tung and Chou

En-lai was being organized from the debris of the betrayal. And although all this was reflected in the secret inward life of Shanghai, nothing of "importance" was happening.

The sulky summer weather, the monotony of the days, and the lack of action and opportunity to grasp at China depressed Carlson to the degree that, for the first time in his life, he felt completely without ambition. He was in China, and yet it seemed farther away than on the day he had joined the Marines and had volunteered for service there. Even the full dress parades for General Smedley Butler who commanded all the Marines in China failed to bring him their customary excitement. Doggedly he fulfilled what was required of him in his duties; routinely he took his daily exercises at the French Club gym to keep in condition in order to ward off the cholera which killed whites with the same dispassion with which it killed yellow men. He read little; he talked less; he let himself slide on the toboggan of slippery days. His resolution to break through the Wall of China had been forgotten.

Through his lethargy and the fogs of inaction his thoughts constantly went back to his father.

"I'm proud of you," he wrote in a birthday letter. "Proud of your ideas, of your high standards of life, of your spiritual achievements; just of you as a father. The earth would be a Paradise if all fathers were like you. . . . Your son loves you."

He heard occasionally from Dorothy and received pictures of Evans, Jr., now ten years old. The boy looked like him, the long face, the light eyes. The nose was shorter, thank God. Carlson wrote an occasional long letter to his son, full of advice and counsel, as his own father had written to him.

He requested duty as an observer in the interior, and was turned down. Only Shanghai was left, and the heat evaporated his blood, the dull duty emptied his mind. He felt only discontent, fatigue and failure. He declined in health and lost fifteen pounds.

Then slowly, as things happen in life, events and people moved in on him and brought a change that was to begin the march of influences which would bring him, ten years later, to a Hankow dinner table with Chou En-lai.

The September weather lightened Shanghai and dissipated the cottony heat. On the 20th, word came that Carlson had passed his examination for first lieutenant. The promotion came exactly ten years to the day of his promotion to the same grade in the Army. In a letter home, he made special mention of this coincidence, for like men who have a sense of destiny, he was always aware of the special juxtapositions and conjunctions of time.

At the end of September Etelle Carlson arrived on the *Siberia Maru,* and with her came a sense of the continuity of the immediate past when Carlson had been so energetic and full of plans. He started to write again, and did two pieces for the *Leatherneck,* the Marine Corps magazine. These articles were not important by themselves but they revived Carlson's interest in what was going on around him.

In June 1928, the sequence of events which stirred him out of his dullness came to a climax. He was given a new job as Regimental Intelligence Officer. And it was this that opened to him the minds of men who, each in his own way, moved Carlson closer to the fulfillment of his destiny.

The first of these was Admiral Mark L. Bristol, Commander in Chief of the Asiatic Fleet, who had taken over the command from Admiral C. S. Williams.

Admiral Bristol was an extraordinary Naval diplomat. Unlike so many of his brother admirals, he was genuinely interested in the well-being of the people to whom he came as America's representative. He was determined to get the truth, and he let it be known that he wanted to meet and talk with everyone, American businessmen, American missionaries, old China hands, and particularly those Chinese who were directing the course of the Nationalist revolution.

Bristol himself was an old friend of China, having been on duty there as commander of the cruiser *Albany* in 1911 when Sun Yat-sen overthrew the Manchu dynasty. It was he who had ordered fired the first foreign salute to the new Chinese Republic. And now, seventeen years later, he could listen with understanding to the aspirations of the Chinese leaders, know their problems and the com-

plexities of their efforts. Bristol's willingness to confer with the
Chinese revolutionists stirred considerable criticism of him by the
old die-hards who, in the ancient tradition of the Tories, persisted
in their gross admiration of the war lords with whom they could do
business. Criticism of Bristol was strengthened by the delay of our
State Department under President Coolidge to recognize the Kuomintang Nanking Government.

Carlson and Bristol didn't get on well at first owing to the inbred
mutual suspicion of the Navy and Marines. At first, Bristol seemed
rather irritating in his insistence that he required from his Intelligence Officers a solid knowledge of China. But gradually Carlson
became impressed with Bristol's humane and progressive attitude.
The Admiral was for admitting Chinese to all the foreign clubs.
"Let's treat them as equals in all respects," Bristol said, "for the
truth is, they are by no means our inferiors." He saw that in the
great reawakening of the Chinese people was enormous progress;
that China was following, in her own time and by her own methods,
the long line of progressive revolutions among which our own in
1776 is numbered. Most of all, he believed that unity would come
to China and that the people would finally assert themselves consciously for full independence. He encouraged Carlson to investigate for himself.

This was new kind of talk for Carlson. He had not yet met among
officers and American officials of responsibility such earnestness,
friendliness for a foreign people, and so urgent a demand for the
whole truth. There was an instant recognition in him, and a re-
versal of his original attitude that all that was required was to teach
the Chinese respect for foreigners.

Natively conscientious, Carlson might have by himself fulfilled
the requirements of an Intelligence Officer to understand and study
the political milieu in which he worked, but with the added com-
bination of Bristol's inspiration, he poured all his energies into
study. He read Chinese history until he could trace the torturous
spirals and interweavings of five thousand years. He studied the
Three People's Principles of Sun Yat-sen, the Bible of the progressive
Chinese, and grasped the thousand-threaded cloth of the modern

revolutionary movement. In order to learn the cast of living characters, he memorized the English translation of the Chinese *Who's Who*. He knew what province every leader came from, what his education was, what role he played in the 1911 revolution and who his friends were. He began the study of the Chinese language itself, that brain-breaking task of memorizing hundreds of distinct characters and inflections and combinations.

He tried to put into words what he had learned. He wrote five articles for the *Walla Walla,* a weekly magazine published and edited by the enlisted men of the Fourth Marines. This series was a serious attempt to describe for his men the organization of the new Chinese Republic. They are little classics of exposition which included, wherever possible, the common experience of the American and the Chinese.

"We of the Fourth Regiment," he wrote in 1928, "if we but pause to realize it, are living in China during a tremendously interesting period. The struggle of a nation to find herself and to evolve an efficient government is an adventure that we in this age are seldom privileged to see. We are occupying box seats for an experiment in government that can best be compared to that made by our forefathers during the period 1783 to 1800 when they struggled against opposition at home and abroad to erect a central government in the United States."

He described the Five Yuan system of the Chinese, in which our three divisions of government, Executive, Legislative and Judicial, are augmented by a Civil Service and a Control with equal rank to the others.

In his fourth article, he expressed a hope that this experiment in democracy would succeed.

"It really depends on the ability of the Kuomintang Party to select for officials, not only in the National Government but in the Provinces, men who are loyal and incorruptible."

These five articles brought demands on him from enlisted men and officers to continue with a weekly feature on the current Chinese political situation. This he did, and his concise and factual reports on those days in which China's Republic was being unified are an extraordinarily rich source of information, much of which has found its way into many books on China.

His writing was not limited to the *Walla Walla,* for in the middle of 1928 he came to know anti-Japanese J. B. Powell, an American who, besides being a correspondent for the *Chicago Tribune,* owned and edited the *China Weekly Review,* an English-language paper published in Shanghai. He was the man who gave many young American newspapermen their first real break in the Orient, and he asked Carlson to write book reviews and articles for the *Review.*

"If I do them," he warned Powell, "I want to do them on my own terms. If I disagree with the author I want to say so. And I don't want anybody rewriting me."

Powell agreed.

Reviewing books is an excellent way of adding to an education. Powell gave him books on the Pacific and on subjects related to American intervention in China, South and Central America. Perhaps it seemed to the editor that it was only justice to have critiques of America's foreign policy analyzed by a Marine Corps Intelligence Officer in China.

Carlson fell for the bait, if bait it was. In all his reviews he took a consistent position that imperialism was evil but that the United States was not an imperialist power. In a review of *The Mastery of the Pacific* by Sir Frank Fox, Carlson wrote:

> The United States has consistently refused to be a party to any agreement or policy which contemplates the use of force to impose governments on a foreign people. Her hand is always extended . . . as to an equal in need of advice and guidance. . . .

It is rather an ironic climax to this peculiar blindness of attitude that within a year from the time he wrote the review of Sir Frank Fox's book he would be fighting to extend American interests in Nicaragua. Only then he would learn, in the black wilderness of Jalapa and Quilili, that truth which Lawrence of Arabia discovered for himself: "To make war upon rebellion is messy and slow, like eating soup with a knife." He would learn there, and later, that our nation was not free of the taint of imperialist greed.

It was through Powell that he met Edgar Snow, who was destined not only to become Carlson's best friend but also to set him finally on the road where he would come face to face with the promise of himself after all his years of searching. Edgar Snow arrived in Shanghai out of the Missouri School of Journalism and the Kansas City *Star*. He was on his way to Madagascar, and intended to stay over in China for a month. His month lasted twelve years. He had a life-hungry yen for adventure that was as huge as Carlson's, and he knew clearly that he wanted to get it by being a good reporter. Younger than Carlson, he had a flexible boyishness and a taste for hell-tearing that had long ago been put down by the tall New Englander. Snow not only had a nose for news, he had a nose for truth. To this he added a deep feeling for people. Comparing him with other reporters of his generation, we would find that where they saw in China a great story he saw a great people. It was this that made his book *Red Star Over China* a reporter's classic of our time, to be remembered when most others, with the exception of John Reed's *Ten Days That Shook the World,* Vincent Sheean's *Personal History* and Duranty's *I Write As I Please,* are long catching dust on the ten-cent box in secondhand stores.

In addition to Snow, Carlson, always eager to know writers, became acquainted with Henry Misselwitz of the *New York Times,* Morris Harris of the Associated Press, Owen Lattimore, and Hallett Abend of the *New York Times.* He got on well with all but Hallett Abend, whose dispatches gave the impression that he was anti-Kuomintang and pro-Japanese. Abend writes of this:

> At the Intelligence Office of the Fourth U.S. Marines my name was anathema in 1929 and 1930. That office was then under the direction of Lieutenant E. Carlson, who later as a Lieutenant-Colonel distinguished himself during the raid upon Makin Island and at Guadalcanal. Carlson instructed his staff to ignore me completely, never to come to me for information

and not to take any of his releases to me. He even intimated to his men that I was probably in the pay of Japan. . . .

Perhaps Carlson's attitude was merely a pale reflection of the hostility shown to me by the late Admiral Mark L. Bristol, at that time Commander-in-Chief of our Asiatic Fleet. I had never liked the Admiral and he knew it, and my analytical articles on the China situation differed entirely from his absurdly optimistical forecasts of the firm establishment of internal peace and harmony.[8]

Abend's activities by his own admission could well constitute sufficient reason for the suspicion that he had a bias in favor of the "die-hards and imperialist-minded groups" who, as he described it in his book, "welcomed my arrival (in Shanghai) warmly." Both Bristol and Carlson could not fail to meet with antipathy anyone who was attempting to win America's sympathy for Japan's moves into China.

Carlson's work as Intelligence Officer, of course, was his first concern; his writing and studying merely augmented and enriched it. Carlson had the qualities which go to make a good Intelligence Officer, discretion, logic and sympathy. A fourth aptitude — shrewdness — was also his, but not in the conventional sense of the word. Rather, as Edgar Snow described him, he gave the impression of being so naïve and so straightforward that one might think he could easily be fooled. This simplicity which was entirely genuine won the confidence of strangers who had important information to give, and the respect of professional peddlers who had information to sell. The former believed in Carlson's unaffected honesty and told him what they knew; the latter, convinced that no Intelligence Officer could be that honest and that Carlson was putting on an act, thought they saw enormous and diabolic cleverness beneath the surface.

When he let it be known through Shanghai that he would not pay one cent for secret information, the businessmen of espionage were outraged.

[8] From *My Life in China,* by Hallett Abend (New York: Harcourt, Brace and Company, 1943).

Free-lance spying, as distinguished from the organized espionage of governments, is the bourse of confusion. Most of it is rumor, watered stock and speculation. Men, women and children in such centers of the industry as Shanghai peddle information like cigarettes. It's a way of making a living, and in this market there is no code of honor.

Carlson tells a story that is an illustration not only of the confusion of the business but also of the way his method paid off.

One day, at Carlson's office appeared a slight red-faced, bald-headed Russian who introduced himself as Mr. Dick. He said that he had been an Intelligence Officer for Michael Borodin, the Kuomintang's Soviet adviser, who had several years before retreated to Moscow as a result of the victory of the right wing under Chiang Kai-shek.

"Lieutenant Carlson, I understand that you do not pay for information," Mr. Dick said.

"That's right," Carlson replied.

"And why not, sir?"

"It's simple," Carlson said. "Information is like every other commodity. If there's a demand for it backed with purchasing power, it will be manufactured."

"But without money, sir, no one will give you anything," Mr. Dick said in the kindly fashion of an elderly brother giving advice.

"None of the manufactured kind, that's true."

"And the other kind, sir?"

"It will be given to me gratis because no one else will have any use for it."

Mr. Dick thought it over while he lit his Russian cigarette carefully. "I think I understand you," he said gently. He then told Carlson that he had given up all thought of returning to the Soviet Union. He didn't like it there any more. And now he was prepared to serve as a spy for any power who would pay him. Carlson was firm, however, about his principle of not paying, and Mr. Dick left.

Several weeks went by and Mr. Dick called on Carlson again.

"This time, sir," he said, "I am willing to make the United States a present of some information gratis. Just to prove my competence."

Carlson accepted it, of course, with thanks, and found that it was rather important.

A week later he received a call from a French Secret Service man who wanted to know if he was acquainted with a Mr. Dick. "I am," Carlson said.

"Be careful of him," the Frenchman said. "He's working for the British."

A month or so after that, a British C.I.D. agent paid Carlson a visit to inform him to watch out for a Russian named Dick who for certain was working for the Japs.

It was about this time that Carlson left China for the States and didn't return until 1933 when he again resumed his duties as Intelligence Officer with the Fourth Regiment at Shanghai. Some time after his arrival, he received a telephone call from a Chinese asking him to hurry over to a certain apartment in a house in the Chinese district where something of great importance would be given him.

When he arrived at the apartment he found his old friend, Mr. Dick. "Do you still retain your prejudice against paying for information?" Mr. Dick asked.

"I do," Carlson replied.

Mr. Dick smiled broadly at that, almost with pleasure. Then he asked whether the United States in the person of Carlson minded walking out of the house with him and driving him into the International Settlement. Carlson saw no objection and said so. Mr. Dick took him to the window and showed him two half-breed Japanese loitering across the street. "They are waiting to kill me," he said without being dramatic. "I had to get help and you are the only man in Shanghai I can trust. Anyone who won't pay for espionage is either a fool or an honest man. I know you're no fool."

Carlson asked him why he was being threatened.

"I have been working for the Japs, sir," Mr. Dick said with an ironic sigh. "But no more."

And then he gave Carlson a small bundle of papers that contained invaluable source material for Naval Intelligence.

"But if you're not working for the Japs, then for whom?" Carlson inquired.

Mr. Dick smiled and said nothing.

"And if you're working for the British or the French or the Dutch why don't you give them this stuff instead of me?"

"I'm not working for the British or the French or the Dutch," he said.

"Then for whom?"

Mr. Dick rubbed his bald head gently. "I'll let you guess," he said, and said no more.

Carlson took him out of the house, and into the International Settlement. And he never saw him again.

And when asked the question as to whom he thought Dick had been working for Carlson gave an Intelligence Officer's discreet smile and said, "I'll let *you* guess now." [9]

By September 1929 the end of his tour of duty on Shanghai was approaching. He had been out there for thirty months. He had done a job which, in the main, satisfied him. In the line of duty he had met fleetingly such personages as Chiang Kai-shek and Dr. H. H. Kung. He had traveled to Nanking and Soochow and seen China beyond its treaty ports. He had learned some Chinese, and something about China. He had studied the Chinese Revolution and saw that with all its weakness it was a good thing for China. He had read a great many books; gained a smattering of Spanish in the event he was sent to Nicaragua. He had written a few things, and they had been liked. He had made friends, Bristol, Powell, Snow. And he would leave behind him a lasting monument to his Intelligence Section — a detailed map of the International Settlement, two hundred feet to an inch. Most of the credit for the map, of course, went to the field men and draughtsmen who made it possible, but Carlson had initiated the work and through months of fret and worry had persisted in completing it.

He was thirty-three, had done well enough for his people to have pride in him, and he knew what his life would be.

[9] My guess was the U.S.S.R.

The Marines, he thought, had brought him all that he had hoped for that day in Oregon five years before when he had tramped the Marshfield trails and asked: What shall I do? He had sought adventure — and received it; strange places — and saw them; time to read and study and write — and it was given him.

But more than all these, he had the beginnings, the glimmer of what, unconsciously, he needed — a cause: China!

A man's progress, said Emerson, is "an unfolding, like the vegetable bud. You have first an instinct, then an opinion, then a knowledge, as the plant has root, bud and fruit."

Carlson was bound by his own speed limit. He would not be rushed faster than his nature's logic could sustain.

5

An eagerness for battle

He had tasted strange places and he wanted more. When Headquarters returned him to the States for duty and sent him from one post to another, he was unhappy. Twice he volunteered for more duty in China; twice he requested service in Nicaragua. They told him he'd have to wait.

In October 1929, the depression moved in on us. We were frightened. But not everybody. Carlson, for example. Nor were many of his fellow officers at Bremerton Navy Yard, Norfolk Navy Yard, Philadelphia Navy Yard or at Quantico.

No, in the officers' clubs and at their field messes there was interested talk about everything except the depression. Occasionally it was mentioned with distaste, as men might speak of a plague in Indo-China. In short, with the rest of his fellow soldiers living in the tight and depression-proof military island, Carlson was unaffected by the national tragedy.

He was at Quantico and near enough to his folks to spend his Christmas with them. It would be the first Christmas in eighteen years. Carlson came home to the same family but to a new parish. In January 1926 the Reverend Carlson had been called to the Plymouth, Connecticut Congregational Church. It was destined to be his last parish, from which he would retire in June of 1944.

Plymouth is a quiet little town of about 6,000. It looks like a model of a Southern New England community with large shade trees, a village green around which are clustered the important buildings, the churches and the schoolhouses. In spirit it was not far removed from West Rutland or Peacham or Shoreham.

It was a good Christmas for Carlson. When he drove up to the white frame house with Etelle Carlson and stamped through the fresh Connecticut snow and saw the bright green holly wreaths in the windows, it was just what he wanted to see.

His father had not changed much. He was still erect and still hearty; his laugh and the great gentleness on his face were yet clear. Joetta, too, had not changed. She had maintained spiritual firmness in the face of continuing phlebitis. From her wheel chair, her pride and aggressiveness were not one whit diminished.

On Christmas Eve, they trimmed the tree together and brought in their gifts. After dinner they gathered around the old Knabe piano they'd had since Shoreham, and sang the old Norwegian carols Father Carlson remembered from his youth.

Thomas Carlson introduced his son to Plymouth which he himself had come to love. They tramped the snowy streets, met neighbors and parishioners, hiked along United States Highway 6 to Terryville, had some johnnycake with friends, delighted in the smell of the blue wood smoke rising warm and sweetly bitter, helped a fellow shovel a path through the snow to his barn, attended a church social where Carlson said a few words about China to the men's club. After five days, Plymouth became his home town just as much as Shoreham and Peacham and San Diego and San Francisco.

It was a good, rich Christmas. Perhaps the best he had ever known or would ever know.

*　　*　　*

When word came in April of 1930 for Carlson to report to the Commanding Officer of the *Guardia Nacional* of Nicaragua, he was delighted.

According to the Historical Section of the United States Marine Corps, the first landing of Marines in Nicaragua for purposes of protecting American lives and property took place in 1853. Then it was the property of the American Steamship Company which seemed to be endangered by "local political disturbances." From 1853 until the establishment of President Franklin Roosevelt's Good Neighbor Policy eighty years later, United States Marines have been the armed instrument of our policy of intervening in Nicaraguan politics. Our reasons for this were the simple reasons of imperialism: we had investments in that country; we bought most of her exports and sold to her most of her imports. Later, our greater national interests were involved in the possibilities of an Atlantic-Pacific canal across Nicaragua. Toward the end of keeping in power Nicaraguans who would deal kindly with our businessmen and State Department we supported any Nicaraguan revolution or counter-revolution designed to protect our $15,000,000 investment. Although Charles Evans Hughes, in 1923, signed a well-intentioned treaty refusing to recognize any government in Central America set up by force, by 1926 our State Department ignored the fact that shipments of munitions were being sent from American ports to a General Chamorro, the front man for Adolfo Díaz whom Carleton Beals called "a lickspittle for Chamorro and American interests for 17 years."

There were many Nicaraguans, of course, who fought against American imperialism. Augusto Calderón Sandino was such a man. In 1912, a young man, he had lost his farm when American bankers took over the Nicaraguan credit and financial system. From that time on he fought the American interventionists. Many times he was tempted with political honors and money with which to buy back his farm. According to Carleton Beals, the foremost authority on Central American politics and men, Sandino refused to be bought off. However, our State Department and newspapers called Sandino and his followers "bandits." Our Naval and Marine forces were called on to exterminate him as a threat to the lives and security of Americans doing business there.

In 1927 President Coolidge, moved by the indignation of his own people against our intervention, sent Henry L. Stimson to Nicaragua to work out an arrangement between the opposing political parties whereby our Marines would supervise the next three elections — and then withdraw. During that time, our Marines would organize a Nicaraguan militia called the *Guardia Nacional* whose mission would be to defend its country from invasion, bandits and rebellion.[10]

Sandino, however, was not in accord with the Accord of Tipitapa. He was a fervent Nationalist and opposed to even benevolent intervention. As Will Rogers had put it: "Our Marines are doing all they can to see that there are fewer Sandino voters to supervise and Sandino is doing all he can to see that there are fewer Marines to supervise."

"Tell your people," Sandino said to Carleton Beals in the first interview he gave an American reporter, "that there may be bandits in Nicaragua but they are not necessarily Nicaraguans."

In May 1930 Carlson landed at Corinto, Nicaragua, was commissioned a Captain in the *Guardia* and ordered by Colonel Robert L. Denig to leave for Jicaro, an isolated backwoods jungle village, with thirty-one men to operate against Pedro Altamirano, one of Sandino's lieutenants.

Carlson had been warned to be very careful, for the week before in Jicaro several Nicaraguan *Guardias* had turned a machine gun on the officers' quarters and killed two.

Before leaving for Jicaro, he told his men in broken Spanish, "I trust you, *amigos*. I will see that you have food and shelter. It is to the benefit of all of us to bring peace and security to your great country."

On the 30th of May he reached his post and moved into one of Sandino's former headquarters.

He waited for a battle. Nothing happened.

[10] The *Marine Corps Gazette* of August 1937 published an article by Carlson, relating the history of the *Guardia Nacional*.

Two weeks later, he was transferred from Jicaro to Jalapa. Here he was in command of thirty-five *Guardias*. The town had about thirty mud shacks which for that part of the country was a good-sized *pueblo*.

> I like the duty [he wrote his young brother Tom]. I am *Jefe* of this part of the country, bandit activity lending a touch of danger, which is stimulating. Problems are constantly arising which call for the use of initiative and ingenuity. I am mastering the language rapidly and give all orders, both written and verbal, in Spanish. I feel that I am accomplishing something.
>
> Our quarters look like one of the stockades of the old western plains. My front door is barricaded and prepared as a machine gun position. The patio in back is surrounded with barbed wire entanglements. I have a heavy Browning machine gun, a heavy Lewis gun and two sub-Thompsons. If I don't get a contact with the bandits soon I am going to be disappointed.
>
> Everything is very quiet. The natives are nervous and think this place is going to be attacked but I have my doubts. Only a fool would try to rush us here.
>
> These *Guardia* are loyal chaps and when properly handled they make good soldiers. I flatter myself that I know how to handle them.

Several nights a week he held a court for the citizens of Jalapa, acting as judge, jury and prosecutor. He refused to use an interpreter and tried every case in Spanish, constantly referring to his big English-Spanish dictionary, and warning the litigants to speak slowly and simply so that he could understand. He played Solomon and Dorothy Dix in disputes that ranged from murder to obstreperous fathers-in-law. His jurisprudence was as just and as simple as he could make it: hear both sides, get as much disinterested evidence as possible, make a decision, persuade the guilty party to admit his guilt and the wronged party to admit either understanding or forgiveness. He never punished a man unless he admitted his guilt.

At eight-thirty on the evening of July 9th, a badly frightened Nicaraguan galloped down the rain-beaten trail into Jalapa yelling at the top of his voice that bandits[11] were looting the town of Portillo. Carlson was notified immediately and sent for the *alcalde* of Jalapa and five other prominent citizens, requesting them to provide him with seventeen fresh horses, his own being tired out and in pasture. Full of hope for combat, he took the trail for Portillo, three miles away, with sixteen enlisted men, leaving nineteen under Lieutenant Walery, the only other American in his force, to defend Jalapa.

He felt uneasy about taking out a patrol. There had been some talk about an attack on Jalapa, and he was afraid that the disturbance at Portillo was a ruse to divide his strength. But he figured he could make the round trip in two hours, and he was confident that Walery and his men could hold out that long against any attack the Sandinistas would be able to make.

It was a dark trail and rain made it darker and slow going. By ten Carlson's patrol reached the outskirts of Portillo. The *pueblo* was quiet, the streets empty, the houses without lights. The sound of the rain was the only life. He ordered his men to enter the houses cautiously. The houses were as empty as the street — except one. Here a family was found, three children and an old man who could not run with their neighbors to hide in the mountains because of illness. They told Carlson that the bandits numbered about a hundred, that their *Jefe* was Simón González, and that they had left about an hour before up the Chusli trail. Carlson informed his sixteen men what the situation was and moved forward in pursuit. He was determined to find the bandits and fight it out with them.

An eagerness for battle had seized him. This would be his debut, though it was hard to realize it. He had been a soldier for 18 years — and he had a keen desire to know what battle was like.

The rain slackened and stopped. A full moon fought vainly with heavy clouds. An hour up the trail, Corporal Vicente Olivas, full of chagrin, reported to Carlson that four men were missing. Carlson

[11] Frequently under the guise of national patriotism, some Nicaraguans actually were looters and bandits. This is a characteristic excrescence on all national-liberation movements.

ordered a ten minute rest. The men didn't come back and it was clear they had deserted. Corporal Olivas was deeply ashamed.

The odds were lengthened with the desertion. A hundred against twelve. He decided to push the pursuit anyway.

"It wasn't merely a question of finding and destroying the enemy," Carlson said later. "This operation, as small as it was, contained rather important morale and political elements. If even partially successful, it would increase the *Guardia's* confidence in itself and prove to the people that it could act promptly in suppressing bandit activity. Moreover, I had confidence in these men. There was a lively farm boy, Teodocia Salgado, who lived near Portillo and loved being a good soldier, and Vicente Olivas, a husky, conscientious and alert sugar mill worker and Huberto Avendano who used to sing on the trails, and at the post would bring me English lessons for corrections in grammar. The risk of meeting a hundred bandits with twelve men was worth taking. There was always a chance of surprising them."

At one-thirty in the morning Carlson, who was up in advance of the patrol, picked up the signs of a body of men. A little while later crossing a river just south of the *pueblo* of Pasmata, Teodocia Salgado sighted the rear of the enemy column, three hundred yards away. Carlson directed his men to dismount, and secure their mounts in the heavy brush.

Silently his patrol moved upon the unsuspecting enemy, now clearly visible by their white shirts against the dark jungle growth. When they came to within 150 yards, Carlson ordered his men to fire. Five of the enemy fell at the first burst. Instantly the others dropped behind trees and opened an intense fire. Carried away by their success, several *Guardias* started a charge, yelling "*Viva la Guardia Nacional!*" But Carlson ordered them back. A few minutes later enemy fire slackened and ceased. The rain started again, and from the darkness up ahead came the pathetic cry of a wounded man calling, "*Mamita . . . Mamita.*"

Carlson rounded up his men, saw that none was hurt, and continued the pursuit. But suddenly the jungle had built a wall around the enemy. All through that night and the day following Carlson and his patrol sought them. But there was no enemy. The *Guardia* would enter tiny *pueblos* and find men working in the fields, but none had seen or heard a thing. The great magic of guerrilla warfare where an army and a people are one angered Carlson. Simón González and his men had vanished.

It was Carlson's first lesson in this kind of war, and he smarted under his failure to match González's skill. Restless until he found out the magic, he returned to Jalapa, left Walery in charge, put on old clothes and went off scouting alone in the thick Nicaraguan jungles. He never learnt just where González had disappeared to, but he learnt how. Guerrilla warfare meant never fighting in a fixed position, always moving, picking out your own terrain. He learnt that it requires special tactics to outflank or surround a guerrilla band. And he learnt other things: how to move in the jungle at night, how to live in it, how to make it a place of protection. He worked out a method of offense against such tactics. Never to stay in one place. To move as often, as far, but faster than the guerrilla enemy. Only then could he be outflanked and surrounded.

On the eighth of December he was transferred from Jalapa to Nicaragua's capital, Managua, where despite severe malaria he assumed the duties of Department Commander of Managua and Corozo, President of the General Court Martial, Commander of the *Guardia* detachment, and later of Chief of Police.

Christmas found him feverish, overworked and homesick. But his longing for home was appeased somewhat when Etelle Carlson arrived from the States.

It was payday at Carlson's headquarters and about fifty men were lined up in the drill field in front of the building waiting for their money. Suddenly the building shivered violently. Walls and ceiling descended in fragments. Carlson was thrown from his feet. He started to get up, was thrown down again. Dust rose in volcanic clouds.

Ten seconds of silence. The earthquake was over.

He crawled out of what was left of his building. The city was silent, then suddenly exploded with cries of pain.

Carlson saw a man covered by the ruins and pulled him out. He yelled for men to search the ruins for other casualties.

Over the city a huge fire hung like a curtain from the sky.

For four days he and his comrades got food and water to the people of Managua, cared for the injured, counted and buried 400 dead. Step by step, a relief organization was built.

When it was all over, Carlson broke down. Hard work, anxiety, sleeplessness and malaria sent him to the hospital. The medicos on the scene thought he'd better return for hospitalization in the States.

While in the Managua hospital, Carlson wrote a letter of confession to his father:

> During certain periods I accepted blindly the precepts of the orthodox churches, hoping for a Divine Revelation which would seal my convictions and eradicate my doubts. The Revelation never came and I berated myself for being a hypocrite, and in order to regain my self-respect I swung to the opposite side of the fence. And yet, there has always been the necessity for thinking the thing through and seeking convictions to which I felt I could subscribe without reservation.
>
> I have come to the definite conclusion in regard to religion.

He said that he believed in God as the Creator and Supreme Being who was also Destiny, Providence and the Simple Principle of Decency. Christ is the greatest moral teacher the world has ever known. His precepts are the standard guide to right living and to universal happiness. He is the son of God as all of us are the children of God, neither divine nor resurrected.

"And now, Dad," Carlson ended his letter, "tell me what I am?"

"You are as I am," his father replied.

Word of Carlson's imminent departure came to José del Carmen Flores, the Governor of the Department of Managua, who wrote a letter to General Calvin B. Matthews, commander in chief of the *Guardia Nacional*. The only record of this letter is the copy made by General Matthews's interpreter.

It has come to my knowledge [Señor Flores wrote] the news that Captain Evans F. Carlson will soon return to the U.S.

Managua has received the foregoing news as a new misfortune, as Captain Carlson with a spirit which insomuch honors him as well as the Army of the United States, has known to sacrify his personal welfare in order to perform his duties with abnegation and disinterestness which makes him creditor of an everlasting gratitude on part of our people.

Managua, through me, request that if Captain Carlson returns to Nicaragua, his services be spared in Managua where he leaves so many debts of gratitude.

The earthquake which destroyed the city of Managua has rendered us an opportunity to know the persons of good will who have been a relief and a comfort in hours of misfortune, among these we shall always count Captain Carlson.

Very respectfully,

(s) José del C. Flores
Jefe Político of the Department of Managua

Carlson received the copy of Flores's letter from General Matthews when he was already back in the States at a Naval Hospital. With it was a copy of a letter General Matthews wrote to the Secretary of the Navy, Charles Francis Adams, giving Carlson's record, a description of his attack on the bandits at Portillo, and his work during the earthquake:

The services of Lieutenant Carlson are a source of extreme gratification to me as Chief of the *Guardia Nacional,* and of honor to the Marine Corps. They assisted in no small degree in meeting one of the most difficult situations we have been called upon to face on one of those few great emergencies which arise in the course of a lifetime and which bring out the qualities of leadership among those who rise to meet the occasion. I earnestly recommend that he be awarded the Distinguished Service Medal for exceptionally meritorious service to the Government in a duty of great responsibility.

A few days later, Carlson was called into the office of the Commandant of the Boston Navy Yard and presented not with the Distinguished Service Medal but with the Navy Cross, an award second only to the Congressional Medal of Honor.[12]

6

High-toned bull sessions

Carlson returned to San Diego in January 1933 and by March he was at sea en route to China again to take over his old job as Intelligence Officer of the Fourth Regiment.

Before Carlson landed in Shanghai on Saint Patrick's Day 1933, two very important things had happened to China. Japan had already put her foot inside the Open Door in Manchuria, and the Chinese Red Army, organized in the southern provinces, had painfully fought off four extermination campaigns directed against them by Chiang Kai-shek. Both these events were moving slowly together like two rivers to catch up with Carlson at their junction.

Shanghai did not satisfy him. He wanted more of China than its foreignized ports. He requested duty in Peiping [13] with the Legation Guard, and was transferred there.

Peiping, the Forbidden City, was a dream to Carlson. It was the China of the books, full of rich color and beauty, untouched by the mark of foreigners in its spirit and architecture. He had never seen so wondrous a city. The thousands of willows and great imperial cypresses, the cool gardens, the tiles, the Tartar walls brought enchantment to him as they had to all others who had ever visited the city.

[12] He also received the Nicaraguan Presidential Medal of Merit and the Medal of Distinction.
[13] Formerly Peking.

It was an immensely crowded place with a universe of sounds: bells and the thousand cries of street vendors and beggars. Each sound was born before the other died. He felt as if he were living in the midst of a huge and strangely instrumented orchestra. And he liked it.

He and his wife rented a charming Chinese house just inside the wall of the Imperial City. As Adjutant of the Post his work was not at all arduous and for the first months, experiencing something new for an old Puritan, he tasted luxury. He went in for polo, playing No. 1 on the team, enjoyed the easy protocol of garden parties, teas, receptions. He found that one could live in Peiping with blinded eyes and deafened ears though the rest of the world fell to pieces.

As always he found it easy to make acquaintances and hard to make friends, and he was overjoyed when Ed Snow came up to teach at Yenching University with his new wife, Peggy.

"I want you to meet Carlson," Ed Snow had told his bride. "He's something you don't see every day in the Marines."

If Shanghai had been Carlson's school of Chinese politics, Peiping was his university of Chinese culture. He studied Chinese ceramics, art and architecture.

He learned the differences in Ming blue, the reds and browns and blues of Ching, the green of Sung, the veins of the porcelain, the touch, the sound, the feel.

This was high "culture," and Carlson enjoyed it. His heart, fearing illiteracy like sin, sang with knowledge. He began to enjoy "learning" for its own sake. And, oddly enough, at the same time he became proud of possessions for the first time in his life. Like any *nouveau riche,* he showed off his home, the old house they had rented, with its moongates fringed in wistaria, the red salvia bordering the courtyard, the bright, red-lacquered door with brass knockers. For a while ease and luxury were not things to be ashamed of. He enjoyed his free, sinless New Englandless year.

Week ends he and his wife went up to an old Buddhist Temple with the Snows and Helen Burton, who ran a curio shop at the Grand Hotel and who had rented The Temple of Flowering Fragrance for $20 a year. He talked porcelains and dynasties and the beauties of Chinese chirography and the aesthetics of Chinese painting, while eating Etelle's un-Chinese chocolate cake and Boston baked beans.

Prominent transients were his guests. Gene Tunney, John Oliver La Gorce, editor of the *National Geographic,* and John P. Marquand, the creator of Mr. Moto, and later of *The Late George Apley.*

"You could never think of Carlson as a great military leader," Marquand said of this time. "When I knew him in Peiping he impressed me deeply as being a scholar, a man interested in ideas and culture."

Never before had Carlson been so free in talking out his thoughts on the universe and nature and men. He was among intellectuals, men who talked a language different from what he had ever known before. There was Owen Lattimore, a Guggenheim fellow, Dr. Flewelling, Dean of the Philosophy Department, University of Southern California, Timperley, an erudite British journalist, Stephen Pyle, pastor of the Peiping Church, Lyman Hoover, a Yale Divinity School man, Lawrence Sickman, Curator of the Kansas City Museum and Dr. Arthur Coons of Occidental College. There were men of science from the Peiping Medical College and Yenching University and the Rockefeller Foundation.

Among these men he could test his ideas at the Monday Club which met weekly at the Hotel Du Nord for dinner. There he entered into high-toned "bull sessions" which, in a compact form, were a belated college education.

In the heat of great resolves and dedication, good food and heady beer, the Monday Club went so far as to draw up a prospectus of a universal creed, in which each pledged himself to practice "honesty, tolerance, justice, humanity and unselfishness."

The rest of the world's problems seemed simpler after that.

His only unhappiness in those days was the discovery of how really ill-informed he was. American literature, for example. He knew Emerson, of course, and Mark Twain, Walt Whitman and the New England poets. But he was unprepared to argue the fine points of literary cause and effect, the influences of region on art, of nationalism on poetry, of folk culture on drama. There was a virtual Tibet of knowledge which he had never explored.

He wanted the latest in literary thought, and he wanted something that tied up literature with the world around it. He found all this in a book by V. F. Calverton that had been recently published. Using Calverton's *The Liberation of American Literature,* he taught a class of the Peiping Woman's Club, for after all no one learns quicker than a man who teaches.

With this class went another; and out of the new one came a revelation which created in Carlson a further conviction about men and leadership, augmenting what he had already learned.

When he first became Adjutant of the Legation Guard he was appalled to discover that as many as a hundred men a month were subject to disciplinary action. He knew that something was wrong in a detachment where morale was so low. He went through the possibilities: food, quarters, lack of entertainment, but in each case the men were well taken care of. He talked with the men but could get nothing from them.

About this time he started his class in Chinese language, history and culture, the first ever held in the Peiping Legation Guard. Specialists in different branches of Chinese culture spoke. The history of Peiping itself was outlined. China's political story was told. Its language taught.

The list of offenders fell from a hundred a month to ten! This was an important discovery for Carlson. He realized with terrific impact that when soldiers are given information about the situation in which they act and live they derive from it a sense of responsibility. . . . He would never forget this lesson.

7

"B for my work"

The Marine Corps brought him back to the States in 1935, made him a Captain, an aide to Major General Charles Lyman, and second-in-command in President Roosevelt's Warm Springs detachment.

This brought him close to his new idol, Franklin Roosevelt. Carlson liked the idea of Roosevelt's forthright acknowledgment that human needs were as important as a balanced budget.

But China was in Carlson's head. It was all he talked about. He wanted to go back as soon as possible. But first he wanted to know more about international affairs. He wanted background.

As General Lyman's aide at Quantico, his chance came. He applied for admission to Professor Charles Hill's class in International Law at George Washington University. He could commute the forty miles from Quantico every night.

Professor Hill, a good fatherly man but a little tired of amateurs, told Carlson that he didn't have the academic requirements for this graduate course, and he couldn't accept him.

"What books should I have studied, Professor?"

Hill gave him a list of ten classics, from Grotius on up to Borchard. In the next two weeks, Carlson read the books, outlined them, presented himself again to Hill and demanded a written examination.

The professor, a little frightened by the Marine's vigor and determination, told him he could take the course without such a test.

And now a world opened, Tibet was crossed. He understood the real meaning of such phrases as "Dollar Diplomacy" and "balance of power" for the first time. He understood now what he had been doing in China in 1927, in Nicaragua in 1931. Embarrassed, he wished he could rewrite some of his book reviews published in Powell's paper.

"I was shocked by what I learnt of our intervention in foreign nations," he said to the author. "I suppose I had taken too much for granted about our American idealism." He paused to think, took his glasses off, moved his hands in front of him in his characteristic way as if he were grappling with something physical. "But I still believe that even while we worked under Dollar Diplomacy we followed a course that was of benefit to others as well as to ourselves."

The Roosevelts invited Evans and Etelle Carlson to lunch in February 1936. The Chief Usher met them at the door, and as they were taking off their coats Carlson saw a couple of Secret Service men he knew. He grinned. They grinned back.

"I feel a little easier," he whispered to his wife.

The major-domo showed them where they were to be seated on a diagram of the table, then led them to the Red Room, where in front of a warm fire stood a group consisting of Lieutenant Colonel Lemuel C. Shepard, who had been in command of the Warm Springs Detachment the previous year and who in 1945 would command the Marines on Okinawa, Mrs. Shepard, Francis Sayre, the Assistant Secretary of State, and Bishop Atwood, an old friend of the Roosevelts. At one o'clock Mrs. Roosevelt came into the room escorted by a beautiful pair of Irish setters, and shook hands with her guests.

"Shall we go into the dining room," she suggested after a while. "Franklin is already at the table."

When they entered the family dining room, Carlson was seated second from Roosevelt's left. There was some lively talk about a speech that Al Smith had just made attacking the New Deal, and the President seemed unaffected by it. Then someone brought up the question of the unfriendly attitude of the newspapers toward the President.

"I used to tell Theodore," Bishop Atwood remarked, "that the editors of the *New York Evening Post* were a bunch of liars."

"T.R. had his own difficulties," the President replied, "but if you have to choose between support of the people and the support of the editors, well — " He made a gesture and laughed heartily.

In his letter home describing the event, Carlson seemed less impressed with being with people who were calling Franklin Roosevelt "Franklin," than he was by being at a table with a man like Bishop Atwood who could call his old hero "Theodore."

"But," he wrote, "nothing, not even having dinner with F.D.R., has happened to me in many a day that has set me up as much as having received a B for my work at George Washington U. Not bad for a non-college graduate, eh?"

He celebrated the B at the Army-Navy Club in Washington. He had proved to his own satisfaction that he could compete with men who had received formal schooling. His old sense of inferiority slipped away. He had three points to his credit as a graduate student in International Law.

By the end of the year he had six points and a thesis on Japanese expansion in Eastern Asia, as well as an article called *Legal Basis for the Use of Foreign Armed Forces in China,* which was eventually published in the *Naval Institute Proceedings.* This was quite flattering, for the *Proceedings* was edited by a board of senior Naval officers who insisted on a high literary standard as well as on originality and authenticity.

The Roosevelt landslide in November of 1936 delighted him. He had been convinced that F.D.R. would win, though he thought the margin would be much smaller.

> I believe that Roosevelt will prove by virtue of his second administration [he wrote home on November 8th] to be one of the greatest of all our presidents. He has the heart and sympathetic understanding of Lincoln. He is well balanced and I believe will remain so.

Roosevelt's victory meant much to Carlson. He had listened to all his speeches, heard him condemn the "economic royalists" and speak up for the "plain man." These words, like chords, set up resonances in Carlson. Since his return from China he had looked around his native land and had seen that there were things wrong with it and things that were being righted. He felt that we were turning a corner in our life at which point underprivileged people would demand and get a greater share of the national wealth.

"Ingenuity, industry and intelligence must be rewarded," he wrote his father, "but not at the expense of relegating the masses to the gutters." An equitable balance for all classes must be found. But how? He saw how American laboring men had joined together successfully in unions and had learnt to work with each other for their common goals. But even here there was disunion, not only among labor, but between segments of the American people. How could unity come about, equity, justice for all?

He was no economist, no philosopher, no profound thinker. He had no recourse to ready-made theories. He wanted merely to see and live with a happy people.

But how make them happy?

Could it be, he asked his father, that this could come about "if the principles of Christianity were practiced in the daily lives of all of us who embrace them"?

Christianity has not failed, his father had preached once, because it has never been tried. Could it be tried, his son asked. Why has it not been tried? Is it being tried in the world now, today, by any large number of people living and working together, ordinary people, farmers, laborers, soldiers?

His father didn't know.

In the spring of 1937, he was informed that his requests to return to China duty were finally approved. He would leave for Shanghai in the summer to study the Chinese language in Peiping.

About a week after he was told he was going to leave, he was invited to see President Roosevelt.

"I understand you are going out to China again, Evans," the President said. "I want you to do something for me while you're there. I want you to drop me a line now and then — direct to the White House. Let me know how you're doing. Tell me what's going on. I suspect there's going to be a great deal going on this summer in China. I'd like to hear what you have to say about it."

Then Roosevelt leaned against his chair and stuck his cigarette holder in the corner of his lips. "Shall we keep these letters a secret? Just between the two of us? Shall we?"

"For as long as both of us live, Mr. President."

Roosevelt smiled broadly. "I've got a lot to do before I die," he said.

May went by, Roosevelt signed the Neutrality Act, Chamberlain succeeded Baldwin. . . . June, Soviet Marshal Tukhatchevsky and seven other generals were sentenced to be shot for treason, Franco's troops occupied Bilbao. . . .

Christianity is failing, Carlson had written home. He yearned to find some place in the world where it lived. Any place — even among heathens.

He left Seattle in late July on the *President McKinley*. For China. His China. The old golden land. Fifteen years before when he joined the Marine Corps they had asked him his choice of duty. He had said China.

Part Four

1

Red poppy

The day he landed a war began.

The S.S. *President McKinley* moved at quarter-speed through the foul yellow water of the Yangtze off Shanghai. An August sun out of a cloudless sky absorbed the river water and made everything sticky. Japanese warships bounced arrogantly in the swells. Overhead, Japanese bombing planes cut the sky swiftly and in single file dove on the Chinese Civic Center of Greater Shanghai.

From the deck of the *McKinley* Carlson saw smoke blooming up from the city where the Japanese bombs had dropped. He frowned, took his pipe out of his mouth and banged the bowl angrily against the rail. That morning he had read in the ship's bulletin that Spanish planes piloted by Germans had bombed Madrid. Now, halfway around the world, he was seeing it. Different planes, different city, but the same barbarism.

The ship swung slowly in the river and entered the Whangpoo. Along the wharves Chinese coolies unloaded Norwegian and German freighters. Somewhere in the city beyond sirens sounded like children crying.

More Japanese planes dove on the city. Great thuds sounded distantly like huge trees falling.

Carlson stared at the city angrily.

Ten years and six months had passed from the day when he had first seen Shanghai. How swiftly the years had gone. He felt a little sad. He was forty-one, old before he had even turned around. Where had the years vanished?

Below him now were the old Standard Oil Docks where in 1927 he and the men of the Fourth Marines had landed, waiting their turn to move against the Chinese mobs, and to put down, once and for all, the goddamned Chinks, the "Reds" who were molesting American lives and property. He groaned inwardly. God in heaven, how ignorant he had been. If he had only known in 1927 what he knew now, how much Shanghai could have meant to him then.

Would the day ever come when people could really see?

His reflections were broken into by the arrival of the tender to take the few disembarking passengers to the Customs Jetty eight miles away.

On the tender he stood by himself, apart from the others. His eyes were turned searchingly to the near shore. China was waiting for him again, as it had waited ten and a half years before. When he had first seen it war lay on its land, and now war again.

There are Chinese who have married, had children and grand-children without knowing a single year of peace, for since 1911 China has been at war.

Up to the present, of the thirty-five years of war, twenty-six have been spent in Chinese fighting Chinese, in civil war, revolution, and counter-revolution. Only for nine years, from 1936 to V-J Day in 1945, did the Chinese as a united nation fight a foreign enemy.

No people have fought so hard, so long and so painfully to win sovereignty over their own lives.

In 1927, when Carlson first came to China, one phase of the Long War had come to an end, and another had begun. The people's revolution led by the combined Kuomintang and Communist parties against their Manchu overlords had been won.

But at the moment of victory the people were betrayed and divided. Chiang Kai-shek's Kuomintang began the fight to extirpate their comrades-in-arms, the Communists and the dedicated followers of Sun Yat-sen. Tens of thousands of the Left were killed, suppressed and exiled. The widow of Sun Yat-sen was forced to leave her native land. Counter-revolution, tyranny disguised as "nationalism" rode the backs of the Chinese people. Civil war began again.

In 1931, Japan, taking advantage of China's disunity and the world's disinterest, created an "incident" in Manchuria, marched in and set up the puppet state of Manchukuo. The Communists, who had established a government of their own in the southeast, in the province of Kiangsi, declared war against Japan. But the Nationalists did nothing. In a world of appeasement Chiang Kai-shek did not want to fight alone. He did not trust his own people enough to organize them for a war against the invaders.

Chiang Kai-shek's relations with Japan continued.

But his own people acted without him. In 1932 the remnants of those Shanghai workers who in 1927 had helped Chiang Kai-shek take the city, and whom soon after he turned upon and purged mercilessly, called for a boycott against Japanese goods. Japan fought the boycott with a land, sea and air attack against the Chapei district of Shanghai. Again Chiang Kai-shek did nothing. Again his own people fought without him. The Nationalist Nineteenth Route Army, acting on its own, kept the Japanese from capturing Shanghai.

But the civil war against the Reds continued.

Thwarted at Shanghai, the Japanese waited a year and created another "incident" in Chinese Jehol. As before, only local patriots resisted. Chiang Kai-shek made a truce with Japan and gave away Jehol. The invader, arrogant with constant appeasement, hungered for even more of China.

Another campaign against the Kiangsi Reds was started.

In 1935 Japan moved into five northern provinces. She now possessed about a fifth of China's territory and about a third of her industrial and natural resources.

Chiang Kai-shek, however, had other battles to fight. Four campaigns against the Kiangsi Reds had failed. The fifth one, planned by German General von Seeckt, must not fail. Nationalist armies, outnumbering the Reds ten to one, drove the Reds out of Kiangsi, drove them across the impassable rivers and giant mountains of twelve provinces, through heat and cold and starvation, through the naked suffering of 6000 miles. The Reds under Chu Teh fought and retreated and fought again for about a year and by the end of 1935 the gaunt and weary remnants of the Long March [1] finally found an insecure haven at Yenan, in the northwest province of Shensi, hemmed in on three sides by the Japanese with whom they were officially at war, and on the fourth side by the still advancing Nationalist troops of Chiang Kai-shek.

But here they stopped; here they had decided that their Long March must end. For a year with weapons captured from their enemies or made in primitive workshops they fought both the Japanese and the Nationalists.

Chiang Kai-shek had insisted that he would not turn against the Japanese until every Chinese communist was either killed or in prison.

In December 1936, he changed his mind. Why?

The tale starts in the little city of Sian, about a hundred and seventy-five miles away from Yenan, the headquarters of the Red Army. There took place that month a fascinating drama which had everything — deaths, kidnapping, high stakes, singularly complicated characters in conflict with each other, Hamlet-like indecisiveness, villains, heroes, heroines, great love.

Consider this: Generalissimo Chiang Kai-shek sends his great friend, Young Marshal Chang Hsueh-liang, to lead an army of his Tungpei troops against the Reds. Friend Young Marshal Chang finds that the Reds are genuinely dedicated to driving out the invading Japanese. He is impressed by them. But his loyalty is to Chiang Kai-shek. He dallies with his offensive against the Reds and tries to persuade Chiang Kai-shek to turn against the Jap. Chiang Kai-shek flies to Sian to scold his errant comrade. "Fight the Reds,"

---

[1] For a magnificent description of the Long March and the life of the Chinese Red Armies, the reader must go to Edgar Snow's *Red Star Over China* published in The Modern Library. Also to Agnes Smedley's *Battle Hymn of China,* Alfred A. Knopf, 1943, to *Twin Stars of China* by Evans F. Carlson, Dodd, Mead & Co., 1940, to the books of Nym Wales, Anna Louise Strong, Harrison Forman, Owen Lattimore, James Bertram, Guenther Stein, Ilona Ralf Sues. To these people, all Americans owe an enormous debt. Their reports of China, through blockade and censorship, have brought to us the knowledge that our own spirit, our own Valley Forge and Revolution, live again on this globe.

he orders. The Young Marshal refuses. Chiang Kai-shek grows black with anger. The Young Marshal pleads with him. Chiang Kai-shek is adamant. The Young Marshal, searching his soul for the right thing to do, finally moves with his brother officers to kidnap their stubborn leader. No, not to kidnap. That would be too scandalous. They will merely detain him at Sian in order to have more time in which to present their arguments for a united China.

At 5:30 in the morning of December 12th the conspirators surround Chiang Kai-shek's house at Sian, and are fired on by his bodyguards who are soon killed. Chiang Kai-shek, taking advantage of the delay, jumps out of his bedroom window sans clothes and false teeth and tries to hide in the hills near-by. Finally, he is found by one of the Young Marshal's officers who apologizes for the indignity, and offers to take the Generalissimo to the Young Marshal. Chiang Kai-shek has no shoes on, and his feet hurt. The officer carries him piggyback to the house. The Young Marshal calls on Chiang Kai-shek who greets him angrily. "You have mutinied," the Generalissimo says. "Finish your job and kill me."

The Young Marshal refuses to kill his Commander in Chief. Instead, he explains why China must be unified; why it is necessary for Chiang Kai-shek to stop warring against the Reds. But Chiang Kai-shek will not listen. "Kill me or permit me to return to Nanking," the Generalissimo demands.

Now some of the Young Marshal's men and officers, the crack Tungpei troops, have come to be much influenced by the Reds whom they had been sent to destroy. They have been convinced that Chiang Kai-shek stands athwart a united China and a war against the invader. They would like very much to take Chiang Kai-shek at his word — and kill him. But the Young Marshal talks them out of it.

Nanking hears about Chiang Kai-shek's kidnapping. Pro-Japanese, anti-Russian General Ho Ying-chin, Chiang Kai-shek's Minister of War, is afraid that Chiang Kai-shek might be persuaded to fight Japan. He orders bombing planes to Sian to wipe out the whole city, Chiang Kai-shek included. But Madame Chiang Kai-shek argues with General Ho, and succeeds in winning time enough to fly to Sian to the side of the man she loves. She will plead for his life; she will free him. She has great and deserved confidence in herself.

In Sian the Young Marshal is in the middle of a vise. He is finding it difficult, on one hand, to persuade Chiang Kai-shek to compromise, and, on the other hand, he can barely keep his own officers and men from murdering Chiang Kai-shek. Madame Chiang Kai-shek arrives. She has a tearful reunion with her husband. They read the Bible together.

And now into the Sian drama enters Chou En-lai, a leader of the Chinese Reds, the man for whose head Chiang Kai-shek had placed a reward of $100,000, and who was number one on his list to be purged that 1927 night in Shanghai. Has he come for revenge? Has he come to destroy the man who was responsible for the murder and torture of ten thousand of his comrades? The Generalissimo and Madame, the Young Marshal and his Tungpei troops wait for the answer.

Chou En-lai talks to Chiang Kai-shek. He addresses him as "Your Excellency" and "Generalissimo." He asks him to continue the country's leadership. He tells him that the Chinese Reds are willing to forego everything, anything, to unite with the Nationalists in order to fight Japan. He reiterates Young Marshal Chang's points, (1) stop civil war, (2) resist Japan, (3) give political freedom to the people.

The radical Tungpei troops of the Young Marshal with the reckless passion of newly won converts are furious with the Reds. "You, yourself," they shout at Chou En-lai, "told us that Chiang Kai-shek is a Judas. That he has betrayed our country and our people. Now that the time is come to get rid of him, you ask him to remain as Premier and ask us to let him fly back to Nanking. Are you betraying us?"

Chou En-lai answers them quietly with the stony wisdom of facing the truth. If they killed Chiang Kai-shek, he says, this would not end civil war, but create the conditions for even more. The Fascist section of the Kuomintang, people like General Ho, would invite the Japanese in. "When we called for a united front," Chou En-lai tells them, "we meant it. We didn't mean a Communist front or a Kuomintang front. But a united front between the two parties. Only Chiang Kai-shek can guarantee the Kuomintang." And then Chou En-lai quotes the words of his great comrade, Mao Tse-tung. "If our country is subjugated by the enemy we will lose everything. We cannot even discuss communism if we are robbed of a country in which to practice it."

Only part of the Tungpei troops are satisfied.

And in the Generalissimo's house at Sian, Chiang Kai-shek refuses to sign any agreement. But he cannot help but be impressed with the sincerity of the Reds. He catches the meaning of General Ho's punitive expedition against the "Sian rebels," which would be really against his own life. He understands, with the help of his wife and W. H. Donald, his Australian adviser, that his "friends" are not friends, and his "enemies" are not enemies.

Young Marshal Chang keeps apologizing for detaining him. Chang has found the Generalissimo's private diary. In it he has read secret thoughts. He has read that Chiang Kai-shek really intends to fight the Japs just as soon as conditions permit him to do so and come out at the end with his power intact.

Now the Young Marshal will detain his old friend no more. He will send him back to Nanking in his own plane, and, more than that, he will return with him to be punished for his extraordinary act of *lèse majesté*. True, nothing has been agreed on in so many words, but an "understanding" has been reached.

With the help of the Reds, the Young Marshal pacifies his muttering and rebellious troops who want to cut Chiang Kai-shek into little pieces, and the Generalissimo, his wife, and Mr. Donald fly back to Nanking. With them, of course, "blushing with shame," is the apologetic Young Marshal.

In Nanking Chiang Kai-shek announces his own incompetence to the people and resigns as Premier. His resignation is not accepted. He resigns twice more. Twice more he is refused. But, as he takes office each time, new decrees come from his pen.

He withdraws his troops from Shensi province where the Reds are. He dissolves his anti-communist headquarters in Sian. He dismisses some influential pro-Japanese cabinet ministers. He supports a new slogan, "Recovery of our lost territories." He sends a quiet directive to the press that the epithets "Red-bandit" and "Communist-bandit" are no longer to be used. Finally, in a speech in February, he asks the Chinese Reds to "surrender" but the terms he offers are practically the same which they proposed at Sian.

As for the Young Marshal Chang, he is sentenced to ten years' imprisonment and pardoned the next day.

Edgar Snow, in describing the Sian "incident" in his book *Red Star Over China,* concludes his summary in these words:

> Now, all this must seem to be an utterly incomprehensible *dénouement* to the innocent Occidental observer unskilled in Chinese politics, and he is likely to make serious errors of judgment in analyzing its significance. Certainly it could happen nowhere else in the world but China. After a decade of the fiercest kind of civil war, Red and White suddenly burst into "Auld Lang Syne." What was the meaning of it? Had the Reds turned White, and the Whites turned Red? Neither one. But surely someone must have won, and someone lost? Yes, China had won, Japan had lost. For the last decision in this profoundly complicated two-way struggle had been postponed once more by the intervention of a third ingredient — Japanese imperialism.[2]

The "third ingredient" struck again on July 7 with an "incident" at Lukouchiao, the old Marco Polo Bridge in Peiping, and in Shanghai on the 24th with another "incident" which concerned an errant Japanese marine in a Chinese brothel. In both cases Chiang Kai-shek, having been Sianized, encouraged his troops to resist, although he did not declare official war against Nippon until four years later, after the attack on Pearl Harbor.

*   *   *

[2] In addition to Snow's book, the Sian story is told in great detail in James Bertram's *First Act in China* and Nym Wales's *Inside Red China,* Doubleday, Doran, 1939. Chiang Kai-shek told his own story in *Sian, A Coup D'Etat,* Shanghai, 1937.

Carlson, of course, knew these last ten years of China's history. He had come to understand the betrayal at Shanghai in 1927. He had scanned with anxiety the Japanese invasion of Jehol in 1933 when he was studying Chinese porcelains in Peiping. He understood more then. By 1937 he was heart and soul with the Chinese in their undeclared war against Japan, but he did not yet comprehend the full meaning of the "last decision" between the Reds and the Whites. Sian, about which he had read, was to him a characteristically complicated Chinese political set-to which had brought a kind of unity to the nation. But he did not yet know on which side lay right and justice. He was soon to find out.

He felt in his element as he left the Customs Jetty. "You're smack in the middle of a war," Morris Harris, the Shanghai Associated Press man told him.

Admiral Harry Yarnell, the Commander in Chief of the Asiatic Fleet, to whom he reported, was a man who saw with impatient eyes the encroachment of Japan upon China. He was no eater of flame, this old Navy man; he did not want to create incidents and make taut the diplomatic strings which held his nation and Japan in polite co-operation. But he hated injustice and he hated Japanese militarism and he wished he could use the guns of his flagship, the U.S.S. *Augusta,* against the Japanese destroyers who were standing off near him and shelling the defenseless city. But if neutrality was his country's policy, he would pursue it conscientiously, though it stuck in his craw.

"You're supposed to go up to Peiping and study," he told Carlson when he read his orders. "But there's a war going on *here.*"

"I don't want to waste my time," Carlson said eagerly. He had hoped for something like this from Yarnell.

"Suppose I modified your orders to stand by here as a Naval Intelligence observer until things quiet down. What about it? We need all the trained observers we can find. We've got to find out how the Chinese fight, and what's more important, how the Japs fight."

"It's exactly what I want to do," Carlson said.

* * *

It was an extraordinary war Carlson was to observe. For a while it was a war within a city; battles that flamed within city blocks and parks and across streets and squares, from alleyways and hotel tops, department stores, market places and Chinese temples. It was the kind of a war you could watch from the window of your hotel room. Carlson and his fellow observers, Commander Overesch, of Naval Intelligence, his immediate superior, Major Eddie Hagen of the Marines, Jim Mills and Morris Harris of the A.P., John B. Powell, Carlson's old friend from the 1927 days and still the valiant editor of the anti-Japanese *China Weekly Review,* and Pembroke Stephens of the London *Daily Telegraph* would watch the battle for the city from roof tops overlooking the Soochow Creek or from the buildings on the perimeter of the International Settlement. They used to rent window space from landlords as if they were seats on the fifty yard line at the Yale Bowl.

Once Carlson watched with bitterness and frustration Japanese tanks and artillery obliterating at a range of sixty yards two thousand poorly armed Chinese. It was hard to watch. He wanted to run over to the Chinese, pick up one of their fallen rifles, fire back. But he was an observer, a neutral. . . .

Did these Chinese, these empty-handed coolies, know what they were dying for, he wondered.

He asked the question of a perspiring coolie, resting for a moment in the hot, scarred street. Wearily he had put down his shoulder pole with its double-ended load of cooked rice for the fighting troops.

"What are you fighting for?" Carlson asked. "What are your countrymen dying for?"

The broad head and the quiet eyes turned to Carlson slowly. Trickles of sweat dropped from the bony creeks. "National salvation," the coolie said.

"But what is national salvation?"

The coolie thought a moment and he frowned; then the words came from his dry lips, words perhaps that he had not heard, nor even thought of before. "The enemy wants to take our homes," he said slowly. "If we work together we can defeat him."

Carlson didn't catch all the Chinese words the coolie used, and he repeated aloud a phrase.

"*Gung Ho*," he said. It was the first time Carlson had heard those words, "Work together." [3]

The coolie smiled and nodded.

An antiaircraft shell landed in the middle of an intersection near by. The coolie left and Carlson ran up. About twenty Chinese lay silent. He ran from one to the other to see who was dead. Ten were beyond human help. Then a police ambulance drove up. Another shell came over and sliced in half a house at the corner.

He moved down the street to a bridge that crossed Soochow Creek. On the other side, at the North Station, where ten years ago he had seen White Russians in an armored train hold off a battalion of Kuomintang troops, Kuomintang troops were now holding off a battalion of Japanese. Machine guns, grenades, artillery were pounding and sputtering away. As he stood on the bridge Chinese planes came over, dropped bombs; from the Whangpoo Jap ships slammed at them with heavy guns. He felt a gripping exhilaration.

> It was a grand scene. [He wrote home that night from the American Club.] It had drama and excitement and imminent death. To me such a scene is the epitome of life. It brings home the futility of life, the closeness of death, the utter folly of worrying about petty details. Those who cringe from death deserve to die, for they lack the faith and the breadth of vision to be useful in life.
>
> The Chinese are magnificent in their fortitude. They have great sources of spiritual strength. I noticed one thing about the Chinese in the course of that incident I never remarked before. The wounded make no outcry. There was no moaning such as Westerners would have made. A little girl about

[3] Later Carlson was to learn that *Gung Ho* was not correct Chinese for "work together." Other words came between the *Gung* and the *Ho*. But in 1939 when the Chinese Industrial Co-operatives took the phrase for its slogan, China accepted it as a contribution to its vocabulary. According to Dr. James F. Bender of the National Institute of Human Relations *Gung Ho*, as a result of its use in the Raiders, has become part of the American language. The *New York Times*, Dec. 2, 1945.

twelve had her knee split wide open in a frightful wound.
She made no sound as a temporary dressing was put on and
as she was moved to the ambulance. You can't down a people
who are so indifferent to pain and death.

The logic was clear to him. "Spiritual strength . . . indifference
to pain and death." Others might say that perhaps this Chinese
characteristic was derived from a life so hard and stringent that
death and pain came as something long expected and familiar. Perhaps pride and fortitude gave them strength. Perhaps the acknowledgment of an inevitability of their fate, where if it is willed
that a man work and marry and breed children and take care of his
own parents and starve and freeze and never have enough, it is
also willed that he should not cry out with pain. Perhaps all of these
theories and more; but to Carlson, it was spiritual strength and
nothing else.

Once he and Ed Snow and Colin McDonald of the London
Times climbed a seventy-foot-high water tower — the highest place
in the French concession — to see a battle. They were on the platform below the water tank around which circled another platform.
Below them were about eight hundred Chinese soldiers in the open
with their backs against a wall of the French concession. Japanese
infantrymen, using houses for cover were massacring the Chinese.
Finally the Chinese wheeled about and scrambled up the wall,
bullets snatching many of them back. Those that escaped the grasping bullets were helped by the French troops on the other side and
were interned.

Suddenly a Jap machine gun started spraying the water tower.
Carlson and his friends ducked for safety behind a concrete wall
that projected off to one side.

Carlson suddenly looked up at the platform above. At that
moment Ed Snow noticed a blotch of red at his feet. "Anybody
hurt?" he asked. "Or is that paint?"

Nobody was hurt, and they went back to watching the remnants
of the surrounded Chinese — those who could not reach the wall
in time — fling themselves against the Jap bayonets.

"I noticed Carlson was missing," wrote Edgar Snow. "Looking around I saw him climbing up the water tower."[4]

Colin McDonald, thinking that the Japs could shoot Carlson down easily as he climbed the tower, watched breathlessly. "Only an absolutely fearless man would take the risk," McDonald said later.

Seven men, head in hands, lay prostrate on the platform when Carlson reached it. He thought they were dead. He spoke, and one man slowly raised his head.

"Are the Japanese here?" he whispered.

Carlson reassured him. Five others rose from the floor. One man lay in his own blood, dead.

"Who is he?" Carlson asked.

"I don't know," one man said with a French accent.

"What's your name?" Carlson asked.

The man took out his wallet with trembling hands and gave Carlson a visiting card. "I'm Dr. Richer," he said.

It was hardly the place to be exchanging calling cards, Carlson thought, but this regard for convention could not be ignored, and he handed Richer one of his own. Then another man turned over the body and looked at the face. "It's Pembroke Stephens," he said. "Of the London *Daily Telegraph*."

By this time Snow and McDonald were upon the platform. Carlson explained why he had left them. "I saw a foot hanging down," he said. "I thought I ought to investigate."

Someone picked Stephens up. Carlson noticed a red poppy in his lapel. He must have bought it at the American Club. It was November eleventh, Armistice Day.

[4] *The Battle for Asia,* Random House, 1941.

2

A patch of America on a dead city

Down into Shanghai, during September, October and November, came clandestine reports that the Red Army, now known, after Sian, as the Eighth Route Army, was fighting the Jap rather successfully, more ably than the Nationalists at Shanghai, and with a new kind of strategy with which, in its first battle against the Japs at Pinhsing Pass in September, it had somehow neutralized the Japanese superiority in fire power and mechanized equipment, and had defeated badly the crack 5th Division under the command of General Itagaki, later Minister of War in Prince Konoye's cabinet.

Ed Snow had a lot to say about the Chinese Reds. He had spent the summer and fall of 1936 with them at Pao An in Shensi province. Following his visit, he had written a book which he was calling *Red Star Over China*. He finished it in Peiping in July 1936 and brought a copy of the manuscript with him to Shanghai. Carlson read it.

Carlson had deep ties of friendship with Snow. He admired his honesty and courage. But when he read his manuscript, he came away almost disbelieving.

"My God, Ed," he said. "Are there really such men as Chu Teh, Mao Tse-tung, Chou En-lai, or have you made them up?"

"I haven't made them up," Snow said. "They are there for anybody to see and talk to and live with." He paused slyly. "Even an American Naval Intelligence officer. One might say, especially." Snow became angry. "There hasn't been *one* foreign military in there."

"But what kind of men are they?" Carlson persisted.

A faraway look came into Snow's eyes. He leaned his short,

muscular body forward in the chair. "They're different, Evans," he said slowly. "They're humble, earnest men, scrupulously honest in word and action."

"In action, too?" Carlson demanded. That was the important thing.

Snow nodded. "Take the Chinese habit of trying to 'save face' for example. They fight it by inviting criticism and by severely criticizing themselves. Just wait till you meet General Chu Teh!"

"Ed, you sound like a Salvation Army preacher."

Snow shrugged.

"You sound like a fellow selling shares in Utopia."

"See for yourself, Evans."

"I'm a hard-boiled Marine, Ed. Generals don't go around inviting criticism and criticizing themselves."

"Chu Teh does," Snow said quietly.

"If I didn't believe you had good sense, Ed, I'd swear you were sending me off on a goose chase."

Snow lifted his eyes. "Then you're going?"

Carlson laughed. "If I can talk Commander Overesch and Admiral Yarnell into sending me, I'm going."

"Good," Snow said, satisfied.

"As much as I'd like to see those 'god-like' men of yours, Ed, if I go it's because I think it's important to learn how they're fighting the Japs up there in the Red Northwest. It'll come in handy some day."

"I'll write you a letter to Mao Tse-tung," Snow said. "He's the chairman of the Yenan government."

Commander Overesch had a stringent and inflexible sense of military duty. To him it was defined as something set down in military orders. It was not open to interpretation. It could not be expanded beyond the immediate mission. Carlson had been ordered to observe the activities of the Chinese Armies. He had not been limited to observation only in the Shanghai area. Therefore, it was quite within his duty to go elsewhere, even to the Red Northwest. Admiral Yarnell concurred.

"But you have to get Chiang Kai-shek's approval to travel to Sian," Carlson was told.

Carlson scoured Shanghai stores for equipment. He figured he'd be with the Armies during the winter, and he bought a sheepskin lined coat, a heavy sleeping bag, and, of course, as strong a pair of hiking shoes as he could find. His pack included a small tea kettle to boil his water in, chopsticks, an enamel cup and a wash basin. He took along a volume of Emerson's *Selected Essays,* and two booklets of the British Three-Penny Library, one on geography and one on law, and the September 1937 issue of the *Reader's Digest.* His health was good; he hadn't had a malaria attack in years. He felt himself ready for anything.

All Shanghai was moving north out of the grasp of the advancing Japanese. The Yangtze which carried boat-borne traffic up to Nanking was filled with refugees on barges, launches pulling strings of boats, small steamers, junks, canoes, houseboats. For Carlson and the few other Occidentals going north, it was hand-to-mouth traveling. In the fight for food and sleeping accommodations men made quick alliances in the swift comradeship of flight. Such an alliance was formed between Carlson, an American airplane salesman, a Mohammedan father and son, and two White Russian brothers. By the time they reached Nanking, five days after leaving Shanghai, the little *internationale* had covered the 200 miles by steamer, barge, put-put launch, rickshaw, and hiking. In the hundred and twenty hours' time, Carlson had about ten hours sleep. But he enjoyed it. He liked the Chinese crowds, the singing actors who traveled the boats for a living, the Chinese soldiers who sat for hours with him on top of a filled coal car that was supposed to take them the rest of the way to Nanking but didn't leave the station at all. His liking for them grew boundlessly, their singing, the jokes, the good-natured tricks, the hardships taken in stride, the sharing of tea and scraps of food. In those five days he had picked up from the Chinese some of their slang, much of their dirt, and more of their spirit.

*　　*　　*

Nanking was a city of the dead and dying in November 1937. The Japanese were too close for the National Government to continue functioning there, and its bureaus and civil servants were on their way to Hankow, four hundred miles to the west, and to Chungking, even further away.

Nanking was empty streets, fear, refugees, barbed wire blockades — the stigmata of a city in war. Chiang Kai-shek and his wife were still in Nanking, as well as W. H. Donald, the Generalissimo's Australian advisor, but they were moving out soon.

Carlson went to see Donald. Through him, perhaps, Chiang Kai-shek could be persuaded to permit Carlson to go into the interior.

Donald lived up on the lower slope of Purple Mountain near Sun Yat-sen's mausoleum. As Carlson drove along the empty highway he felt again the speed of passing time. He had marched up that highway eight years before behind Sun Yat-sen's cortege. He had been Admiral Bristol's guest at the reinterment of China's greatest leader. Then the highway had been crowded with marching people, full of hope for the future. And now, he asked himself sadly, where had all those tens of thousands of human beings vanished? Where had their hope gone? Along what newly crowded roads gray with fear were they now marching, fathers and grandfathers and sons, grandmothers and mothers and their children, with the packets of pathetic property on their backs? And some were dead, he knew; and some were fleeing this city now; and some were perhaps up in the Northwest; and some, sucked of all hope, were staying in Nanking until the Japs came, believing it could not be worse under the conqueror.

W. H. Donald is always described in books and articles as a man of mystery, a legend. The one thing clear is that he was a man of enormous influence in Nationalist China.

John Gunther says that Donald was a "most extraordinary human being," who had done everything in his time in China from combing out the pigtails of the Soong sisters when they were children to writing some of Sun Yat-sen's proclamations. He was a man, Gunther relates, who knew more Chinese state secrets than any foreigner who ever lived in China.

When Carlson was introduced to Donald, the integrity and kindliness of Donald's expression — characteristics which Carlson always sought for in meeting strangers — made him favor the man.

Carlson presented his request for a pass to go into the interior. He told Donald forthrightly that he hoped to be able to get to the Red Armies.

"Do you think you have something to learn from them?" Donald asked.

"I won't know until I see them," Carlson replied.

"You know," Donald said thoughtfully, "that travel in the interior is risky and difficult at this time."

"I know."

"The Nationalist Government can't assume responsibility for your safety."

"I don't want it to," Carlson said. He was glad this came up. He wanted no strings other than those that bound him with his Intelligence mission. "I'm willing to take care of myself and give the government a paper releasing it from any responsibility."

Donald ran his fingers through his graying hair, and grinned broadly. "I'll talk to the boss," he said. "I'll let you know."

"Mr. Donald," Carlson said, "can I hope that you'll present my request to the Generalissimo with, shall I say, sympathy?"

Donald bellowed with a laugh. "Hell, Carlson," he said. "If I had a brick for every time the boss turned down one of my sympathetically offered requests, I'd have enough to build a new Chinese Wall from Peiping to Tibet."

While waiting for the word on the pass, Carlson opened himself up to the talk, opinions, theories and gossip of the men in Nanking who knew more than he did. There were quite a few China hands left: the consular attachés, Jimmie McHugh, Frank Roberts, George Atcheson and Hall Paxton. There was Colonel Claire Chennault, who had resigned from the American Air Force to help China's. The newspaper crowd, men whom he respected, helped him considerably; Tillman Durdin of the *New York Times,* Weldon James of the United Press, Yates McDaniel of the Associated Press, and Colin McDonald of the London *Times* who had just come up from Shanghai with stories of the disintegration of its defense.

They were all together at meals and at night, talking, swapping anecdotes, singing familiar songs, getting homesick, interweaving one with the other a patch of America on the dead city. Months later many of them would be together at Hankow in what they would call the Last Ditchers' Club, hanging on to the doomed city, waiting like tired doctors for its death. Now, in Nanking, they were "interning" for it, so to speak. By duty or job or from the sheer perverseness of human curiosity, they wanted to see how long they could remain in the city before the Japs moved in. They were always Last Ditchers, in those days, and out of them ran the black thread of news of China's defeats to our own crossroads. They were, within the limits of their tasks, Jeremiahs calling out doom to their native land eight thousand miles away.

Carlson learned a great deal from all these men, and from Chinese like J. L. Huang, and from Americans like George Fitch, head of the Y.M.C.A. Both Huang and Fitch were the directors of the Chinese Officers' Moral Endeavor Association (a name which, almost by itself, was enough to win Carlson's interest). This association, along with Chiang Kai-shek's New Life Movement, was admittedly an attempt to create for the Nationalist armies the reputation for incorruptibility which the Communist armies had won. Both Fitch and Huang made out an excellent case for the high morale of the Nationalists, and Carlson was convinced for a time. Later, however, he was forced to reconsider when he visited the little Yangtze city of Kukiang. There he saw a large group of Chinese men in chains, with armed guards in front and to the rear of them, being marched toward a barracks. He asked the officer in charge who these men were, criminals or traitors.

"Recruits," was the answer.

He was shocked to discover that many Nationalist soldiers had to be impressed into service, and that obviously nothing or little was being done to explain to the Chinese the reasons for the war. Nothing was told them about how their lives could and would be improved with the defeat of Japan. In short, if the war was being fought for a democratic China, the mass of Chinese didn't know it, didn't see it, and didn't experience the practice or even the promise of democracy.[5]

On November 26 Donald telephoned Carlson saying that the Generalissimo had approved his trip and a pass would be sent over to the Embassy. By seven o'clock that night Carlson was aboard the crowded *Tuck Wo* en route to Sian, via Hankow.

In Hankow, he stayed long enough to pay his respects to Ambassador Nelson T. Johnson who gave him some fatherly advice on how to take care of himself; to the quiet and gracious Paul Josselyn, the Consul General; to thoughtful Admiral Marquadt, Commander of the Yangtze patrol, who told him to go down into the sick bay of the *Luzon,* his flagship, and help himself to as much medical supplies as he thought he might need; and finally to Tung Pi-wu, the Eighth Route Army representative in Hankow, later to be one of China's delegates to the United Nations Conference at San Francisco. Tung Pi-wu looked like a conventional mandarin with thin drooping mustachios and heavy-lidded eyes. He was cordial, if somewhat uncommunicative, and informed Carlson that when he got to Sian he should look up a comrade, Lin Tso-han, who would arrange transportation up to the Yenan headquarters of the Eighth Route Army.

"Lin Tso-han is one of our oldest comrades," Tung Pi-wu said. And then he added with a broad smile, "The Party always sends him into danger spots whenever it is uncertain whether our delegate will come back alive. If we lose an old man, it's not as bad as losing a youngster." He winked at Carlson. "That's why I'm here at Hankow. I'm an old one too."

Before leaving Hankow, which Carlson found too European for his taste, he borrowed one of the Embassy typewriters and

[5] Lin Yutang describes the abuses of Chiang Kai-shek's methods of conscription in *The Vigil of a Nation,* John Day, 1945. Mr. Lin Yutang is a defender of the Generalissimo against the Chinese Reds.

brought his diary up to date. He promised himself that once he left Hankow he would make entries every day before going to sleep, no matter how late. He was determined to keep a full record of his trip.

3

Among the heathen

Excerpts from Carlson's diary:

3 December

Our train arrived in Sian at 11 P.M. A representative of the Guest House was at the train and took charge of me. A military officer took my name and looked at my passport. A customs inspection was made to determine whether or not there was contraband arms in my luggage.

The Guest House was more than I anticipated. A modern building with well-appointed rooms and private baths. It was good to boil out in a bath and roll up in a bed for a good night's sleep.

4 December

I arose late this morning. I spent an hour reading in bed before arising. James Bertram's book *First Act in China* about the Sian kidnapping of Chiang Kai-shek is extremely interesting, especially now that I am on the ground where the main scenes were enacted.

I had no difficulty finding the headquarters of Mr. Lin Tso-han. He was not there, but a Mr. Wu. He will wire ahead to Mao Tse-tung at Yenan about permission for me.

5 December

I learned much to my surprise that today is Sunday. At Eighth Route Army Headquarters, I met a Mr. Li Po-chou who speaks English very well. He volunteered to go to Yenan with me as my interpreter providing Mao Tse-tung approves my entrance.

Spent the rest of the day in bed. Malaria is back on me. I don't feel natural, and I must get myself in shape.

6 December

I sent my card over today to General Chiang Ting-wen, commander of the area, and a Nationalist, of course . . . I must get some quinine . . .

7 December

Chairman Mao Tse-tung sent a radio here today granting permission to travel to the Shansi front. An officer is on the way to meet me here. That's grand news.

Tonight I dined with the Swensons, she from Connecticut, he from New Jersey, both missionaries in China for the last 25 years. Wonderful people, and the food was old home and marvelous.

8 December

Almost every wounded man I see, and there are about 10,000 of them in Sian, has one or both legs amputated. Dr. Clow of the British Missionary Hospital tells me that this is because local hospitals are not equipped with the men and appliances to attempt to heal serious leg wounds, so amputation is prescribed.

The entry of December 10 was not typed but written. Surrounded by a bodyguard of eight men, each armed with a Thompson sub-machine gun, Carlson wrote it in a rocking, smelly, crowded third-class coach bound for T'ungkwan.

It had been quite a day.

At 10:45 that morning a call came from the Eighth Route Army Headquarters to hurry over there. As he approached the building in a rickshaw, an orderly ran out and told Carlson to continue down to the railroad station where an officer waited for him. The train for the front would be leaving in half an hour.

"I'm not going to the station," Carlson said to the orderly. "All my equipment is still in the Guest House."

"That doesn't matter," the orderly said hurriedly.

"I'm not going."

"You'll get new equipment."

Carlson shook his head stubbornly. He wasn't going to take the chance on spending a sub-zero winter in Shansi without his sleeping bag and change of clothing. He ordered his rickshaw to take him back to the Guest House.

As he finished packing, a young officer with an Eighth Route Army sleeve badge, entered the room. He was smiling.

"I was waiting for you at the station, Ts'an Tsan," the officer said, giving Carlson the official title of "attaché."

"I'm sorry," Carlson said.

"We try to be prompt in executing orders," the officer said. "In old China, it would have taken a week to leave," he added proudly.

"And in new China you don't give a man a chance to take his clothes with him," Carlson retorted with a laugh.

The young officer remained silent a moment, then joined Carlson's laugh. "You know, Ts'an Tsan, the Eighth Route Army would not permit you to go naked."

He traveled up the gorge-rimmed Yellow River, into the Red Partisan territory in Shansi, and was led on horse to the secret headquarters of the Eighth Route Army near Hungtung.

Just before evening the little patrol of Carlson, his bodyguard, and a guide, entered an innocuous-looking village and followed a sheaf of telephone wires to a compound. The patrol stopped. Carlson dismounted, tied his horse to a post, and looked around. The sun was all but gone, but the afterlight illumined the scaling white compound walls and the dark-green single shrub that grew behind it and over its edge. He turned around to look off from whence he came, and he saw coming toward him a stocky man of medium height wearing the plain horizon-blue uniform of a Chinese private soldier. His face was broad and bronzed, beaten by the weather like a sea captain's, with sun wrinkles at the corners of his eyes. The man's bronzed face was smiling, and in the semidarkness his white teeth shone. He came toward Carlson with his hand stretched out in welcome.

Excerpt from Carlson's diary:

As he came toward me, I recognized the features of Chu Teh, the famous commander of the Eighth Route Army. Immediately and intuitively I felt that I had found a warm and a generous friend, and a man who was a true leader of men.

He led me into his living quarters, a simply furnished room with a sleeping k'ang in an alcove. The walls were covered with maps of the Shansi-Hopei district with the Eighth Route Army and Japanese positions marked out plainly. We talked in Chinese for a few minutes, he being exceedingly tolerant of my inadequate vocabulary. After a while, an interpreter came in, and it turned out to be my friend, Li Po, who had volunteered to interpret for me in Sian but who had to leave before Mao Tse-tung had sent permission.

From Edgar Snow Carlson had heard the life of Chu Teh whose name, given to him by his unsuspecting parents fifty years before, oddly enough means "Red Virtue." It is pronounced "Ju Deh" in English. Chu Teh, as Snow pointed out, was unique because for forty years of his life he was the perfect example of Chinese corruption. The son of wealth, he rose to power as an able and respectable General under Sun Yat-sen, became an opium addict, plundered his province's treasury, collected a harem, and seemed to approve a dog-eat-dog life where he was top dog. "He had, in fact, only one really bad habit," Snow said wryly. "He liked to read books."

Books, the influence of several Chinese students who had returned from study abroad and a native idealism brought to him a "sense of shame" and a passionate desire to overcome his own ignorance. He pensioned off his harem and fought ceaselessly and with a steel will to conquer his craving for opium. He traveled to Germany where he first found Marxist and Leninist books, and joined the Chinese Communist Party Branch in Berlin. After a few years in Berlin, Paris and Moscow of humble, hard, conscientious study, work that required the kind of demoniac strength with which he had downed his hunger for narcotics, he returned to Shanghai and turned over his fortune to the Communists. After the betrayal of 1927 and the Kuomintang-Communist battles of 1931 to 1933, he and Mao Tse-tung led the Long March to the Northwest.

Carlson had heard all this about Chu Teh, but the one element in Chu Teh's history which made Carlson open his heart to the man "immediately and intuitively" was the fact of his change of life at forty. This had meaning to Carlson. He saw in Chu Teh the clear image of what in his own life was yet faint and blurred.

Before these two men were to part, the Yankee Carlson would come to love the Chinese as he loved no other man except his father. His whole life would be a renewal after Chu Teh.

Few men are won by principles alone, but rather by other men who preach and live them. We are not followers of the word as much as we are of the deed which emerges from it. It was the example of Christ, not merely His sermons, the living humanness of Lincoln, not only his proclamations, which conquered their followers.

"Just as our courage is so often a reflex of another's courage," wrote William James in his essay on free will, "so our faith is apt to be, as Max Müller somewhere says, a faith in someone else's faith. We draw new life from the heroic example. The prophet has drunk more deeply than anyone of the cup of bitterness, but his countenance is so unshaken and he speaks such mighty words of cheer that his will becomes our will, and our life is kindled at his own."

This is what Carlson came to feel.

Yet, as he and Chu Teh talked in the little room at headquarters, Carlson stood off within himself, not quite aloof, but with the native skepticism of a man who fears evil so deeply that he must hesitate before grasping what he thinks is good lest his own desires mislead him.

"You are the first foreign military officer to visit our army, Ts'an Tsan," Chu Teh said. "We're glad to have you here, but just what would you like to see?"

Carlson replied that he wanted to go into battle with the troops, to live and march with them, to study their partisan tactics. He said he had learned a little about guerrilla war in Nicaragua. He wanted to learn more.

When Carlson finished Chu Teh waited.

Li Po, the interpreter, turned to Carlson to inquire if there was anything further he wanted to say.

"Yes," Carlson said. "Tell Chu Teh I would like to know something of the doctrines which govern the conduct of the men of his army. That's as important as their military tactics."

When Li Po was halfway through translating Chu Teh smiled broadly and pushed back his blue forage cap in a gesture of decision.

"Good," he said. "Tomorrow, I will call a meeting of my staff and you can ask them all the questions you want. The trip with the army we'll discuss later. Now let's eat."

There were talks with the Staff, with the political director, Jen Peh-hsi, whom Carlson describes as a man with "bird-like alertness," with Tso Chuan, the acting Chief of Staff, with a Korean who was the director of the Enemy Works Department (Intelligence), and with many others, senior and junior officers, non-coms and enlisted men. For ten days he moved through the life of the camp, talking, listening, asking questions and being asked eager questions about the world outside. He learnt — and he taught. They asked him to tell them the faults and weaknesses of the Chinese, and in turn they laid out their ideas in front of his mind for him to study, to reject, to modify, to refute. He heard Chu Teh speak of the inevitability of a war between Japan and the United States. They discussed the meaning and effect of President Roosevelt's "quarantine the aggressor" speech, the situation in Spain, the Italian recognition of Manchukuo.

The Eighth Route Army had simple rules for the conduct of their guerrillas: soldiers must ask permission before entering a house; they must keep the house clean, speak kindly to the people, pay for all they used at the market price, never commit a nuisance but dig latrines; must not kill or mistreat prisoners.

"The Army might be compared to fish, and the people to the water through which we move," Jen Peh-hsi, the political director said. "The water must be cleared of obstructions, and the temperature must be conducive to the efficient movement of the fish. The people, as well as the Army, must learn why we fight Japan, and how they can help. They must learn how to govern themselves, and how to live and *work together* in harmony."

"Work together . . ." Gung Ho! There it was again. Not quite as it was in the Chinese, but it was the second time he had heard the phrase.

"How do your officers and men Gung Ho?" Carlson asked in pidgin Chinese. The question was crucial. This was the knot of military life which he had not yet been able to unravel.

"By political work," Jen Peh-hsi said. "It is the life line of our army. Indoctrination. . . . First, we must teach our soldiers to read. When units are on the march lesson papers are pinned on the back of the man ahead, so that our illiterate soldier may study as he marches. By every device we can think of, meetings, plays, games, cartoons, and of course, by example, we try to teach our men and ourselves the principles of honesty, humility and co-operation."

Political work? Carlson wondered how that might apply in his own army. Could it be done? Could it have been done during the World War? In Nicaragua? Ah, there were problems. The cause must be morally just or else political indoctrination is perversion, empty phrases for a crusade that is dishonorable. As he turned these thoughts over, he prayed that if ever again his country went to war, its morality would be so clear that he could with full heart teach his men the reasons for their sacrifice.

He turned to Jen Peh-hsi and Chu Teh urgently.

"What about your officers and men?" he demanded.

"Our officers," Jen Peh-hsi said, "are, as you have seen, in daily and intimate contact with the men."

"Aren't there any distinctions between them?"

"None."

"Not even social ones? Different messes? After duty?"

"See for yourself, Ts'an Tsan," Chu Teh said.

"What are officers?" Jen Peh-hsi asked. "They are leaders. And how do we tell whether a man is a leader? He is a leader if he has given his men convincing proof of his ability to lead, his correctness and swiftness of decision, his courage, his willingness to share everything with his men. If he proves all this, then he is respected. His

men have confidence in him. But men and their leaders are comrades. Off duty, they are on equal social basis. They salute only on
duty — and only when they are addressing each other formally for
purposes of transacting business."

"How much of your plans of the battles do you tell your men?"

"Men who know most fight best," Chu Teh said.

"Yes," Jen Peh-hsi added. "That's another thing, Ts'an Tsan.
Before our troops go into battles the leaders hold a meeting with
them and explain the reasons for the engagement and the tactics
that will be used. After the battle another meeting is held at which
time we discuss our mistakes, for only by knowing our mistakes,
men and leaders together, can we learn how to correct them."

"Do you have a name for your way of doing things?" Carlson
inquired. There was a need in him to be precise about this method
of life.

Jen Peh-hsi looked at Chu Teh and then back at Carlson, and
shrugged. "Political indoctrination, perhaps. We don't have a
name."

"Military political indoctrination," Li Po suggested. "Does that
help, Ts'an Tsan?"

Carlson thought a minute. "No," he said. "It's more than that.
What you do does more than help win battles or inform people as
to the reasons of their condition. You're teaching yourselves and
people how to live like decent human beings. It's more than
politics, military tactics, mass spirit, sacrifice . . ." He was searching for the right word. It was important! He could invest his
whole life in words that men *acted* upon! Finally it came and
clanged like a bell inside him.

"It's ethics!" he cried. "That's what describes it. Ethical living,
ethical politics, ethical tactics. It's *ethical indoctrination!*"

It was as if he had known it all along. Fifteen years before he
had written an essay for his officers' class in Quantico. He had
said that ethics was the conscious striving of men for the welfare
of society as a whole.

His father was an ethical man. Franklin Roosevelt was an ethical
man. There were millions of ethical men in the world. He had

once wondered if he'd ever find them together, living, working,
striving together. Where existed a society of ethical men? he had
asked. And now he had found one — in the hills of Shansi province
in China, in the sprawling areas of the Eighth Route Army. He
could say without equivocation he had come on it like a Columbus.
Here, among the heathen were Christians, among the atheists were
men loving men as dearly as Christ would have wanted them to.
Here, with all its primitiveness, human weaknesses and imperfec-
tions, was a community which practised the Sermon. It was what
he had wanted to believe was possible somewhere in the world,
among any kind of men.

It was possible.

And so it went, the talk and countertalk, the learning and the
asking. And Carlson never felt so alive and so hopeful of himself
as in those clear, sharp, bright December days.

This by-the-book Marine Corps officer, this tough-fibered Yankee
soldier had looked around the world for something he didn't know
he was looking for; for New England, for Emerson, for Thoreau,
for John Brown, for William James — in short for a community of
men in which there was a day-to-day translation of democratic
ideas into democratic actions. He had been a man drunk with the
hope that some day, somewhere, he would find men weary of
words and passionate for their practice. In essence he had been
searching for America — for the promise of his own country. And
he found it — not in his native land of which, through the "accident" of his work, he saw little. But he found it by the same
"accident" in a country with an alien tongue, among men who but
to a few were outcasts.

He had reached a point in his life where his social conscience
required a catalyst. His vague, naïve and subjective humanitarianism
was not satisfying him. Unconsciously he was greeting every new
experience and every new leader he met with a longing and a hope.
Through trial and error, sometimes by will and sometimes through
the sheer momentum of his life, he had been seeking for a way to
make practical his Utopian longing for an ethical society. In Chu
Teh and in Red China he found what he needed. Without them

he might have gone on harassed by a profound discontent, without knowing the reasons for it. Now, his life could become meaningful and thus satisfying.

He went around to see the words in practice. He saw with his own eyes that Chu Teh, the commander in chief, lived no better than the cook; that no officer aggrandized himself or held himself apart; that among these people were selflessness and brotherhood. He saw with his own eyes how men came directly to their officers, to Chu Teh, their commander, with complaints, with criticism, with suggestions. And on what a high level these were! For there was a spirit of mutual and interwoven responsibility, and most of the complaints, suggestions and criticisms were for the good of all and not for the personal satisfaction or comfort of the critic.

He felt alive in the very special sense which William James in a letter to his wife so magnificently described:

> I have often thought [James wrote] that the best way to define a man's character would be to seek out the particular mental and moral attitude in which, when it came upon him, he felt most deeply and intensely active and alive. At such moments there is a voice inside which speaks and says, *"This is the real me!"*

Carlson could say now, at last, *"This* is the real me!"

4

"Silent Night"

He was not the lone American among the Chinese Reds. There was another, a woman, one of the most extraordinary "womanly" women of our times. Her name was Agnes Smedley.

In her book, *Battle Hymn of China,* she writes of their meeting:

When I heard that Carlson had arrived, I decided to give him a wide berth. My experience with American officials in China had not been enviable. Most of them thought of the Chinese as "Chinamen" who took in washing for a living; I didn't like their religion so to speak. Because I regarded the Red Army as a revolutionary organization of the poor, some Americans considered me a glorified street-walker; and after the Japanese invasion their women in particular had looked on me as a camp follower, a creature who lowered the prestige of the white race.

One day I was sitting on a mud bank watching two Army units in a basketball game when Chu Teh came up behind me and asked me to meet one of my countrymen.

"I've long wanted to meet you, Miss Smedley," Captain Carlson said.

"Well, now you've met me," I remarked, and turned back to the ball game.

Carlson records the same incident in his book, *Twin Stars of China*, and he adds that when Agnes Smedley replied, "Well, you've met me," there was considerable and puzzling belligerence in her tone.

"I doubt if he knew that, when we first met in the Eighth Route Army Headquarters," Agnes Smedley wrote in a letter to the author, "I considered him a military spy sent by the American Embassy and the Marine Corps . . . I regarded him not only as a spy against that army, but a traitor to the principles on which the American republic had been founded.

"Because of Evans' background in Nicaragua and with the Marine Corps generally, I had little faith that he would understand the Eighth Route Army. He did not know my deep-seated hostility to all that he represented. We had only coffee in common, it seemed. I talked and explained everything I knew of that army, and the headquarters did the rest. Then the troops in the field and the common people who were their strength and support opened Evans' eyes."

Agnes Smedley looked woefully grim in her military uniform, Carlson observed. Her face had the signs on it of suffering. But he saw that there was no vanity in Agnes Smedley. "Absolute honesty in thought, speech and action was written all over her," he recorded in his diary that night.

He had heard of Agnes Smedley before this, from the Snows and, through them, from her autobiography, *Daughter of Earth*.

Roughhewn out of Missouri poverty, out of Colorado mining camp poverty, she fought her way to self-knowledge and independence in a world where a woman who wanted the same freedom as men was branded a maverick. Maverick she was proudly. She fought for the rights of women, and it followed that she fought for all oppressed people. Capitalists called her a Red, and Reds, because of the way she went about it, called her an idealist, a bourgeois democrat. She went to China in 1928 and found a whole people being treated by the world like the world treats a woman. She grasped the symbolism of foreign invasion, of Chinese integrity, of the feudal pigtail, of the binding of the Chinese women's feet, in short, of "the rape of China" by its own masculine and barbaric past as well as by the ruthless "running dogs of imperialism" (male dogs, to be sure). She became an ally of every Chinese who made a stand for decency among men and equality with women. In the Chinese Reds she found what she was looking for, though even here, as we shall see, her victories were not without struggle. In the days of misery for the Chinese Reds, during the Long March and the retreats, she risked her life to bring them aid. Almost entirely alone, she sent out news from the heart of the heart of China to the world outside. She had suffered for this from the anti-Red Chinese and from her own countrymen, but her pain was made easier by the thought that perhaps one more Chinese woman had won the respect of her husband, and that somewhere else, perhaps tomorrow, another would be freed of the bondage of the dray horse.

Smedley and Carlson spent a great deal of time together in this headquarters village, walking, talking, exploring each other's lives and ideas.

To him, as he wrote in his diary, "she was grand, attractive, alive, animated, wise, courageous, a wonderful companion, impetuous, wants things done right away."

To her, as she wrote much later in her book, he was "as firm as the farmers of his native New England. . . . His principles were deeply rooted in early American Jeffersonian democracy." And he reminded her of the words of the "Battle Hymn of the Republic," "As He died to make men holy, let us die to make men free."

They were in love with each other, not as a man and a woman, but as two equal humans, as comrades.

Their friendship became one of the "firmest in my life, welded in the fires of war," Agnes Smedley wrote.

As for Carlson, his admiration grew not merely because she knew many things he didn't or because her physical courage was unsurpassed, but because she, this American, "had forsaken the comforts of what we regard as civilization for a primitive life among an alien people. Her one desire," he wrote, "was to remain with these people who were making such a valiant effort to realize the ideals for which she had consistently fought."

Giving up comforts for an ideal! There was nothing in human experience which won his respect so quickly. Chu Teh had done it, Mao Tse-tung and the others whom he met or would meet soon, had done it. A whole army had done it! To Carlson such people almost literally proved the life and sacrifice of Christ.

It is perhaps this selfless element in Communist China which explains why, as Nathaniel Peffer described it, "There is something in Communist China that captures the imagination of all sorts and conditions of men. Emotional radicals, objective intellectuals, neutral correspondents, diplomatic officials, military officers hardly given to excessive sympathy for radicalism — regardless of occupation or class or previous attitudes or social convictions, they all come away from Yenan ardent defenders if not enthusiasts." [6]

One evening at dinner, Carlson remarked to Chu Teh that it seemed to him about time to get out to the front.

"I've learnt your ethical indoctrination," he said. "But I want to learn your guerrilla tactics."

Chu Teh nodded abstractedly without saying anything and Carlson felt resistance.

[6] *New York Times Book Review,* October 28, 1945.

Chu Teh went on slowly. "Ts'an Tsan, it's difficult. Very dangerous. Our front is so often changed."

"I'm willing to take the chance."

Chu Teh shrugged and changed the subject.

Later Carlson said to Agnes Smedley, "Chu Teh is concerned
over my safety. He doesn't want me to take chances."

"Reassure him," Smedley said. "I don't know how, but find some
way. I know he's always trying to keep me from stopping a Jap
bullet."

That night Carlson wrote a letter to Ambassador Nelson Johnson in Hankow.

"I'm going to the front soon," he wrote, "at my own request, and
against the advice of Commander Chu Teh. If I should be killed
or wounded I want it distinctly understood that no blame is to de-
volve on the Eighth Route Army or on the Chinese government."

Next morning he brought the letter unsealed to Chu Teh and
asked Li Po to translate it for the general. When Chu Teh heard
the letter, he smiled.

"I would like you to mail it, General," Carlson said. "I want
you to be satisfied that it has been sent."

"We trust you, Ts'an Tsan," Chu Teh said, but he was obviously relieved. "Now, what part of the front do you want to go
to?"

"To Wu T'ai Shan."

Chu Teh frowned, wiped his furrowed forehead unhappily.
"Why do you pick the most dangerous front?"

"Because it's dangerous."

Chu Teh pulled over a map and showed it to Carlson. "At this
moment, Ts'an Tsan, eight Japanese columns are trying to smash
into that area. You'll have to pass through tight Jap lines."

"In that way I'll see more action."

"You know, Ts'an Tsan," Chu Teh said, laughing, "if I weren't
a soldier like you, I'd think you were crazy." He rose and offered
his thick, creased, hard hand to Carlson. "Next week, you go to
Wu T'ai Shan. You can take Li Po with you for interpreter. And
I'll send a bodyguard and an orderly with you, too."

"Just Li Po, General," Carlson said with a grin.

Chu Teh shook his head stubbornly. "We'd like to keep you alive, Ts'an Tsan."

Diary:

I told Agnes about my trip to the front, and at dinner to-night at 4 P.M. (our usual hour) Agnes asked Chu Teh for permission to go to Wu T'ai Shan with me. Both Chu Teh and Jen Peh-hsi demurred. They offered various excuses. Said that those who went to the front had to be prepared to shoot.

"I'll shoot!" said Agnes. "I was raised in the West."

"But you are a woman," they objected.

Well, that raised Agnes' ire. She went for them with all the fire she possesses which is considerable.

"I'm not a woman because I want to be," she said. And as an afterthought, she flung out with biting sarcasm, "God made me this way!"

Well, that brought down the house, for, of course, they were all atheists.

Chu Teh finally explained that though Agnes was right about equality for women, it was really a question of weighing which way she would be more effective, as a soldier in the field or as a writer on behalf of social justice.

"I'll decide that for myself," Agnes Smedley cried.

"It's too important for an individualist decision," Jen Peh-hsi said.

"I propose we vote on it," Chu Teh said. "That's the democratic way. Who, but Agnes, feels she should go?"

Jen Peh-hsi said, "I vote against risking her life needlessly."

Agnes Smedley looked at Carlson appealingly.

"No electioneering at the polls," he said. "I vote to keep you here."

"I vote to go," Smedley said firmly.

"You lose," Chu Teh said.

"But I still want to go!"

"The election's over," Carlson said with a laugh. "Let's go out and light a bonfire."

.

Christmas Eve. Agnes came into Carlson's little room with some coffee to celebrate. With a half a pound of peanuts which he had bought for the occasion, the feast was laid.

"I leave for the front tomorrow," Carlson said. "I've never been so excited." He went over to the charcoal stove to get some hot water for the coffee.

"If I don't see you before you get back to civilization, Evans," Smedley said, "I warn you that there's one question which all our fair ladies in the foreign colonies will ask."

"What's that?"

"What does the Red Army man do for women?"

Carlson laughed aloud. "Well, what does he do?"

Smedley got serious. She put down her cup. "The virtue of continence is taught in this army," she said. "I've been with them a long time and I never heard of a case of rape. Nor is there prostitution. That's considered exploitation of women, and the Reds are against exploitation of any human being."

Carlson thought that over a moment and picked up his enameled cup and sipped some coffee. "It would be a nice thing, Agnes," he said slowly, "if back home tomorrow morning in every church the minister preached a Christmas sermon on the exploitation of human beings."

"Would they be against it?"

"Real Christianity is against it. Jesus spoke against it."

"Jesus is dead."

Carlson smiled sadly. "There are many for whom He lives."

"You, for example, Evans?"

"There are many, Agnes. Just think what a world we'd have if all of us practiced the Sermon on the Mount."

Smedley smiled. "I never heard your father preach, Evans. But I'll bet you sound like him."

"My father comes as close to being a practicing Christian as a man can be." He laughed as a memory returned to him. "I guess that's why I ran away from home."

"Where were you last year Christmas?" she asked him.

"Quantico. Civilization. Of a sort," he added. "We celebrated in style."

"Let's celebrate in our own style," Smedley said.

"Do you know any carols?"

She thought a moment. "No. Not a one."

There was a silence. The steam from the pot on the stove made a hissing noise, accompanied by the crackles of the burning charcoal. Outside, in the cold winter streets, a group of soldiers sauntered, singsonging their Chinese loudly.

"I know some Negro spirituals," Smedley said, after awhile.

Carlson opened his little pack and took out a chromatic harmonica. "You sing the spirituals," he said. "And I'll play some carols on my harmonica."

Agnes Smedley took off her soldier's cap and moved to the side of the warm stove. She rubbed her hands together briskly, and looking into the glow began to sing softly.

> When Israel was in Egypt's land,
> Let my people go . . .
> Oppressed so hard, they could not stand . . .
> Let my people go.

Carlson's harmonica joined the chorus.

> Go down, Moses, 'way down in Egypt's land.
> Tell ole Pharaoh. Let my people go!

They were silent after that. Carlson took a poker and stirred the fire. He was thinking of Plymouth.

"Do you know 'Silent Night'?" Smedley asked him. "If you do, I'll sing. As much as I remember."

He cuddled the harmonica against his lips, then closed his eyes a moment to remember the opening chord.

> Silent night, holy night,
> All is calm, all is bright
> Round yon virgin mother and child . . .

Afterwards, Carlson played, "From the halls of Montezuma, to the shores of Tripoli . . ." Then he grinned, took a swig of coffee, and swung into "Oh, How I Hate to Get Up in the Morning."

"Do you know 'My Country 'Tis of Thee'?" Agnes Smedley asked. "I love that song."

She stood up and joined Carlson at the stove. Loudly the words came from her lips.

> My country 'tis of thee,
> Sweet land of liberty.

They stood at attention until the song was over. Then, afterwards, they sat down again and were quiet.

Chu Teh and others came in. It was a good thing. The Americans were too lonely.

"We want to celebrate with you," Chu Teh said.

They drank more coffee, and talked, and proposed toasts, and made jokes, then Tso Ch'uan did a sword dance, and Chu Teh sang a ballad of longing, a sad, stirring, homesick song which he had learned in his Szechuan birth province.

When it was time to leave, Chu Teh said what Carlson had been thinking, "Tonight we have the brotherhood of man."

5

If a man has only legs

It was the day after Christmas, cold, clear, bright.

Two squads of fourteen men each, all carrying Tommy guns, lined up in front of Chu Teh's headquarters. With them were a half a dozen *hsiao kweis* (little devils), Red Army apprentices, clucking with excitement. Behind the two squads came a train of fourteen pack animals with medical supplies for an Eighth Route Army division at Wu T'ai Shan 200 miles to the northeast. Carlson took his place in line, his heavy pack slung over his left shoulder.

Chu Teh had offered him a mount, but he said he wanted to march. With him was his interpreter and friend, Li Po.

The patrol leader gave the command to march, *"Tsou Pa!"* The advance guard started down the trail to the east. The rest of the patrol followed in single line.

Among the crowd watching them go was Chu Teh and Agnes Smedley. Chu Teh waved farewell and then gave Carlson the American military salute.

But Agnes called out at the top of her voice, "Good luck, Evans."

Down at the head of the line a voice started singing an odd melody, defiant and bitterly sad. It flared along the marching men like an incendiary fire in a high wind.

> Here we were born and here we were raised,
>> Every inch of the soil is ours;
> Whoever tries to take it away from us,
>> Him we will fight to the end.

Through the villages they marched.

"Everywhere I went, I seemed to be a curiosity," he wrote in his diary. "I inquired about it and they told me that I was the first foreigner through these parts. If I stop for boiled water, a crowd gathers. I resented this at first but I got used to it."

They marched at the rate of about three miles an hour for the first days, to get into trim. The men sang and made loud jokes. One lad of 13, just graduated from a radio school, dogged Carlson's steps, muttering the code to himself, "Dit-da-dit, da-da-da, dit-dit-da-da."

28 December

Had a miserable night last night. Sciatica in my right thigh. Getting old, I guess. Up at 0600; a few hours later we started to cross the Hei Fen (Black Tiger) Mountains. A climb of five miles put us on top.

29 December

Climbing another mountain today. I gradually worked up to head the column, because I was feeling particularly fit and because I wanted to see what the troops would do. Well, it

wasn't long before one of the escort with a Tommy gun inched
his way ahead of me and stayed there the rest of the climb.

The days went by, swiftly duplicating each other. The early start,
the long march, the climb, the breaks for boiled water and rice, the
little villages, the hospitable people lining the road and cheering
them, the puffy magistrates full of ceremony. And toward evening when the patrol leader, T'ien, finding a village, would call on
the chief, ask for billeting and receive it in friendly style, the men
would spread their blankets in the little houses, wash their feet,
and eat their second meal of the day, usually of millet, bean curd
and cabbage soup.

The weather was cold and the men suffered, for their clothes
were thin and their feet badly shod. Carlson taught them how to
gargle their sore throats with warm water and salt, and doctored
the sickest ones with the supplies Admiral Marquadt had given
him.

It was bare mountain country, woodless and cut grotesquely by
the geological knife.

Fighters from divisions in the field joined the patrol for days at
a time and from their leaders Carlson added to his knowledge of
guerrilla tactics. Guerrillas must never remain at one place for a
long time. They must augment their forces by men from the neigh-
borhood, by winning their respect. Guerrillas never enter a battle
without very strong indications that they can win it. They avoid
static warfare, for they have no reserves, no line of supplies, no
rear. Surprise is their chief weapon. Decoys, feints, distractions, pretense are vital. "We stop at nothing," the men said. "We wear
women's clothes, Japanese uniforms, we'd go naked if it helped
disguise us."

"Comrade Peng Teh-huai, our great guerrilla leader," he was
told, "once said that important as tactics are, we could not exist
if the majority of the people did not support us. They are our eyes
and ears. They hide us and feed us. We are nothing but their fists."

Everywhere there were schools: schools for partisans, for women,
for children, self-defense, national salvation, agriculture, peasant

handicraft, machinists. Carlson visited them all, for he soon came to see how much his presence helped the students. The fact that a foreigner and a military man had deemed them important enough to march all those miles to see them expanded their pride and morale.

And at each school, as well as with the soldiers of the garrisons and the Eighth Route Army whom he met, he had to answer more questions than he asked. What would Chiang Kai-shek do after the victory? What was Hitler doing now, Russia, Great Britain, and of course, most important, would America help them?

By the tenth they approached the war zone. They had a mixed force of about 600 men. Chen Hsi-lien was in over-all command.

The terrain roughened now. The mountains were higher. Villages along their route had been evacuated, and were empty shells of poverty.

Ahead was the Chengtai railroad which ran from Sian to Peiping. They would have to cross it to get to Wu T'ai, and march through an area nominally in Jap hands.

On the morning of the day they were to cross a peasant came in to the village where they had spent the night with news that a Japanese column was moving eastward down a valley which joined theirs a mile and a half away at the little village of Tung Yen T'o.

15 January

Chen Hsi-lien left to investigate. Ten minutes later he returned. The news was correct. The situation was serious. He had decided to go forward to make a personal survey while the rest of the patrol would move back to Chen Ai, a mountain about three miles away. I asked his permission to go with him. He said that nothing of importance would occur. I did not want to embarrass him by my presence and I left with the patrol for the mountain. While we were packing to go, Japanese artillery was heard in the direction of Tung Yen T'o. A 75mm howitzer. This was the Japanese favorite means of reconnaissance — reconnaissance by fire.

The whole village went with us across the little valley and up to Chen Ai. Twenty minutes after we left the village, Li Po turned around. He grabbed my arm and told me to look. Below us, entering the town we had just left, was a troop of Japanese cavalry.

We made a billet on the mountainside but kept everything in readiness to move. More artillery came from Tung Yen T'o.

At 7 P.M. Chen came in with a map. By candlelight, we studied it. 500 Japs were at Tung Yen T'o, and another detachment was en route there from the north. We talked over the situation. The mission of our patrol was to get us across the railroad, so it would not attack the Jap unless forced to. But it would remain in position between the Jap and its own base at the county seat of Kao Lu.

For three days the patrol remained at Chen Ai while guerrilla forces and regular troops from Kao Lu engaged the Japanese. Feverishly Carlson followed the course of the battle by means of Chen's map and reports from the couriers which came to them from the headquarters near Tung Yen T'o.

The Japanese marched back and forth across the valleys in the hope of trapping the Chinese. But Chen always knew exactly where the enemy was from the peasants who trailed the Jap columns with the skill of Red Indians. One night Chen led his men over a mountain to the rear of the Japanese position, and attacked. Surprised, the Japanese withdrew, leaving fifteen dead. Chen lost one dead and two wounded.

During the three days on the mountain, between studying the battle reports and figuring out what he would do if he were Commander Chen, Carlson read Emerson to allay his impatience and tried translating some of the passages to the Chinese soldiers who told him that much of Emerson sounded as if he had plagiarized Confucius.

19th January

Arose early and prepared to depart. There was a cry of *pu tso* outside. Bad news for us. The Japs tried to pull a fast one by hiding half their column in a ravine while the other half made the withdrawal. The partisan spies had them spotted before they made camp. But it means the trail is not clear, and we must wait.

20th January

Told this morning that tomorrow we leave. At 1230 we were informed we will leave immediately. There are fifty students with us now, among them one girl, Chang Hsueh-hwa, the wife of Nieh Yong-sen, the commander at Wu T'ai.

21st January

Went through Tung Yen T'o which the Japs had captured and then left. There was ample evidence of what such occupation means. The town was ruined, every piece of woodwork taken from the houses and burnt, leaving only mud walls. A few old men were burying the bodies of three of their number who had been shot by the invader. One had not understood an order quickly enough, one refused to k'ou t'ou (kneel to the ground) for an officer, the third had been killed for no reason at all.

After leaving Tung Yen T'o, we moved into the heart of the mountains. One company covered our western flank by following a parallel mountain ridge. Climbed three mountains today. Tomorrow four, they say. Weather about 35 degrees by day, 25 by night. It is quite a sight to watch our lengthy column of blue-clad figures wind up and down the mountain trails as far as the eye could reach. I was upset today by the abominable way our pack mules are handled. No one can pack them efficiently and they are always in difficulties.

On the 22nd they were too near the railroad and the military highway which ran parallel to it to light fires, and they ate cold rice.

At three o'clock that afternoon the chief guide, a battalion commander named K'ung, called the men together and gave his final orders. No talking, no smoking, no coughing. Keep as close together as possible. An advance guard would capture the town at the highway until they passed through. The next company would then become the advance guard and seize the rail crossing. That was all. Good luck.

"*Tsou Pa!*"

The column curled down a slope.

The setting sun flared beautiful designs on the sky behind them.

Ahead was a river bed and a 3000-foot mountain on the other side.

Night came when they reached the summit, and the darkness fingered each man nervously.

A tall fire suddenly bloomed brightly against the black shank of a near-by mountain. Was it a signal or merely a peasant burning off his winter terraces? There was no talk of what it was. Each man speculated silently.

Now, down the trail. . . . Smooth round stones turned easily under foot. It was walking in an earthquake. Men fell and cursed softly, but got themselves up again and took their places. The deep panting of the lungs, the soft pattering of felt-soled shoes, the sharp burst of trickling stones were the only sounds.

The moon came up late that night and the stars were very bright. Carlson tried to watch them. But he couldn't watch them and keep his feet.

Dogs, barking like trumpets against their straining ears, told them the village at the highway was close by.

K'ung, the guide, dropped back to Carlson, took his hand, and ran with him up to the highway. Black against the night were figures of the advance guard lined up on both sides.

K'ung and Carlson sped across.

"The motorcar road," K'ung whispered when they were on the other side.

Five miles ahead on the other side of a mountain was the railroad.

The column moved swiftly. They were in a trap that might yet be sprung. The village, held by the Japs, was behind them. There was ample time for word to get to the enemy garrison near the rail crossing. Perhaps, thought Carlson, that is why they let us across the highway so easily. He suddenly wished he had a cigarette or a pipe. It was in Peiping four years ago that he had stopped smoking. It had been a matter of health. But now he wanted to smoke more than anything else. He laughed at himself. A man has only one life. He should never give up small pleasures even if they hurt him a little. One life, that's all a man had . . .

He wondered, too, at the speed of the column. Five miles up a mountain at double-quick. Stonewall Jackson's foot cavalry, he reflected, was a mere turtle compared to this. The five miles were five hundred miles. The sweat on his face stayed wet in the freezing air.

Suddenly K'ung appeared out of the darkness and took Carlson's hand again. Together they scrambled down a slope, across a footbridge, up an embankment and through a culvert beneath the tracks.

K'ung stopped short, perked up his round, sensible-looking head to listen, then shook Carlson's hand.

"I go back now," he said. "Company Commander Teng will escort you the rest of the way."

He saluted punctiliously and glided back into the darkness.

Then came the sound of scuffling and a falling body. Someone grunted, "Your mother!" and figures ran up.

"We've captured four Chinese traitors," a man whispered to Carlson. "They were guarding the tracks for the Jap."

Commander Teng sought out Carlson.

"We must move fast now, Ts'an Tsan," he said. "The Japs are in a town a half a mile away. They will know that we have crossed when they miss their Chinese guards."

So no rest now, but putting one foot ahead of the other and ahead of the other and ahead of the other until he could not feel his feet or know he was walking. The breath sliced his lungs like razors and his arms and face became numb and seemed to float free of the body.

A thought came to him slowly, struggling into his mind through a sargasso sea of fatigue.

This was the eighth mountain they had climbed since eight o'clock that morning. The eighth mountain in twenty hours. He tried to figure the time they had rested. Five minutes here. Ten minutes there. Perhaps no more than a half-hour that whole day.

It suddenly came to him that during these twenty hours not one man had straggled or dropped out. This was exceptional endurance. Beyond any he had known before.

He glanced at a soldier next to him. What made him endure this?

The soldier smiled. "A long march, eh?" he said between the pushes of his breathing.

"Tired?" Carlson grunted.

"If — a man — has — only — legs — he get tired," the soldier said, gasping out the words.

The words kept time in his head with his slogging feet. He tried to get their meaning. Why if a man has only legs?

But now he noticed that he was lagging, falling behind. Men were streaming past him.

Ahead of him was the main body of the patrol. Only Li Po and Ching, his bodyguard, were at his side.

"Damn it! I can't let the Eighth Route get the better of a Marine," he thought, and plowed forward.

But the men in front seemed to be speeding away from him as at the finish of a hundred-yard dash.

Finally, as if in a nightmare, the summit. A plateau swept by a bitter wind from the north. He saw the bodies of men stretched out on the bony top, groaning in their sleep as, but a few minutes before, they had been groaning in the climb.

"It's safe here for a few minutes," Teng said.

"Do you have a cigarette, Teng?"

Teng smiled and gave him one. Carlson sucked in the smoke, bitter now to his taste. "I'm never going to give up smoking again," he said.

The moon was rising. He sat down and looked around him, suddenly not so tired, suddenly feeling the sense of his own life and that of the men around.

He would never forget what he saw, for with all its terror of a man chase, and the obscenity of bottomless fatigue, it was a beautiful scene.

It was bitterly cold [he wrote in his book]. Out of the eastern horizon a full moon was rising, its rich glow giving the adjacent hills a pale yellow hue and creating the illusion that we gazed into a phantom world. Overhead familiar constellations twinkled cheerily in a blanket of unbelievable blue. And all around was silence, save for the heavy breathing of the prostrate forms. But for these sleeping figures I might have been on a mountain-top in Europe or America, so universal is the topography of night. But they were Chinese, and this was China, and those blue-clad forms were here because they sought to save this China from those who labored below to take it from them.[7]

And why was he here?

That was simple. He was doing his duty.

Was it any more than that?

It was simply that the accidents of duty brought him here, he told himself. And, of course, he was lucky to have such duty, to open his eyes to such newness of spirit, to bring him into so dedicated a community of men.

"I wonder if they have started to follow us," Commander Teng said. Then he sighed, arose from his crouching position and started waking the men.

In a few minutes, the familiar command was passed. "*Tsou Pa!*"

Carlson gave Li Po a couple of aspirin tablets and took some himself. It would help keep them going.

Five hours later they reached a village. They were hungry for food and sleep, and happy they were safe. But before they had a chance to eat a peasant galloped up with a report of a pursuing Jap column.

Weary beyond bearing, the men repacked the mules and, uncomplaining, slung their own packs over aching shoulders.

"*Tsou Pa! . . .*"

Fifteen burdensome and infinitely long miles later, in the late afternoon, they found security in a village garrisoned by a strong unit of the Eighth Route Army. Now they could rest. "O good sleep!" the men yelled. "O my mother!"

Carlson was beyond tiredness and after he and Li Po and Ching ate their fill he wanted to talk just a little while before going to

[7] *Twin Stars of China* (New York, Dodd, Mead & Co., 1940). This book has been an invaluable aid in describing Carlson's Chinese trips.

sleep. He wanted to tell them how extraordinary the 600 men were. They had marched fifty-eight miles in thirty-two hours. They had done the first stretch of forty-three miles in twenty hours. And not one had fallen by the way, not one had straggled. Did these men know what they had? Did they know why they had shown such endurance? What was it? Where did it come from? How was it related to ethical indoctrination?

Carlson wanted to talk to them about this but Ching and Li Po were snoring lightly, and he too closed his eyes and fell into a dreamless sleep.

"If I ever have an outfit of my own," Carlson told Li Po the next morning, "I'm going to give them ethical indoctrination. I'm going to show them how they can find the will to sacrifice, and the desire to endure. This is not a Chinese thing but a human thing. This is what makes great soldiers."

Fifty-one days and one thousand miles passed from the time Carlson said good-by to Chu Teh and Agnes Smedley to the time he saw them again. His left shoulder on which he had carried his pack had a half-inch callous growth on it.

During his time in Shansi he learnt many things. He had met and lived with peasants, shared their food, heard their complaints. He had talked with provincial leaders like General Yen Hsi-shan, Chiang Kai-shek's representative, whose troops were listless and sullen, and indifferent. "What are you fighting for?" he had asked them when his patrol met a column of General Yen's men. "Your mother!" they cursed. "Who knows what we're fighting for?" The General himself was a tired old man, more merchant than soldier, who was forced to tolerate the Eighth Route Army in his province because they were fighting the Japs for him.

Yes, he had learnt the Chinese people, but he was conscious only of very immediate things. These Chinese were fighting a hard war. The population among whom they fought was starving, but more important, the fighters themselves, though fierce, unyielding and loyal, were without the sustenance to fight.

They went into battle with ancient weapons, with battered rifles, often with less than half a dozen rounds apiece. They had only a paltry supply of demolitions, and time and again they were beaten back because they didn't have a single stick of dynamite to blow up a bridge. The wounded among them were as good as dead, so lacking in medical supplies they were. Carlson visited their makeshift hospitals and saw men bleeding their lives out on straw mats, because there were not enough bandages and clamps. He saw men black with gangrene for want of antiseptics. He watched operations done with crude knives and scissors, and without anesthesia.

But, withal, he was convinced that the Japanese machine, modern as it was, "could hardly prevail against a populace inspired and trained to endure the hardships which such resistance might entail. It could not destroy an army geared to outmarch and outsmart its opponent in a protracted guerrilla war. Its effort to conquer Shansi was about as effective as an attempt to plow the ocean."

In this opinion he was in the minority of the foreign observers in Shanghai, Nanking and Hankow.

But Shansi, he realized, was only one small part of the nation. If China was to survive, the whole Republic must learn from the Shansi guerrillas, and from the Eighth Route Army, and in turn the Republic must help them. But did the rest of China know what was being done there? Did the Kuomintang in Hankow and Changsha and Chungking know? Did Chiang Kai-shek know? And if they knew — even if they knew — would they do anything about it? Or would they permit their hatred of Chu Teh and his Reds, of Jen Peh-hsi and his indoctrination, of the Eighth Route Army's democratic alliance with the peasants of Shansi to blind them?

> As I turned my face toward Hankow [Carlson wrote when he left Shansi] I speculated as to the willingness of Chiang Kai-shek to undertake the task of indoctrinating his subordinates with the spirit of practical self-sacrifice which animated the leaders of the 8th Route Army. Would he be willing to mobilize the people for resistance and afford them the civil rights and social equality which alone could command their unqualified devotion?

6

Before I die

When he arrived in Hankow, he found that somehow a report
had gotten out back home that he had been killed by the Red bandits, and he hastily cabled his father and mother in Plymouth, re-
assuring them that he was still alive.

He was full of the fire of what he had witnessed, and wrote his
report for Admiral Yarnell and Naval Intelligence, and he sent
several letters to President Roosevelt. But the rest of his time, day
and night, was spent in talking to whomever he could find about
the men fighting at Wu T'ai Shan, their achievements, their dis-
ciplines, and most of all their heartbreaking sacrifices.

Ilona Ralf Sues, author of *Shark's Fins and Millet,* and once
private secretary to Madame Chiang Kai-shek, met Carlson at this
time. She wrote:

> The skinny, bony six-footer, with his tanned, deep-lined
> face, his strong nose, his kindly twinkling eyes, became part
> and parcel of our little group. Anyone looking at Carlson
> once could not possibly miss the rust-colored riding breeches,
> the rough tweed jacket over a thick hand-knitted pullover,
> and the big pipe he either puffed or handled as a Chinese
> storyteller handles his fan to express an idea, a thought, a
> situation. Carlson had the tough health of a trapper, the staunch
> heart of a soldier, and the pure sweet soul of a saint. Add to
> this a deep love for mankind, freedom and democracy, and a
> well-tempered sense of humor, and you will have a more or
> less complete picture of the man.
>
> He came back from Wu T'ai Shan [Sues relates] with
> wonderful stories of courage, and horrible accounts of con-
> ditions there. Lack of ammunition, lack of virtually every-
> thing a human being needs to continue alive — food, clothing,

blankets . . . No doctor, no medical supplies to take care of some 3000 wounded or of the desperately undernourished population.

He had an appointment with Chiang Kai-shek. He went to headquarters full of hope, to present the case and get some help for the heroic outposts, strategically so important. We warned him . . .[8]

They had warned him. They had said that Chiang Kai-shek would not help, that he was the prisoner of his own hatred of the Communists and of those advisers around him who preferred to be puppets of the Japanese than servants of their own people. But Carlson had a naïve faith in himself. How could any man resist what he would tell him? How could Chiang Kai-shek deny the pleas of his own countrymen for help to fight their common enemy? His friends at the Hankow Hotel Terminal, Agnes and Ilona, and Dr. Norman Bethune, head of the Medical Aid Unit sent to China by the Canadian and American Leagues for Peace and Democracy, told him that the pattern of the nations of the world these days was to give up everything, including their own sovereignty, rather than make an alliance with Reds. Carlson disbelieved them. When they referred to Great Britain's, France's and America's betrayal of Spain, Ethiopia, and Austria, now in the process of being sold to the Nazis, he said that Chiang Kai-shek was no Chamberlain. Had he not made a united front with the Reds at Sian? Then he would keep it. It was only that his advisers were deceitful. If Chiang knows, he'll help, Carlson affirmed.

He had last seen the Generalissimo in 1929 at the reburial of Sun Yat-sen on Purple Mountain in Peiping. Then he was youthful, uncertain of himself, almost reed-like in his eagerness.

Hollington Tong, the Vice-Minister of Public Relations, escorted Carlson to Headquarters in Wuchang, across the Yangtze from Hankow.

"How much time have I got, Holly?" Carlson asked.

Tong made a polite gesture. "Perhaps fifteen minutes, Captain.

[8] *Shark's Fins and Millet,* by Ilona Ralf Sues (Boston: Little, Brown and Company, 1944).

Or as long as the Generalissimo desires to keep you. He's a busy man."

"I understand," Carlson said, pointing to a large roll of maps he was carrying. "But I've got a lot to tell him."

They waited in the Generalissimo's office for a few moments. It was rather sparsely furnished, Carlson noted. He put great weight on the trappings with which men surrounded themselves. He so despised ostentation and luxury himself that he felt these vices could not adorn any honest man. In this his puritanism was the border of priggishness.

Madame Chiang Kai-shek entered first. Carlson's first thought was that she had the great ability, for a lady of importance, of putting people at ease, but as they chatted, he couldn't evade the feeling that she was too conscious of herself as not only a lady of importance but of high historic destiny as well.

The Generalissimo came in. He greeted Carlson with a cheery smile and a handshake. While Carlson's greetings were being translated for him, Chiang Kai-shek stood erect watching him closely.

Carlson thought that the man had aged greatly in the nine years that had lapsed. His hair was graying and his face had thinned. But the nine years had brought enormous poise and confidence in himself. That he was the Chief of State he left Carlson in no doubt, despite all his friendliness. His brilliant black eyes, once insecure, now held Carlson's own. "Relentless," was the way Carlson put it. "Here was intelligence, loyalty, stubbornness."

Carlson laid out his maps on a table.

Madame Chiang turned to her husband who was still standing and suggested that he sit down.

"The Generalissimo," she told Carlson, "is still troubled by the back injury he got at Sian, and it's unwise for him to stand long."

"Generalissimo," Carlson began, "Madame Chiang Kai-shek. The first thing I want to say is that I bring greetings from the leaders of the Eighth Route Army, from Chu Teh especially, and from the commanders of the 120th Division and the Fifth Partisan Group. I bring to you their sincere expressions of loyalty. The words I heard most among the leaders is that everything is past, the civil war, the bloodshed among brothers. All Chinese are brothers, and Chiang Kai-shek is our leader."

The Generalissimo nodded and glanced up at his wife.

"They firmly hope, Generalissimo, that this feeling of good will can continue after the victory over Japan."

Chiang Kai-shek murmured something to Hollington Tong who translated.

"The Generalissimo wants to know if the Communists have any conditions for a postwar China?"

"I'm not in a position to speak for them, sir. I can only say that from my observations the only conditions would be a democratic China with freedom for the people to select their own leaders, and the indoctrination of the people for an understanding of democracy — political and economic."

Chiang Kai-shek ignored the reply and requested Carlson to give him a military picture of the situation in Shansi.

For about an hour Carlson described the disposition of forces in Shansi and answered the Generalissimo's questions.

"Sir," Carlson said at the end, "I believe that the will-to-resist of the people in the Wu T'ai mountain area is stronger than any I've seen elsewhere. The co-operation between the army and the people is better than I have seen in other parts of China."

"Why do you think this is so?" Chiang Kai-shek asked.

"Because of two things: they are completely surrounded by the Japanese, and the common danger inspires them to subordinate certain individual liberties to the common cause. They are also inspired by the self-sacrificing character of their leaders."

Chiang Kai-shek was silent.

"Generalissimo," Carlson continued urgently, "they need help. They need medicines and bandages and food and ammunition and dynamite for demolitions."

The Generalissimo rose stiffly from his chair and thanked Carlson for giving them his opinions. He failed to mention the appeal.

Carlson did not speak though he knew it was his place to offer his thanks in turn. He felt set down, dismissed, and he minded it, not for himself, but for those Chinese brothers of Chiang Kai-shek in the freezing North who were fighting their common enemy with skill but with empty bellies, with fierceness but with empty guns and few of them. Two lines of an Emerson poem slipped on the screen of his mind as apt for this moment of desperate disappointment:

> Things are in the saddle,
> And ride mankind.

He tried to find some way of re-opening the discussion, of asking the Generalissimo in another way for help, but he realized that his official position as an American naval attaché permitted only a diplomatic suggestion, and he had already done this.

In the hope that something might come if he delayed Chiang Kai-shek's departure another minute, Carlson opened his notebook to a blank page and asked for Chiang's autograph.

The pencil Chiang was using had a red lead in one end and a blue lead in the other. He bent down to write, saw that the red point was down, then quickly flipped the pencil over and wrote with the blue point. "It was a split-second gesture," Carlson wrote later, "but it implied much."

Carlson came back from Chiang Kai-shek's headquarters utterly discouraged. "He was almost aged," Ilona Ralf Sues wrote. "The lobby of the Terminal was full of people. He put his big hand on my shoulder, towering over me.

"'Let's have a drink in the dining room,' he said. 'I'm chilled to the marrow of my bones. He and the Madame listened to me with that impenetrable, icy indifference. . . . They won't do a thing for Wu T'ai Shan.'"

But Carlson did not give up. In the dying city, raided three to ten times a day by Japanese bombers, he and Agnes Smedley and Episcopal Bishop Logan Roots, who had been in China forty years, and Dr. Richard Brown of the Canadian Church Mission, and Dr. Norman Bethune, the stocky Canadian chest specialist who had laid the groundwork for the use of blood plasma in Spain, scrounged, stole and saved to raise money. They begged. They organized lotteries. They threatened everyone shamelessly. And within a month

Dr. Brown, following Carlson's route, reached Wu T'ai Shan with some medical supplies.

Carlson saw other Chinese leaders, and within the frustrating and restrictive limits of his diplomatic position he tried to interest them in the fate of the Shansi guerrillas.

"They are fighting in the most strategic area of North China," he argued. "Japan's conquests there will be without decision and costly. With your help, the Eighth Route Army will not only resist, but will also drive out the 100,000 Jap troops." [9]

Carlson could not seem to get the Kuomintang and Government leaders at Hankow to see it. He talked with "Christian" General Feng Yu-hsiang, Vice-Chairman of the Military Affairs Commission, of which the Generalissimo was Chairman. He talked to the Minister of War, General Ho Ying-ching, he who had wanted to bomb Sian and Chiang Kai-shek included. He pleaded with Dr. H. H. Kung, Minister of Finance. And with the exception of Dr. Kung, they were all polite and indifferent. Kung was polite and interested.

Carlson did not underestimate their patriotism, but he was impressed with their shortsightedness. He disliked the comfortable way they lived, their clothes and food and homes and offices. He constantly compared these with the primitive conditions of life among the leaders in the North. If he had not seen the front soldiers, he might have lost his faith in China.

During this time in Hankow he was invited by Agnes Smedley to meet Chou En-lai, the Communist leader, who in the post-Sian United Front had become a member of the National Government. He was the son of a Mandarin family, slender, gentle, shy, whose private ambition might well have been to be a poet. With Chu Teh and Mao Tse-tung, he was one of the three most prominent Reds in China. It was he who had helped his old enemy Chiang Kai-shek at Sian.

At dinner, they talked. Carlson had the advantage, for Ed Snow had told him Chou En-lai's history.

[9] Confirmed by such observers as Owen Lattimore, T. A. Bisson, Guenther Stein, Edgar Snow, Nym Wales, Harrison Forman and others.

"I was in Shanghai in April 1927," Carlson told him. "The time you were there."

"When I was arrested?" Chou inquired.

"Yes."

Chou became thoughtful, as if he were trying to recall something deeply obscured in the past. "We never met then, did we?"

"No," Carlson said.

"Of course, we didn't have much to do with the American Marines," Chou said. "We used to see them marching down the streets trying to frighten us."

Carlson changed the subject, for he was a little ashamed of his attitude toward the Chinese in 1927, and he didn't want Chou En-lai or Agnes Smedley to question him. He was proud of his new maturity. He did not want to explain his own growth, the slow development of his ideas.

That night in his diary, Carlson wrote:

> *26 March 1938*
> Tonight I went to a dinner party with Chou En-lai, Agnes, Po Ku (once Chairman of the Northwest Soviet), and Li Po. Agnes raved about newspaper correspondents who send home inaccurate dispatches. Chou listened quietly for a long time, apparently paying no attention, then sat up, cupped his chin in his hand and said softly, "If journalists always published accurate accounts of current events, there would be no need for the historians."

Ten days later, he visited the battlefield of Taierchwang still warm with the dead.

> *7 April 1938*
> I will never forget this day. We went on an inspection of the area just held by the Japanese. Destruction and desolation were everywhere. Dead bodies, dead horses, dogs, ducks — At one place lay the body of a woman with a child in her abdomen. At another place was the body of a peasant, two dead ducks lying near. I have not seen such destruction since France, Shanghai not excepted. Joris Ivens presented me with a diary of a Jap soldier with a bullet hole clean through it.
> At about 5:30 P.M. we returned to Hq. in the city for tea

and Japanese biscuits. Then we set out for the front — some
two miles north of Taierchwang. I shall not soon forget this
walk. Three Chinese Generals and I walked abreast down the
road, they singing a Chinese patriotic song, I trying to learn
it and humming it. They were in high spirits as a result of the
victory. We were walking into a magnificent sunset. Ahead
an armored train was silhouetted against the setting sun.
Behind us was a charred city — and around us were Chinese
soldiers preparing to retire for the night in their dugouts.

The *History Today* boys and I found a barn to spend the
night in, and we sang songs of all our countries.

It was a great day and a sad one.

The "History Today" boys, a group of camera men, were Joris
Ivens, a dark, energetic Hollander, who is one of the greatest docu-
mentary film makers in the world, John Ferno, another Hollander,
and Robert Capa, who had made magnificent camera studies of the
Spanish fight for independence, and was now working for *Life*.
With them was Israel Epstein of the United Press. They had lain
on the dry, bitter-smelling straw, talking of China and Spain, when
Carlson took out his old harmonica and softly blew a few melan-
choly chords. The last time he had played was Christmas Eve at
Chu Teh's headquarters.

Carlson played some American songs. Ivens and Ferno sang some
Dutch working songs; Capa took the stage with a lonesome sounding Hungarian peasant tune; and Epstein, not to be outdone, came
forth with a rousing Polish march. Before the songfest was finished,
they joined together to sing *Chee Lai,* the great song of the Chinese
partisans.

> Everyone who works for freedom is crying,
> "Arise! Arise! Arise!"
> All of us with one heart,
> With the torch of freedom,
> March on!

A week later he was back in Hankow where he met his senior
officer, Commander Overesch, who told him that he could remain
as an observer as long as his health could stand it.

Again he made the rounds of conferences and dinners. He talked with the British Ambassador, Sir Archibald Clark-Kerr, who with extraordinary modesty presented a letter of introduction from Edgar Snow. He talked with Captain Frank Dorn and Colonel Joseph Stilwell of the War Department. "Pinkie" Dorn was a quiet, sensitive man, an artist, but Stilwell was a scientist. His mind and his face were one, firm, knotted, realistic and skeptical. Like a laboratory technician, he despised theory and obeyed facts. He twisted Carlson's memory for hours to get out of him what he had seen, and he was impressed by the flexibility and ingenuity of the Red guerrillas.

"It looks to me," Stilwell said dryly, "that the success of the Reds against a more powerful enemy is the Red officers' habit of saying, 'Come on, boys,' instead of 'Go on, boys.' "

He and Carlson talked over their own future as observers. The Chinese were fighting a strenuous battle at Hsuchowfu, and Stilwell indicated that he was going there.

"There's no point to having two American observers," Carlson remarked. "You go to Hsuchowfu, and I'll go up to Sian and then to Yenan. I want to learn more about the Northwest."

They agreed to divide the war.

7

John did baptize . . .

From a letter home:

SIAN (SHENSI)
30 April 1938

DEAR DAD AND MOTHER AND THE REST OF THE FAMILY:

After a lapse of two months I am back here, ready for another jaunt. I'm afraid I've neglected you all lately. I spent three weeks of March writing my report.

One of the major sacrifices that goes with my work is the failure to get news from home. Letters are a long time coming through.

I picked up a few good books at Hankow. "Education of Henry Adams" and Irving's Sketchbook. Always I have my Emerson. And for your particular information, Dad, I carry a copy of the New Testament.

Have come to be quite good friends with Bishop Logan H. Roots, Anglican Episcopal. We have wonderful chats. Fort Logan H. Roots in Arkansas was named for his uncle.

I haven't forgotten you all. I'm ashamed of myself for not writing.

In Sian the end of April he sent his card over to General Chiang T'ing-wen, the Governor of the area and Chiang Kai-shek's appointee. The General requested Carlson to call on him.

Chiang T'ing-wen had a reputation as a Red eater. He hated them, had killed as many as he could in the Civil War, and had purchased the enmity of many of his own people by his ruthlessness. He greeted Carlson cordially, hiding his suspicion of the admirer of the guerrillas behind a warm interest in Carlson's health.

"I have been afraid for you, Ts'an Tsan," he said. "It isn't everybody who has the stamina to march as much as you have. After all, we Chinese are used to it."

Carlson smiled.

"I hear you are one of the few foreigners who think that we will beat the Jap."

Carlson smiled again.

Chiang T'ing-wen tried another tack. "You are seeing a great deal of war. But not enough, eh? Is that why you are back here?"

"Yes."

"And where now do you propose to see more?"

"I want to go up to Yenan to observe the organization which Mao Tse-tung has up there. And then I want to go into Mongolia. The Japanese say that their control is supreme in the occupied areas of Shensi, Chahar, Hopei and Shantung. From what I have seen, I don't believe them. On the contrary, I believe that the Chinese partisans as well as organized armies have considerable control over these provinces. But the world doesn't know that. If I see this for myself, I'll be in a position to testify to the truth."

The General looked at Carlson wonderingly.

"But such a trip is extremely dangerous," he remonstrated. "Why do you do it? Why is it important to you to inform the world as to its ignorance about our war?"

Carlson relates in his diary that when the General asked him this question, he was unable to reply for a moment.

> I had not stopped to examine the urge which prompted these expeditions, being conscious only of trying to place my finger on the key elements of this conflict. But now I realized that behind the desire to fulfill an official duty there was a deeper urge.

And then slowly he told the General that he had come from a country where ordinary people as well as their leaders regarded liberty and equality as inalienable rights. "We've had a Revolution and a Civil War for them. In the Chinese people I have seen this same love of liberty and equality, and I am convinced from what I have seen that they are ready to sacrifice comfort, homes, and their lives so that their children, at least, will enjoy these rights. My country, the United States, can't take sides in your war, General. Not now. Not this year perhaps. Maybe not for a couple of years. It will come, I'm sure. But until that time I, as one American, can see how you resist the invader, and make my report to the world. The risk is one which any of my countrymen would gladly take."

He realized as he finished that he had not intended so melodramatic and sentimental a speech. He had wanted merely to speak out his heart — and this is what had come. But these concepts, equality and liberty, budded into his life from the very beginning, had now borne a spirit that would not be denied.

Chiang T'ing-wen was quiet after Carlson spoke, almost in a reverie, and then, to Carlson's amazement, tears came into the General's eyes.

"Ts'an Tsan," General Chiang said huskily, "I had no idea that any American understood us so well, and what we fight for. I approve your trip. I will see that passes are given you, and I will personally write letters of introduction to my Generals in Yulin and Inner Mongolia."

He made the two-day trip from Sian to Yenan in an open truck with a Miss Jean Ewen, a nurse from Vancouver, British Columbia, who had spent five years working in a Catholic mission in Shantung, and had then volunteered to work with Dr. Norman Bethune for the Eighth Route Army. With them were several Chinese students on their way to study at one of the Yenan training schools. These students were part of the flood of young people from every province in China who gave up comfortable homes and modern universities to make the pilgrimage to the new Mecca, there to study under leaders and teachers who, fabulous to the Chinese ear, were neither slaves of opium, bribery or personal aggrandizement.

Yenan had been the capital of the Provisional Central Government of the Soviet Republic of China. But after the Sian incident when the Communists, in order to make the United Front workable, dissolved the Soviets and subordinated the Red Army to the National Government, Yenan became the headquarters of a pro tempore Border Government consisting of the three provinces of Shensi, Ninghsia and Kansu. This Border Government, highly influenced by the Communists who kept the central office of their party in Yenan, proclaimed itself a democracy, and gave to the people, "without regard to classes," Edgar Snow reported, "the right to elect officials — the first attempt of this kind ever made in China." [10]

In Yenan, the United Front worked. Although subsurface tensions existed — and made co-operation difficult — Communist officials worked with Kuomintang officials and with old war lords who, loving their power, reluctantly submitted to the expedient of a new way of things. No anti-Japanese party was banned. But in Hankow and Chungking the United Front was more a name than

[10] *The Battle for Asia,* by Edgar Snow (New York: Random House, 1941).

a fact, for in the Central Government areas, Communists, as Edgar Snow reported, were rigidly excluded from the army, public office and participation in the general civilian mobilization.

More than that, nearly all Chinese progressives had been suppressed, works like *Carmen,* novels of Gorki and Romain Rolland were prohibited, and the free speech of anti-Japanese expression was restricted. It is no wonder then that Chinese students who were outspokenly passionate in their hatred of the invader should prefer the openness of Yenan with all its primitiveness, its caves for schools and dormitories, its paltry diet of millet and rice. They understood what old Lu Hsun, China's great writer, meant when he said to them, "The road to Yenan is for China's youth the road to life."

Yenan, then: a city of 25,000 in the desert land of northern Shensi, cupped by grassless yellow mountains and pitted with ancient and newly made caves. Nym Wales describes Yenan in the late afternoons when the desert atmosphere reflects every sound. She could hear the cries of the goat herders mixed with the shouts of soldiers at bayonet practice, the cheers of spectators at a basketball game and the strains of the American song, "Dixie," to which some unnamed Chinese versifier had put stirring words for action.[11]

His first night in Yenan Carlson wrote his diary in a cave, high on a cliff which had recently been vacated by Dr. Norman Bethune.

5 May, 1938

Yenan is a city of caves. Three valleys come together here. When more space is needed to accommodate the growing student bodies, they dig out a few more caves. The town has a friendly air. There are more *tung-hsis* (little hors d'oeuvre - pastries) for sale than I expected.

I sent my letters of introduction to Mao Tse-tung by one of his staff, and at 7 P.M. word came around that Mao was ready to receive me.

[11] From *Inside Red China,* by Nym Wales (New York: Doubleday, Doran, 1939). Nym Wales's book surpasses all others — including Edgar Snow's, her husband's — in the detail with which it describes the life in Yenan in those days.

Who was Mao Tse-tung? If Chu Teh, the ex-war lord, can be considered the Reds' strong right arm, and Chou En-lai, the scion of Mandarins, the skilled conspirator and negotiator, then in these overly simplified terms, Mao Tse-tung, who came from the peasantry, can be described as the intellect, the dialectician, the scholar who grew out of grass roots. Like the others, this Lincoln-esque man of 45 had a gentle tongue and a mild manner and was, as far as Carlson could see, utterly without pretense. In 1911, when he was 18, Mao saw his first map of the world, and discovered at the same time its humanitarian and scientific contours when he read Adam Smith's *The Wealth of Nations,* and Darwin's *Origin of Species,* and books of John Stuart Mill, Rousseau and Spencer. In 1920, after a meeting to celebrate the third anniversary of the Russian Revolution had been broken up by the police, he read *The Communist Manifesto,* the first Marxist book ever published in Chinese. The next year, at about the time that Chu Teh in Berlin joined the German branch of the Chinese Communist party, and Chou En-lai in Paris joined its French branch, Mao Tse-tung became one of its founders in Shanghai. His history, after that, paralleled the others; membership in the Kuomintang, of which he was one of the Central Committee; then the period of hiding and organizing the first units of the Red Army, after the 1927 split between the Kuomintang and the Communists, the resistance against Chiang Kai-shek's anti-Red campaigns, the Long March of 6,000 miles, up to Yenan in Shensi province, and finally the war against the Japanese.[12]

Carlson described Mao's office in his book:

"The pale light of the single candle which lit the room in which Mao worked, the simple furnishings of a k'ang, a wooden table and a few shelves of books, and perhaps above all the abstract air of Mao, himself, gave the atmosphere a quality of otherworldliness."

"Welcome, Ts'an Tsan," Mao Tse-tung said in a low voice. "I've heard of your wanderings with our armies and I'm glad to welcome you here."

[12] Mao Tse-tung's biography, as well as Chu Teh's and Chou En-lai's, are brilliantly set down in Edgar Snow's *Red Star Over China.*

They shook hands warmly.

"I must apologize for asking you to come over at night," Mao said. "I sleep by day — and night's my time for feeling alive."

For a while they talked of personalities, Chu Teh, Chou En-lai, General Chiang T'ing-wen and the Generalissimo, during which time tea and peanuts were brought in by a guard.

Then began the real talk, the talk for which Carlson had come, the talk by which he sounded the mettle of the man. Much of their conversation which, it must be remembered, took place in 1938, dealt with prophesies and analyses now, in some part, outdated. Mao Tse-tung, of course, predicted that Japan and the United States would one day go to war, but his guesses as to its terrain and duration were far from the mark, for he could not foresee that the atomic bomb would do away with an American landing on the China coast.

Carlson said that he thought Britain would fight if Germany invaded Czechoslovakia; Mao Tse-tung emphatically disagreed, a point of view which five months later was confirmed by the betrayal at Munich.

"How long will China resist?" Carlson asked, assuming that she would have to continue her struggles alone.

"China," Mao said, "is like a gallon jug which Japan is trying to fill with a half pint of liquid. When her troops move into one section, we move into another . . . and when they pursue us, we move back again."

Mao filled his pipe with some dried, stringy, yellow Chinese tobacco, and Carlson made a note to send him some American kind.

"What are the plans," Carlson asked, "of the Chinese Communist party for the postwar period?"

The Chinese took a long time answering, for Communists are notorious for their reluctance to speculate on the future. He rose from his chair and stalked up and down the room puffing his pipe strenuously.

"It's hard to tell," Mao said finally. "As you know, we do not think that Communism can come to China right away. It's a long way off. Our immediate goal is democracy in China, but a real one,

with actions, not words. We shall never come to blows with Chiang
Kai-shek and the Kuomintang over the issue of Communism or
Socialism. If we differ, it will be over the issue of a genuine people's
government in China. We hope to keep the United Front with the
Kuomintang. We are for a two-party government. We believe that
the state should own the banks, the mines and should reduce taxes,
interest rates and rentals. We're for the development of producer
and consumer co-operatives, though we have no objection to private
enterprise. And, of course, we are for friendly relations with all
foreign powers on a basis of equality. Those are our immediate
hopes, for which we will fight. They are not, as I said before,
Communism. But they are the requisites for a united China and
for peace among us and for a chance to rehabilitate our country.
Communism will come in China — some day. But we are not ready
for it now."

Carlson hurriedly put down the words in his notebook. He felt
that there was nothing very radical about Mao's proposals. Most
of China's banks, mines and communications were already owned
by the government, in part or whole. In his own country, the co-
operative movement had many followers, and many who thought it
might be the answer to the conflict between capital and labor. As
for the friendly foreign relations, no one, at home, could disagree.
The Communism that would come? If the people of China desired
it, it was *their* lives, *their* fate, *their* future to be determined as they
wished. His own beliefs were that a genuine democracy in which
none were exploited for the enrichment of a few was the most
powerful system in the world. None could surpass or conquer it.

"What about America?" Carlson inquired. "Have we helped
the Chinese people?"

"Yes," said Mao firmly. "You and the Soviet Union have helped
us more than any other nations." Then he paused and took his pipe
out of his mouth and looked down at the dancing candle flame.
"Yet, according to our figures and your own government's figures,
you have provided Japan with over half of the war materials she
purchases abroad."

Carlson was stunned. He asked Mao to repeat what he had said, and for the second time, he shook his head as if someone had hit him hard. The otherworldliness of the dim cave he had felt earlier in the evening came back to him. Mao's words had shattered an outer rampart of Carlson's self-respect.

"Have you the figures here?" he demanded sharply.

"No, but our Embassy in Washington has them."

"It isn't possible!" Carlson said stubbornly. "Our people are sympathetic to China."

"People frequently are so blinded by the sun of profits," Mao said slowly, "that their eyes see neither their country nor themselves."

Carlson was outraged. Mao Tse-tung's remonstrance rang in his head like a tuning fork.

When he left Mao Tse-tung's cave dawn was breaking over the yellow hills. Confusion within him spoiled the beauty of the scene. To Mao he had replied with big, empty words. He had spoken of the slowness with which the will of the majority in a democracy shows itself. But the answer had been inadequate.

He stalked angrily down the hill toward the town. His muscles ached with rage. A pride he had never known he possessed had been humbled. His dignity and self-esteem as an American had been hurt.

"Am I such an innocent, such an ignoramus," Carlson thought painfully, "that I don't know what's going on in my own country?"

"Slow, Evans, slow," he warned himself. "You haven't been in your country since this war started. You haven't read your own newspapers and magazines."

"But if Mao's right, how shameful!"

When he returned to his own living place, he couldn't sleep, though he had been up the whole night. He looked around for something to read and laid out the books he had brought with him. There were Emerson and the booklets of the British Three-Penny Library; and there was his copy of the New Testament. He had bought it because on his earlier trip to Shensi and Wu T'ai Shan he had seen a resemblance between the practices of the Eighth Route Army and the doctrines of Christ. He had planned to read the four gospels systematically and compare them with the life around him.

He had never had the time, and now he opened to Mark and read aloud by the light of the morning coming in through the open entrance.

"The beginning of the gospel of Jesus Christ, the Son of God, as it is written in the prophets, Behold, I send my messenger before thy face, which shall prepare thy way before thee. The voice of one crying in the wilderness, 'Prepare ye the way of the Lord, make His paths straight.'"

But Mao was probably right. And if he was right? What then?

"John did baptize in the wilderness . . ."

He tried to read further but the question kept repeating itself against the words. If Mao was right, what then?

But Mao *was* right! He would not lie. Of course he was telling the truth.

And when Carlson faced himself with that, he became consumed by a gigantic guilt rising in him like a malarial fever. Here he was, traveling with the underarmed and undernourished Chinese armies, raising money for their sick and wounded, and within the limit of his position and often beyond it, committing his sympathy, by word and action, to their cause, when his own America, whose democracy he had described so often and so passionately to the Chinese as worthy of their emulation, was proven to be divided, shortsighted and greedy. This contradiction sickened him, for he felt personally responsible for his country's evil.

How could he stand aside and wash his hands of it? His duties as a citizen and a soldier prevented him. How could he draw a line between himself and his blind profit-hungry fellow Americans? Had he not told the Chinese he talked to that every citizen in a democracy shares in its deeds, good or evil?

That morning, oppressed by his guilt and wanting confirmation one way or another, he wrote letters to President Roosevelt and to his father. Was it true that Americans were supplying Japan with arms and the materials of war? he asked. Who condoned them? Who condemned?

But before replies could come to him at Sian, he was on his way again to the front.

8

The growing guilt

Diary:

14 May

I am going North soon. Met the five boys who are going with me. Liu, the oldest, about 29, is a novelist; Auyung, the son of an actor, is a dramatist. He has a beautiful singing voice and can speak English. Lin San is a poet and looks like one, Ching is a journalist and as practical and down to earth as any Downeast Yankee I've ever known. He's even got that kind of wry, twangy humor. Wang is the youngest. He's a cameraman, and until recently he was completely disinterested in politics. But he fell in love with a girl-student and followed her to Yenan. He is now learning the facts of life, politically as well as otherwise.

15 May

Today we left Yenan. Our truck broke down 30 miles outside of the city, and we spent the night there. Auyung plays the harmonica.

And so it went, through the provinces of Shensi and Suiyuan, and into the Yellow River country of Inner Mongolia, and south again through Hopei and Shantung and Anhwei. May went by and June and July, and his mind and his heart and his diary were filled with the scene, the people, and the struggle. And, as in his earlier trip, he learnt more of the people of China. He slept in their houses and barns and marched with them, doctored them and shared their food. He listened quietly while peasants and soldiers, Kuomintang

and Communist, regular and partisan, spoke. And he listened to
their generals, the Manchurian, the Eighth Route Army, the Nationalist. He asked questions of them all, and of the Tibetan Great
Lama and the Living Buddha who had their own partisan anti-
Japanese groups. He observed the military schools where young
men trained with spears and staffs for want of any other weapon.
He visited the hospitals, and cried within him at their poverty. He
talked with Japanese prisoners and learnt their military life; he
studied battles with the men and the leaders who had fought them.
He heard the opinions of Spanish padres and Lutheran ministers
and Franciscan Brothers from California who were seeding souls in
the back wastes of China and harvesting them only when their own
lives and acts merited it.

He shared everything with the Chinese, even their diseases, for
he became sick with dysentery and trachoma and relapsing fever.

And with him as he went stalked the growing guilt. He had not
heard answers from home to his letters of inquiry. And he found
that he could no longer talk to the Chinese so glibly about America
and her help.

Finally the confirmation of Mao's accusation came to him. He
was in the little Hopei town of Nanking, and he was talking to a
soldier.

"We like Americans," the soldier said. "But why do you help
our enemies?"

"How do we help them?" Carlson demanded.

"You give them war materials, Ts'an Tsan!"

"How do you know?"

"I have seen it."

"Where?"

"In a newspaper."

"What paper?"

"Your own."

"Show it to me!"

The soldier nodded and took out of his pocket a torn, sweat-
greasy clipping, and gave it to Carlson with the gesture of a prosecutor handing over the key exhibit of his evidence. Carlson read it.

It was an AP dispatch from an American newspaper. It had the facts. We *were* sending to Japan over half the war supplies she received from abroad.

"Can you read this — it's in English?" Carlson asked.

"No, Ts'an Tsan. But I know what it says."

Yes, the soldier knew what it said; and so had Mao Tse-tung and so also Chu Teh and Chiang Kai-shek. They all had known it, but not he. What sublime and ridiculous innocence! How ignorant this citizen had been!

Yet, he had a rootlike faith that President Roosevelt did not condone these men; and that there were other Americans, like Henry L. Stimson, who fought against them. In Carlson's mind it came down to a question of the ignorance of his fellow citizens. They, as he, did not know the facts. They were uninformed. And a democracy was capable of great evil when its citizens did not know the truth.

When he had thought of these things, he made a vow that he would bring the truth to his fellow countrymen. It was his duty, when he returned to the States, to tell all who would listen what he had learnt in China. He would persuade with fact and figures and the unalterable statistics of his personal experience. His countrymen must learn where evil lay, and where justice and their own future security lay.

He would not let anything stand in his way.

On August 7, seventy-seven days after he left Yenan, he returned to beleaguered Hankow, found a place to stay in a Lutheran mission, found that all his mail sent to him via the Embassy had moved with it to Chungking. He sought out Americans, Mac Fisher of the Associated Press, Tillman Durdin of the *New York Times* and Arch Steele of the Chicago *Daily News*. They gathered in his little room in the mission.

Carlson asked a question. "Do you fellows know that we're supplying the Japs with most of their war stuff?"

The newsmen knew.

"It's a shameful thing, isn't it?"

They agreed, perhaps a little wonderingly, for Carlson seemed blazing with anger.

"It's got to stop!" he said.

And with the characteristic weariness of men who have seen too much of the world, they said it had to stop but they'd be damned if they knew how. And then they hastened to ask Carlson questions. What were the Reds doing? Was there order in the areas they controlled? Did they get on well with Kuomintang? And then they came to the *big* question: Did the Japs control all that they said they did?

And Carlson told them! He quibbled with nothing. He gave them all he knew. Manchukuoan troops were deserting to join the anti-Japanese Manchurian leader, General Ma Chan-shan. The Eighth Route Army guerrillas were crossing Jap lines with ease, issuing their own money, conducting their own schools, maintaining their own small arsenals. "The Japs possess nothing outside of the ground they stand on literally; a few cities, railroad and highway junctions, and county market towns."

"This is terrific," Fisher said. "In the States everyone thinks the Japs have really conquered North China."

"They think so even in Hankow."

"The Japs don't have a chance in China," Carlson said. "If we'd stop putting guns in Jap hands."

"And scrap steel in their mills," Fisher said.

"Is it your considered judgment, Captain," Steele asked, "that the Japs really don't hold those four so-called conquered provinces of Shensi, Hopei, Shantung and Suiyuan?"

"Hell, Arch. The only Japs I saw were prisoners. Here's my route map. I lived in these towns and cities. You can see for yourself."

"If only the people back home knew it," Durdin said.

"Evans, it's a shame we can't quote you on this," Fisher said. "Every time we get a good story it's off the record."

"Off the record!" Carlson exclaimed. "Off the record nothing. I want the States to know what's going on here. I want 'em to know the truth. You can quote me!"

Excited by the break, the correspondents started writing down their notes, getting direct quotes from Carlson, checking up on the facts.

On August 9, the Chicago *Daily News* ran a special radio dispatch with Arch Steele's by-line.

Japan Controls North China Only As Far As
Guns Reach, U.S. Officer Says After Visit

The story spoke of the complete ineffectiveness of Japanese control in North China which was "demonstrated in a remarkable fashion by an officer of the United States Marine Corps."

On the same day the *New York Times* ran Tillman Durdin's wirelessed report.

FINDS CHINA RUNS
"OCCUPIED" AREAS

Capt. E. F. Carlson of U.S.
Marines Makes 2,000-
Mile Trip, Much
of It Afoot

CROSSES JAPANESE LINES

Officer Says the Chinese Have
Arsenals, Factories, Bank
of Issue and Schools

And the Connecticut papers, including Plymouth's, ran the AP story, and it was the first word Tom and Joetta Carlson had of their son since April when they received his letter from Sian.

Time on the twenty-second, calling Carlson "tall, bristly-haired, up and coming," gave his story two columns and ran a picture of him and Chu Teh.

It is not possible to say who protested Carlson's story first, the Japanese Foreign Minister in Tokyo to our Mr. Joseph C. Grew, or the Japanese Ambassador in Washington to our Mr. Cordell Hull. At any rate, word reached the Navy Department that Carlson had talked out of turn, and the Japanese didn't like it. But, for the moment, the Navy Department did nothing.

Carlson, in Hankow, knew nothing of this. He kept on talking to whomever he met, especially to the members of what was called

"The Hankow Last Ditchers' Club." This unofficial group was not really a club but rather an atmosphere, a hail-fellow bravado in the face of a city doomed to die. It consisted of journalists from all countries and foreign observers who were their friends. During the months of August and September when each day might bring the Japanese into the city, they met and talked and drank and exchanged sentimental farewells to each other as, one by one, they left Hankow. Each, of course, had vowed to be the last of the Last Ditchers but their home offices and their duties decided otherwise. Among its members were Walter Bosshard, a Swiss journalist, two American newsreel men, George Krainaikov and Eric Mayell, and George Hogg, blooming fresh from Oxford, who was to die of malnutrition and lack of medical attention in 1945 while working for the Chinese Industrial Co-operatives in the interior. There was *Life* photographer Robert Capa, Carlson's old comrade from the Taierchwang battle, and the American correspondents, Richard Watts, Victor Keen, Jack Belden, Arch Steele, Tillman Durdin, Mac Fisher, Yates McDaniel. Agnes Smedley, who was working with the Red Cross, was one of the prime organizers of The Last Ditchers — literally the last of them, and its only woman member until Freda Utley, who hated both the Japanese and the Soviets, arrived. Occasionally, some temporary members flew in and left after a few days, Edgar Snow and John and Frances Gunther, Edgar A. Mowrer and Vernon Bartlett from England.

As kind of ex officio members were the staffs of the embassies and men like Stilwell, who even then was called "Vinegar Joe," and "Pinkie" Dorn, the American Consul General, Paul Josselyn, and Rear Admiral Le Breton of the American Yangtze Patrol.

Carlson literally had the press of the world with him in the Last Ditchers. And he did not let the chance go by. He admired these men. And he knew now why he had wanted for so long to be a writer. Who else was there who could inform the people of the world so well?

To live in Hankow in those days, Carlson felt, was like watching at the bedside of a dying friend. Man's disease of war was choking out the life of the city. Every day there were air raids, and every day more death and dying, more ruins, more refugees. The small band of the Last Ditchers were passengers on a sinking ship. Agnes Smedley described how they drew close together, searching each other's hearts and minds for the best way of life:

> Our old values seemed to vanish and we lost regard for material things, for no one knew whether there would be a tomorrow. . . . In the tense atmosphere of war even poetry, song and wit blossomed among us and a magical glow shone over our friendship.[13]

Carlson saw Chiang Kai-shek again, and again he pleaded for help for the Eighth Route Army and the partisan and guerrilla groups. He told him what Mao Tse-tung had said were the Communist postwar demands.

"How do they compare with your ideas, Generalissimo?" Carlson asked.

"*Ch'a pu to,*" Chiang Kai-shek replied. "About the same."

But no help was forthcoming.

Carlson felt depressed again. There was too much suspicion of the Reds. Too many authoritarian elements in the Kuomintang. If victory came, and the Reds did not give up everything, civil war would follow. And, he asked himself, if he were a Chinese Communist would he give up everything? Would he give up his fight for lower taxes, lower interest rates? Would he give up his army which had been shaped from the people's passion for independence and a better living as long as there were other autonomous armies in China headed by dictators, backward provincial leaders, old hankerers after long-lost feudal rights? He'd be damned if he would!

Civil war seemed inevitable unless Chiang Kai-shek willed it not to be. It was he alone who had the strength to break the boycott against supplies to the Eighth Route Army. He alone could dissolve the mutual distrust by the deed of recognizing who were the

[13] *Battle Hymn of China,* by Agnes Smedley. (New York: Alfred Knopf, 1943.)

enemies of his people and who their friends. Sian had taught him something. But Carlson wondered whether it had taught him enough.

Carlson's time was running out. There were more interviews, more dispatches.

His friends warned him that he'd get into trouble. He did not disregard them. He wanted to avoid it. He was a Marine officer, accustomed to discipline, ambitious to win the approval of his seniors and of Washington.

And yet, by God, he would argue, the people at home must be informed. Some one in authority must tell them. No one else had seen what he had. A man had a responsibility not only to himself. Did he take democracy to mean something real — or was he just fooling around with words?

9

"You'll starve to death!"

The seventeenth of September was just another day in the slow dying of Hankow; more Japanese air raids, more streets packed with corpses, more government officials moving out to Chungking. In the foreign cocktail bars and sports clubs, it was just another day too. People lunched, drank, made dates for dancing that evening, exchanged business references, signed contracts.

On that day, Carlson received a dispatch from his immediate senior, Commander Harry Overesch:

RECENT ARTICLE WHICH APPEARED TIME OF 22 AUGUST REGARD-LESS OF AUTHENTICITY MUST UNDER NO CIRCUMSTANCES BE RE-PEATED. THIS RESPONSIBILITY IN FUTURE WILL BE STRICTLY YOURS. STAY IN VICINITY OF HANKOW AND KEEP TAB ON POLITICAL IN-FLUENCE ON MILITARY

That night, Carlson wrote in his diary:

> Received rather a nasty radio from Overesch today, saying
> that any future references to me in the press would be my
> responsibility regardless whether or not they were authenti-
> cated. At first, I was inclined to ignore the implication, and to
> outline to him another trip I had planned. On second thought
> it seemed too serious to let pass. It means that any third party
> reference to me can bring me disciplinary action.
>
> I am tired of attempting to adjust my action to the arbitrary
> whims of a superior officer. Self-preservation seems to be the
> first thought of an officer of the U.S. Army or Navy. His whole
> training tends to accentuate that inclination. As a result he in-
> evitably takes the short view of things, considering each prob-
> lem in terms of his personal economic security. He will take
> no action which may jeopardize his career. He is continually
> thinking about the next selection board, and of how his
> superiors in Washington will consider the decisions and ac-
> tions he has taken. Consequently, it seems to be indicated that
> I should separate myself from the service if I am to continue to
> think and act in accordance with my own convictions. With
> this in mind, I today sent in my resignation to the Secretary of
> Navy, via the Naval Attaché at Peiping.
>
> It is quite a wrench to break the association of so many years.
> I might retire, but the Naval restrictions would continue to
> apply should I remain on the retired list. No, resignation is my
> only solution.

Although he put his act on the high plane of principle, beneath
was considerable emotional struggle. There was first his pride which
had been considerably shaken. He felt that he was no longer trusted
by his superiors, and to a man who takes himself and his work
seriously this was unbearable and considered by him an attack on
his integrity. Second, the military life which had satisfied at least
one of the requirements of his personality in the past — his need for
discipline — no longer seemed capable of continuing this. In 1922,
when he had decided to join the Marines, he had few convictions
about himself and about how he wanted to use his life. Military
discipline then seemed security and a strong crutch in an unstable

world. But now that he knew exactly what he wanted to do, now that he had an overwhelming conviction about himself, military discipline became oppressive, a Moloch of narrow-minded dictation from above.

Yet with all this there was his career to consider. He had a distinguished record, China and Nicaragua. Tommy Holcomb, the Commandant, admired him. Franklin Roosevelt had confidence in him. If he kept his health, he would go far. Even now, he was high on the captains' list, would soon be major. With the war, which he knew was inevitable, he would go up even faster. He might get a regiment, then a division. There was no uncertainty in his own mind that he would get a general's stars before his sun was set.

He had twenty-five years of service in the armed forces. Twenty-five years of living a kind of life which, whatever failings it had and with whatever frustrations it had brought him, had been his only life. He had few friends outside it; he had no interests beyond it; he had no way of making a livelihood away from it.

Agnes Smedley whom he had expected to approve his decision to resign was frightened.

"You're crazy, Evans," she said. "You're naïve. You're innocent. You don't know anything about the capitalist system. Do you think it has any use for men of principle? You won't get a job. You'll starve to death!"

He bucked under her words. "Don't plague me with starving, Agnes! The only thing I'm worried about is whether I'm doing the right thing? Am I?"

"Yes," Smedley said.

"Then that's enough."

Smedley warned him that his would be a bitter life.

"*You* have lived it, haven't you?" Carlson said.

"Yes, but that's different. Look at me — an outcast, never certain from one day to the next of my living."

"If you can do it, I can," Carlson said angrily. Then he added: "Don't insult me."

Sure, he was afraid he wouldn't get a job. He was not that naïve. He worried whether he'd even have a chance to say his say about

China. Who would listen to him? How could he get an audience?

He would write a book. That was certain. He would tell his story and get it published if he had to publish it and sell the book himself on the street corners. His father had once told him that decent principles were not enough. A man had to have the courage to live by them.

But he didn't want to permit himself to think of security. Am I right? he had asked.

Was it important for his country to know what was happening in China?

It was important.

Why?

Because war with Japan was coming, and China would be our ally.

Something must be done to bring light to Americans. They must know who their friends are. They must stop helping their enemy. He had made a vow that he would tell them and let nothing stand in his way, not his own career, nor his own chances of starving. Agnes with all her fervor did not have his confidence in the American people. He believed in them. God in heaven, he believed in them. They would see the right; they would act on it. Slowly, to be sure. Confusedly, contradictorily. But they would see the right. Agnes had been hurt too deeply by only one segment of American life. He had not been hurt yet. He knew only the great tradition. "I — will — not — equivocate!" Had he ever forgotten that time in Boston at Garrison's statue? Well, he would not equivocate now!

There was another reason, too, that he resigned and would not accept retirement. To retire meant that he would be living on three-quarters pay for his rank. He could be accused of living off the government while attacking some of her policies. That was too doubtful a position for him. He wanted his motives to be unassailable, his act to be seen purely for what it was. If the people to whom he talked of their responsibilities toward China were to be persuaded, they would have to have confidence in him. Confidence is given only to men who have proven their selflessness. It was Mao Tse-tung's secret, and Chu Teh's.

But it was hard. It would be hard. He hated to give up everything, his friends, his life work, his career. He knew that his brother Marine officers would find it hard to understand him. They'd consider him a traitor to the Corps. Comradeship of years, of the field, of battle, the deepest comradeship a man can have, would be gone. No matter how hard his old friends tried, he'd be fair dead to them, for there would be little left to share together. Of course, they would defend him against the pipsqueaks in the Corps who would charge him with treason, with being a Red, with having gotten the "Moscow religion." His friends would defend, but in their hearts they would be saying, "Poor old Evans . . . threw his life away."

That's what Stilwell was saying.

"I admire what you're doing, Carlson," Vinegar Joe commented. "But you're throwing away too much. No Chinese would do for our country what you're trying to do for theirs."

Carlson shook his head, tried to grin, tried to find some light reply. He liked Stilwell, admired him. But even he didn't see the issue.

"I'm not resigning for the sake of the Chinese, Colonel," Carlson said awkwardly. He hated talking about motives. "I'm doing it for ourselves. I may be wrong, but I think I'm trying to help our stake in the world."

"I respect you for it anyway," was Stilwell's reply.

Six years later, Stilwell, General in the Army, would remember Carlson when it came his turn to decide between his own career and his duty to his country. Within a week after his recall from China where he had sought to aid all Chinese armies, regardless of politics, in their fight against the common enemy, he wrote Carlson a letter in which again he acknowledged his admiration and added his admission that Carlson had been right.

Carlson did not forget his father and his home. He knew, without asking, that his people would approve his act. The old, deeply felt ambition to be a success for their sake had vanished. The years had laid over the green eagerness to be the rich returned home-town boy. His people would think him a success for what he was doing now, rather than for what he might be doing in five years from now as a famous general. His father and mother would have to say "Yea" to his stubborn demand to do what he thought was right.

According to protocol, Carlson had submitted his resignation to Admiral Le Breton (COMYANGPAT), Commander of the Yangtze Patrol, to forward to the American Legation, United States Naval Attaché (ALUSNA) in Peiping.

That was on the seventeenth. On the eighteenth a dispatch went from COMYANGPAT to ALUSNA with a copy to Admiral Harry Yarnell, the Commander in Chief Asiatic Fleet (CINCAF):

> FROM CARLSON COLON REQUEST THAT THE FOLLOWING DISPATCH BE FORWARDED TO THE SECRETARY OF THE NAVY QUOTE RESPECTFULLY REQUEST THAT I BE RELIEVED FROM PRESENT DUTY AND RETURNED TO THE UNITED STATES AS EARLY AS PRACTICABLE AND THAT ON MY ARRIVAL THERE THAT MY RESIGNATION AS AN OFFICER OF THE NAVAL SERVICE AND CAPTAIN IN THE MARINE CORPS BE ACCEPTED EVANS FORDYCE CARLSON UNQUOTE DESIRE RETURN SHANGHAI TO SETTLE AFFAIRS IF PRACTICABLE BEFORE RETURNING STATES

Early morning of the nineteenth brought a Shanghai dispatch from Admiral Yarnell to Admiral Le Breton, requesting Le Breton to withhold action on Carlson pending further instructions.

Yarnell liked Carlson. He had read his reports; liked them enough to send an enthusiastic letter of commendation to the Chief of Naval Operations in Washington. He had no idea what was eating Carlson. Something big, he decided. Carlson wasn't a youngster to go off in a tantrum. He'd have to find out what it was and stop the man from leaving the Navy.

He wrote a dispatch to the Naval Attaché at Peiping:

> SINCE CARLSON GAVE NO REASON FOR RESIGNATION AND IN VIEW HIS OUTSTANDING SERVICES WHICH HAVE MERITED AND RECEIVED THE WARM APPRECIATION AND COMMENDATION OF ORIGINATOR AND VALUE HIS FUTURE SERVICE SUGGEST YOU REQUEST COMYANGPAT CONTACT CARLSON IF PRACTICABLE AND ASCERTAIN BASIS OF REQUEST AND URGE HE CAREFULLY RECONSIDER SAME

ALUSNA forwarded Yarnell's request to Admiral Le Breton, who showed it to Carlson.

Carlson was deeply touched by Yarnell's confidence in him. But he knew that Yarnell could do nothing to relieve the oppressive restriction.

In his diary for the nineteenth Carlson wrote:

Today Yarnell held up my resignation. Asked me for a reason. I replied both by letter and dispatch that I wished to be free to speak and write in accordance with my convictions. I thanked him for his thoughtful consideration of me. Overesch came through with a half-hearted expression of regret of the action I had taken. I have made my decision and will stick to it.

Carlson's message to Yarnell was carefully worded:

DEEPLY APPRECIATE CONSIDERATION SHOWN ME BY YOU AS COM-MANDER IN CHIEF THROUGHOUT MY YEARS OF SERVICE ONLY THOUGHT HAS BEEN TO PERFORM EACH TASK TO BEST OF ABILITY DURING PRESENT ASSIGNMENT HAVE CONTINUOUSLY CONSIDERED EACH PROBLEM WITH VIEW TO ATTAINING SOLUTION WHICH BEST SERVED NOT ONLY NAVAL SERVICE BUT OUR GOVERNMENT AS WELL DECISION TO REMOVE MYSELF FROM THE SERVICE AND ASSOCIATES OF OVER SCORE YEARS MADE ONLY AFTER CAREFUL DELIBERATION AND AS RESULT OF DEEP CONVICTION MY DUTY TO EMBARK LITERARY CAREER UNFETTERED DESIRE IF PRACTICABLE TO RETURN SHANGHAI VIA CHUNGKING IN ORDER VISIT AMBASSADOR ALSO ON ARRIVAL U S SUGGEST I BE SENT WASHINGTON FOR CONFERENCE EARLY ACTION WOULD BE SINCERELY APPRECIATED

Yarnell knew at last what was hurting Carlson, and he forwarded the resignation to the Secretary of the Navy. He hoped that action would not be taken until Carlson came to Shanghai. There might still be time to talk him out of it.

On the twenty-first, the day on which Yarnell reluctantly sent off Carlson's resignation to the Secretary of the Navy, the situation was made ironic by a dispatch which Overesch in Peiping received from Marine Headquarters authorizing him to examine Carlson for promotion to Major on his record. This meant that Carlson would not have to take any examination.

Carlson, however, requested that the promotion be suspended. He did not want to accept it in view of his resignation.

On the twenty-third he received his orders to leave Hankow for Shanghai, via Chungking. Word passed swiftly that Carlson had resigned. Correspondents sent the news back home. They reported that Carlson, "bowing to Japanese pressure," had resigned.

"Everyone here very sympathetic," he noted in his diary. "I do not want sympathy. Right now all I want is a release from a situation which has become intolerable."

On the night of the twenty-seventh between air raids, the Hankow Last Ditchers had a farewell party for Carlson. They rigged up a mock courtroom and charged Carlson with "desertion" of The Last Ditchers. Everybody got passably drunk and sentimental. Agnes Smedley presented the case for the prosecution, and Mac Fisher of the Associated Press, who was trying to defend the "culprit," heard himself making a speech that was not excusing the "desertion" but rather eulogizing the courage of this Marine officer who was willingly giving up his "whole god-damned career because the god-damned Japs had forced the god-damned State Department to force the god-damned Navy Department to force him to keep his mouth shut."

Carlson expressed himself fully on the subject of the Japanese but he defended the State and Navy Departments. What else could they do? After all, our policy in the Pacific was to appease the Japanese, for we were not ready to go to war over China and we did not yet see how our own interests were challenged. It was for this that he had resigned, so that he could show us our own interests. He predicted that they'd all be together again soon, somewhere. They'd all be covering the American-Japanese war, which was as inevitable as tomorrow.

But the serious talk faded against the sentiment, and the farewells were sad. The party broke up to the strains of "Auld Lang Syne" which was started by a world-weary, completely unsentimental American correspondent, who denied ever having a feeling more emotional than waiting for his next check.

The next day, Carlson's last in Hankow, Hollington Tong, Chiang Kai-shek's Minister of Information, gave him a dinner. The speeches were long and laudatory, full of diplomatic nosegays. Tong pointed out that Carlson was one of the few foreigners who believed in China's victory. Carlson replied that he himself had derived strength from China, that its people had revealed the wonderful dimension of the human spirit. Yes, he had confidence in the Chinese, he said. "And their leaders," he added, making sure to use the plural.

On the twenty-ninth of September, the day Mussolini, Daladier, Chamberlain and Hitler met at Munich to partition Czechoslovakia, Carlson was conducted across the river to Wuchang and thence to the lake where he boarded a Chinese National Airways Sikorsky. On the lookout for raiding Jap planes, they took off at 5:15 and headed west. At Chungking Ambassador Nelson T. Johnson invited him to stay with him in his new Embassy offices in the Standard Oil compound.

"Carlson," Johnson said when they got talking, "tell me about these Chinese Communists. Are they really Reds?"

"In my opinion, Mr. Ambassador," Carlson replied, "their political doctrines are representative democracy, their economic doctrines are the co-operative theory, and only in their social application are they Communists, for they place a great deal of emphasis on social equality. They are not like the Russian Reds for one simple reason. China is not Russia. Each country, they tell me, must move toward socialism in its own way, at its own tempo, and with its own peculiarities. Russia, for example, had a revolution — and then ten years afterwards had to reinstall private enterprise for a while. The Chinese Reds are not against private enterprise from the very beginning. They say that's the way it has to be in China. They're realistic men. They're not trying to superimpose something unworkable. They want a democracy in China, free speech, free press and the rest. As an American, that's what I want to keep alive at home. I can't help but sympathize with any Chinese who wants it in China."

5 October

Johnson is a remarkable man and deserves a large place in the history of our diplomatic relations with China. Certainly

no other man of my acquaintance could have handled this
situation with his judgment, patience and diplomacy. For over
a year now he has been living under abnormal conditions. He
saw the Peiping coup (Marco Polo Bridge incident which was
used by Japan to take Peiping). Then he spent three months
at Nanking during the heavy bombing. At Hankow he set up
a provisional Embassy and again went through the suspense
of frequent air raids. Here at Chungking he is more isolated
than ever, living on such food as is available locally. Yet there
is never a word of complaint from him. Other Ambassadors
cruise around from here to Hongkong and Shanghai. But he
sticks to his post. His friendship has meant much to me.

Before leaving Chungking Carlson talked with Dr. H. H. Kung,
the Generalissimo's brother-in-law and Finance Minister. Kung was
getting over a malaria attack but he seemed eager to talk, an eagerness coming from a desire to communicate certain ideas to the
United States without doing it through official diplomatic channels.
Telling them to Carlson would, in effect, be telling them to Ambassador Johnson, for Kung knew that Carlson would report on
their conversation.

Tentatively, barely suggesting, Kung presented his feeling — personal feeling, mind you — that President Roosevelt, whom everybody trusted, might be in a position to call a peace conference. Kung
believed that Japan would welcome such a conference. Naturally the
Japanese-Chinese war would be on the agenda, the position of
Manchuria, and so on. It was merely a suggestion, Kung remarked
casually. As for Manchuria — well, perhaps the Chinese government would grant it dominion status under the Chinese flag but
with certain economic privileges to Japan. China might also
guarantee Japan annual consignments of rice, cotton, iron. Just as
concessions for a peaceful settlement.

As Kung knew would happen, Carlson related the conversation
to Ambassador Johnson, who undoubtedly relayed it to the State
Department.

The air raid sirens were sounding as his huge Douglas transport took off from Chungking for Kunming, but they made it safely. From Kunming to Hanoi he took the Michelin, the rubber-tired train.

Finally he reached Hong Kong which sat as smug as a fat cat with the warmed milk of colonial exploitation in its belly.

He had a talk with T. V. Soong, who was a brother of Madame Chiang Kai-shek, Madame H. H. Kung and Madame Sun Yat-sen. Soong was head of the Bank of China, a liberal by emotion and a conservative by interest. He had no diplomatic suggestions to make, as his brother-in-law, H. H. Kung, had. But, like Kung, he reflected what Carlson heard everywhere: "We don't expect America to fight our battles. But we don't expect her to help Japan either."

The guilt which once Carlson had felt about his country had diminished. He was en route to fulfilling his obligation.

"Not many foreigners think we will win," Soong said. "It means a great deal to us when one does, like yourself who is a military man and has seen so many of our people and so much of our land."

"Anybody who believes in the people," Carlson replied, "has got to believe that China will win."

The crown of his interviews was with a woman he had never met before, but whom he had come to admire from afar — Madame Sun Yat-sen, the widow of China's greatest leader. She was, as he noted in his book, the fitting finale to his years of observing the Great Chinese Drama. The last time he had seen her was at her husband's re-interment in Peiping in 1929. Then she had been deep in mourning, at a distance from him, slowly following the body of her husband up the highway to the Purple Mountain. And now he was seeing her in a small apartment in Hong Kong, where she was living in retirement, a critic of her brother-in-law, Chiang Kai-shek, and his Kuomintang Party whom she called traitors to the principles of Sun Yat-sen.

"I sensed something of the spirit of this woman," he wrote, "in the severity of the simply furnished room. She was allowing herself no luxuries." His Yankee soul warmed to such abnegation.

To Carlson Madame Sun was a beautiful woman, the most attractive of the Soong sisters. She had all of Madame Chiang's graciousness but was more sincere and more outspoken. In his diary he noted that Madame Sun's face told of a love for humanity and a lack of thought of self. There was no pretense about her, no *k'e ch'i* (standing on ceremony).

Carlson told her of all his experiences in the Northwest, in Hankow and Chungking, and his words were like lights on her relaxed, unmasked face. She frowned at his tales of lack of help for the partisans, laughed when he told her of his meeting with Agnes Smedley, was taut with suspense at the trials of the Eighth Route Army, and nodded with high approval at Mao Tse-tung's plea for postwar unity.

She herself was rather bitter. She argued that the time was long past when representative government should have been established by Chiang Kai-shek who, it seemed, was more concerned with winning loyalty to himself than to the principles of a democratic China. And if the people were not yet prepared for the voting franchise, then why hadn't steps been taken to prepare them?

Madame Sun didn't say much about what she was doing, but Carlson knew from friends in Hong Kong that she was the strength behind the China Defense League which raised money for hospitals and for the care of refugees.

"And she saw to it that every dollar was honestly spent," Carlson recorded. "Under her eagle eye there was no diversion of funds to the pockets of unscrupulous officials."

Earlier that day T. V. Soong had made a rather flattering offer to Carlson. He asked him to return to China after his resignation went into effect and advise the Military Commission of the National Government. And now the offer was repeated in a different way by Madame Sun. She asked him to return and advise the Canton Defense Council.

He could not deny that both offers were pleasing to think about, but he was not leaving the Marine Corps to become another W. H. Donald, as valuable to China's cause as the Australian was. Rather — and he must keep it clearly in front of him — he was leaving because his country was unwittingly undermining its own chances of survival.

And so he refused both T. V. Soong and Madame Sun Yat-sen.

His last stop in China was Shanghai to see Admiral Yarnell.

"Are you still set on leaving us?" Yarnell asked.

"Yes, sir."

Carlson went into the details of his feelings.

"Fine, Carlson, fine," Yarnell said. "But I don't think you're a good judge of the situation."

Carlson bridled respectfully.

"You're too close to China. Your nose is right up against the stump of a tree and you can't see the forest behind it. Give yourself time and distance. China is only part of the world. This war is only part of the war that may come. There'll be a place for you in that war. An important place, Carlson. I'm not telling you this to flatter you. You're a very competent officer — and you've got a fine record. I ask you: what's more important — to resign now or to stay in and throw your weight around on the side of the best elements in the Naval and Diplomatic Service? What do you think?"

Carlson was silent.

"Whether you like my arguments or not," Yarnell went on, "you've got to admit that you need time and objectivity before making a decision to throw away a whole life work."

Carlson lit another cigarette, and he saw that his fingers were trembling. These damn decisions, he thought. They are always more complicated and more difficult than a decision on a field of battle. Yarnell had a point.

Yarnell saw he had a point, for he pressed it against Carlson. "You wrote me that you had given your decision deliberate thought. Nonsense! You received Overesch's dispatch on the seventeenth of September and you — " he referred to some papers on his desk "You sent in your resignation on the eighteenth. One day! One day isn't time enough to make that kind of decision!"

Yes, Yarnell had a point. . . . He wasn't attacking the decision itself but rather the speed and situation in which it was made. . . .

Perhaps he was too close to China. . . . Perhaps he had moved too swiftly, too temperamentally. . . . Yet he knew his act was correct. The people at home had to know what was going on. That thought he must keep unclouded. He could tell them only if he were a civilian again. . . . *Again?* When had he ever been a civilian?

Breaking into his own reflection, Carlson said, "Admiral, I appreciate your interest in me — "

"My interest is primarily in keeping good men in the Navy," Yarnell interrupted.

"But I've got a job to do that may be bigger than the Navy, Admiral."

"I agree. But who says you can't write or speak as a Marine officer? Just because Overesch objects? Because Japan objects? Take it up with them in Washington. Something can be worked out. But at any rate, wait! Don't be hasty. When you get back to the States, don't press your resignation. Let it slide. Washington will hold off until you force the issue. Agreed?"

Yarnell rose from his chair.

Frowning, Carlson followed his senior officer and stood up. He walked over to the corner of the cabin and looked out of the porthole to Shanghai beyond.

There was China, the foster-mother country which had brought him renewed love for his own mother country. There was his destiny, his fate, the prod into his heart which had brought him to the end of his search. Shanghai, Hankow, Chungking, Yenan, Jehol, Peiping . . . All the tortured and blessed cities . . . And Mao and Chu Teh and Li Po and Chou En-lai and Auyung and Nieh and Agnes and Donald and the Generalissimo and the wondrous Madame Sun. . . . All the tortured and blessed people . . . They had given him himself, brought into sharp focus the blurred image of what he had wanted to become.

But how had it been possible? His job as a Marine had made it so. Otherwise, there might have been nothing. . . . Otherwise he might have ended his days a fruit salesman in Montana. . . .

The Marines had given him an education, the time to study, the chance to see other lands and other people. . . . Had he not determined that some day he would have his own outfit inspirited with ethical indoctrination to prove to the world that men who knew and loved what they knew were men who fought best? Out of the service, how could he do this? Was it not perhaps equally important to his country to have military men devoted to making its armies democratic?

Perhaps he had not thought this act of resignation out thoroughly enough. Perhaps Yarnell was right. He could always resign again.

Carlson turned to face Yarnell and smiled grimly.

"Admiral," Carlson said with a dryness in his throat, "I've never heard you called a seagoing lawyer, but if you weren't seagoing, I'll bet you'd have been a lawyer."

Yarnell laughed. He had won. He felt he had done a service not only to Carlson but to his country.

"I'll think it over," Carlson said, "I'll hold off on the resignation for a while." He wondered as he spoke whether it was only a question of time.

Later that day Commander Overesch added his plea to Yarnell's. He said that he had meant his telegram to Carlson to be merely a warning, and regretted that it gave him the wrong impression. "I had not intended it to be so severe," Overesch said.

Carlson boarded the old transport *Chaumont,* the ship that was like home, the ship on which he had traveled so often. On board he found a copy of a letter of commendation which Yarnell had sent to him to read:

UNITED STATES ASIATIC FLEET
U.S.S. *Augusta* (Flagship)

SHANGHAI, CHINA,
16 November, 1938

From: The Commander in Chief, ASIATIC FLEET.
To : Captain Evans F. Carlson, U.S. Marine Corps.
Via : The Major General Commandant, Headquarters, U.S.

Subject: Commendation.

1. Upon your detachment from duty on this station, I wish to take this opportunity to again express to you my ap-

preciation and admiration for the very valuable and efficient
services which you have rendered during the past year.

   2.   Your duties as an observer with the Chinese military
forces have required you to travel thousands of miles in the
interior of China, often on foot and horseback over the most
difficult and hazardous terrain, and under primitive living
conditions similar to those encountered by native troops. During this time the nature of your duties not only subjected you
to the immediate dangers of active warfare but to those of
pestilence and disease as well.

   3.   Your willingness to suffer privations and endure
hardships, and the courage and zeal displayed by you in the
performance of your difficult duties merit and receive my warm
approbation and commendation, and are in keeping with the
best traditions of the naval service.

   4.   The Major General Commandant will be furnished
a copy of this letter with the request that it be filed with your
official record.

(signed)
H. E. YARNELL

Copies to: ALUSNA, Peiping
          MarPac

10

Salt-and-pepper tweed

He arrived in San Francisco the end of December 1938 and spent
Christmas with his wife there. He had a month's leave before re-
porting to the Marine Corps Base at San Diego. He wanted the
month; it would be his time for thinking things out.

   The whole Marine Corps had heard of Carlson's resignation. Old
friends moved in on him to show him the error of his ways.

"If you want to write you can write," said Lt. Col. John Thomason, Jr., who had written many short stories and several books on the Marines. "I write. No one tells me I can't."

"But you write stories. They're not controversial, John. You don't deal with live issues. I don't want to write what you write."

General Lyman, whose aide Carlson had been, talked to him.

"Why don't you at least take your retirement pay, Evans," the General pleaded. "If you think that Eighth Route Army of yours is so great and needs so much help, you can send them your pay. If you resign, you have nothing to send."

"I'm still thinking it over, General," Carlson replied.

He heard President Roosevelt's speech to the Seventy-sixth Congress. Carlson was stirred by F. D. R.'s words, and horrified at the apathy in the States. They didn't know what's going on! They lived in a fool's world! "You go to the movies," he cried, "play bridge, bet on horses, get excited over polo and football — and, God in heaven, human beings are starving to death across the world, are dying by inches fighting our battles for us."

He told them all, and they said that poor old Evans had gotten religion, and what he needed was a long rest from China.

His wife tried to persuade him not to leave the service. "You love military life," she said. "When you resigned from the Army, you couldn't wait to get back. You will lose all your friends. They won't understand your reason for leaving. They'll think less of you."

"Let them!" he cried savagely. "Let them. If I lose such friends, I don't want to keep them."

From Plymouth came letters from his father and mother, Tom and Karen. "Do what you think is best," they wrote. "We're behind you in whatever you decide."

Yarnell had told him to put distance between himself and China. Well, he was doing it. He was six thousand miles away. But China was right next door to him, in the same room, in the same bed. He couldn't pull the shade down on Yenan and Wu T'ai Shan . . . On Madame Sun Yat-sen . . . On Chu Teh.

They were expecting something from him. They had shared their food and their minds with him. They expected him to act.

Yet . . . What was the right thing to do?

Etelle Carlson got the brunt of his anguish. She stood with all the others against him. She and General Lyman and Major Thomason. It wasn't that she didn't understand or was unsympathetic or wouldn't have gone with him in any life he would choose to live; it was only that she and the others did not know the vocabulary of idealism in action. One can understand the words, "good citizenship," but few can grasp the necessity for acting on such words. It is not practical; it is not sane; it is not effective; it gets you nowhere. Can't you do these things you want to without sacrificing? they asked. In essence they wanted him not to do anything!

On February 20, 1939 he was assigned as Intelligence officer to the Headquarters of the Fleet Marine Force in San Diego.

Three days later he put to test the possibilities of whether he could continue in the Marines and live with himself or whether there was no choice but to leave.

On that day he sent a communication to the Secretary of the Navy, via the Commandant of the Marine Corps:

> 1.   I have been invited by Mr. Olin D. Wanamaker, on behalf of the Associated Boards for Christian Colleges in China (150 Fifth Avenue, New York, N.Y.) to address a group of influential people in Washington, D.C. on an undetermined date between March 20 and April 7, on the subject of the present situation in China. The group would be assembled by Doctor William McClellan, President of the Potomac Electric Power Company. Reporters would not be present, and it would be stipulated that no publicity would be given the talk.
> 2.   Information is requested as to whether there would be any objection to my making a talk.
> 3.   The talk would be objective, would not reveal any material received in confidence from Chinese leaders, and would be designed to acquaint the group with actual conditions existing in China.
> 4.   There would be no expense to the government.

His reply came two weeks later, signed by Admiral William D. Leahy, acting for Navy Secretary Claude Swanson. The first paragraph repeats the facts of the request. It was in the second paragraph which Carlson found his answer — to everything:

2. The Navy Department has no objection to the proposed talk *provided it reveals nothing that you learned by reason of being language officer or because of other duties assigned to you by the Naval Attaché in China.* [Italics author's.]

"Nothing you have learned . . . because of duties assigned to you . . . in China!"

This was absurd. Anger flourished in Carlson. This was more than absurd; it was dishonest.

How could he talk five words about China without revealing what he had learned in the course of his duties there? He had never been there except on duty.

Leahy meant simply that he could not talk.

And he would talk!

All the fine words of Yarnell, his wife and friends were empty sounds now.

All he heard was his own vow: Americans must be informed. They must stop sending supplies to Japan. They must see their own interests.

He had thought it over — and here was the answer.

His resignation, this time to be followed through, was sent on the seventeenth of March, one day after he received Leahy's reply.

He arose late from bed the next Sunday morning, put on a salt-and-pepper tweed suit, drove out into the country in back of San Diego with his wife and said, "Don't you notice how happy I am?"

She noticed it. But she was not so happy.

Before Leahy's letter reached him, Carlson had been given the professional examination for promotion as Major, had qualified, and his name had been sent to the United States Senate for confirmation. As before in Hankow, he pressed his resignation before the Senate could confirm him. He wanted no one to accuse him of waiting until he became a Major before leaving the service.

As it happened, his resignation was accepted by Major General Holcomb, Commandant of the Marine Corps, "with regrets and appreciation . . . and with hope for a happy and successful civil life" to become effective April 30, 1939. On May 3, the Senate, slow in its own way, confirmed the appointment of Carlson as Major.

Marine Corps Headquarters asked Carlson to take his commission in the Reserve, but he rejected the offer for the same reason he had refused to retire. He wanted no strings.

Now he was free. He was free to go where he wanted, to speak, to write, to say what he knew without requesting anyone's permission.

The Institute of Pacific Relations, an unofficial and nonpolitical organization founded in 1925 to study the peoples of the Pacific Area, was conducting an inquiry into the problems arising from the Sino-Japanese war. Edward C. Carter, the Secretary-General, asked Carlson whether he would undertake to write a nonpartisan study of the Chinese Army in all its aspects.

He gladly accepted.

He didn't have much money saved, and would have to live on borrowings from his insurance policy and the infrequent sale of an article to a magazine — usually one that didn't pay very much. The Institute of Pacific Relations gave him a grant of $500 to write the Chinese Army book.

He and his wife rented a house in San Diego, and he began a life which for so long he had wanted to live.

It was a simpler life than the one in the Corps. No calls to make, no entertaining, no going out evenings for dinner. It meant all his meals at home, at odd hours; it meant, most of all, a new kind of self-discipline — at the typewriter. For so active a man physically the typewriter might have ordinarily been a prison. His portable lay black, inert, metallic and uninviting against the bright outside, the banks of flowers on the lawn, the low hills beyond, the beaches near by, the country walks.

He pounded it, possessed.

Mrs. Carlson wrote about their life to his people in Plymouth. "Our only relaxations," she said, "are the movies. We go once or twice a week. We were very enthusiastic about *Alexander Graham Bell* and *Pygmalion*. We're looking forward to seeing *Juarez*. With the European situation the way it is and the China business still unsettled, I know Evans will be getting the urge to be doing things. He already has it but he wants to do more on his book."

He had to write like a man possessed, for the wars were calling.

In between articles for *Asia* and *Amerasia* on his experiences in China, speeches at churches, conventions, American Legion Posts, he worked on his Chinese Army book.

It is not a long study, about thirty thousand words, and it is filled with facts of logistics, finance, chain of command, strength of companies, regiments, etc. It contains a brief but complete historical background of the Chinese military.

Although the book, in all respects, is an objective piece of work, Carlson could not avoid judgments.

He announces, in the beginning, his own unworthiness for the task confronting him but hopes that his experience, shared by few other foreigners, might have some significance.

"Intimate association with the Chinese soldier," he wrote, "evoked in the writer a feeling of profound admiration and respect for this unorthodox but effective military man."

The average Chinese, to Carlson, is resourceful, intelligent, loyal to his family, "and faithful to the point of death to a leader who treats him with consideration."

He contrasts the morale of the Kuomintang forces with those of the Eighth Route Army, the differences between a group of men trained primarily to obey and a group trained by the "rule of reason" in which understanding and volition are primary. The men, he says, of one army "become automatons without spiritual convictions. When the men of such an army are pitted, in a long and arduous war, against troops which are fighting for an ideal, the spirit of the latter enables them better to endure the strain."

When his manuscript was finished, it was submitted through Edward C. Carter, to such authorities as Mr. T. A. Bisson, Mr. George Atcheson, Jr. of our State Department, and Lieutenant Colonel Philip R. Faymonville of the War Department. They made many valuable suggestions, and Carlson gladly made revisions. The book was published in the Spring of 1940, received few notices in the general press, but among soldiers and diplomats, it was taken as an authority.[14]

That summer, relieved of his first big writing job, he was happy to accept an invitation from the Institute of International Relations at Mills College in Oakland, California.

Here he was among men who had made a profession of the study of international affairs, Harry Gideonse of Columbia University, Stanley Hornbeck of the State Department, Samuel Guy Inman, specialist on South American affairs for Cordell Hull. Others who participated were Norman Thomas, the socialist, and Gerald Heard, the anthropologist-philosopher-pacifist.

He felt himself flowering in the round-table debates. He was matching the fact of the school of his eyes and ears and heart against pedagogical fact, theory, and doctrine.

To many of his colleagues he may well have sounded strange, a messiah of contradiction. He was Major Carlson, recently resigned from the Marine Corps, saying, "I do not believe in the use of force . . . in international differences." Saying: "We must begin with the self-discipline of the individual." He was against an International Police Force. He called it good in theory, unsound in practice. How could its component parts and its leadership be divorced from representing the power interests of their respective countries? he asked.

He argued with Frederick Libby of the National Council for the Prevention of War. Libby said that we should not interfere in the Sino-Japanese war. Prohibiting trade with Japan would not help.

But Japan gets 54 per cent of her war materials from us, Carlson insisted. We are taking sides. The wrong side. We must force Congress to pass embargoes stopping such trade with Japan.

Whenever he had a chance to speak, he played the same tune: We must stop helping Japan. China can win. Japan has only a finger-hold on China. Our national interests are bound up with China's victory.

[14] *The Chinese Army* by Evans Fordyce Carlson; Institute of Pacific Relations, 1940.

And he showed his contempt for phrases like "balance of power," "spheres of influence," "power politics." He admitted them as facts, but he refused to accept their permanence. He wanted to go beyond them; self-discipline, sacrifice . . .

He was, in this aspect, alone at Mills College.

From Mills College, he wrote a letter describing the Institute and the talks he was giving:

> Besides my lectures here, I have one at the International House in Berkeley, one for the San Francisco Junior Chamber of Commerce, and one for the Pacific Coast Conference of the Committee Against War Shipments to Japan.
>
> Hope I can get away with all this. If I do, Dad, pat yourself on the back. Any speaking ability I have, I inherited from you.

He was certainly keeping his promise to himself.

On March 10, 1939 Joseph Stalin had made a speech to the Eighteenth Congress of the Communist Party of the Soviet Union. In it he criticized the appeasement of Hitler at Munich, and warned those in other countries who hoped for a Nazi-Soviet war that Russia will not pull other nations' chestnuts out of the fire. On the 5th of May Foreign Commissar Litvinov resigned. Molotov took his place. One month later Great Britain, somewhat frightened by what she was hearing in the foreign offices of Europe, sent a minor diplomat, William Strang, to Moscow to work out a British-Soviet agreement. Strang had little authority; nothing much was done. On the 22nd of August the world was shattered by the signing of a Soviet-German Nonaggression Pact.

Americans did not know what to make of it. No one, least of all the American Communist, had anticipated the move. And confusion, heartache, malconstructions emerged in the next five or six days. Carlson was one of the few who grasped quickly a point of view on this enormous event. His estimate of the Russians, derived from talks with the Chinese Reds and Soviet citizens he had met in China, had convinced him there was a fundamental difference between Soviet life and Fascist life. Munich had shown him that the non-Fascist, noncommunist, democratic capitalisms of the West were trying to encourage a war between Russia and Germany in the hope of destroying both without cost to themselves. It was the same kind of shortsightedness, he felt, which permitted the United States to help Japan against China. He did not believe that Russia would permit itself to engage in a gladiators' contest with Germany while the rest of the world jeered both sides and hungered for the day when it could pick the carcasses of Russian and German dead.

The day after the nonaggression pact was announced he took the time to write a long letter to Plymouth. He knew that his folks would be interested in his opinions, now that he had worked up a little reputation in international politics:

> Well, Russia evidently has the boys guessing now. The Russo-German Pact was one of the shrewdest moves made in many a day. I am inclined to believe that it may mean the end of the old type French and British imperialism as I have known it in China. It also means the dawn of a new social and economic era in Europe . . . America will be well advised to keep out of Europe and turn her face to the south and to the west.
>
> If things get hot in Europe I will probably head for New York and try to get a job as a war correspondent there. I am eager to see you all but I am sailing pretty close to the breeze right now and don't want to spend any more money than I have to.
>
> Bishop Roots is here in Frisco, and we had several soul-searching talks. He is trying to win me over to the Moral Re-Armament movement, but I can't reconcile their deeds with their words.

No, MRA was not for him. He distrusted its "works" even while he heard its protestations of its "faith." He would distrust the angelic choir, if they did not match with their deeds the sinless seduction of their song. No Loreleis for Carlson.

11

The shadow of his home

Carlson's mother, Joetta, had been a bed and wheel-chair invalid for fifteen years. It was something the doctors weren't too sure about: neuritis, phlebitis — something that sallowed her body and sickened her. Carlson, who was lecturing here and there, the West, the South, the East, felt he ought to go home. His mother was 74. She could not live much longer.

Perhaps Joetta Carlson knew she was dying when her son returned. Perhaps because of this, or because she wanted to show off in her beautiful, proud, pathetic Evans way, she appeared to him to be more energetic and more spirited than he had ever remembered her.

They had some good times together. They kept telling stories of the past on each other. Carlson told them of the people he had known in his life. (Make up for lost time.) He described the places in China he had lived in and marched through.

He joshed his mother a lot, especially about his first enlistment in the Army.

"I told 'em I was six years older than I really was, mother," he would say with a grin.

His mother always was baited by the story. "But, Evans," she would protest, "that would mean you were born in 1890, and your father and I weren't married until 1893. *How could you?*"

The son would laugh and the father would laugh. But Joetta was still scandalized all these years.

"Did Dad ever tell you we received a telegram from Orville Kellogg when you joined the Army?" Joetta asked.

"Yes," Carlson said.

"We could've pulled you back, you know," Joetta said. "Underage. It would have been simple."

"I know," Carlson said.

"But we didn't. Your father and I talked it over. We thought you ought to have a chance to make yourself — the way you wanted it." She tightened the blue silk shawl around her shoulders.

Carlson was silent. The cards of memory were being shuffled. He remembered coming down the hill behind the parsonage at Peacham when he embraced his mother, arm around her shoulder, and he looked across the hills and thought how wonderful it would be if he could have all the adventure in the world and never leave home.

"It was hard to have you leave us, Evans," Joetta Carlson said. What could he tell her now?

It was a week or so before Christmas, and Carlson was down at Virginia Beach, Virginia, at a convention of the Institute of Pacific Relations. The mimeographed manuscript of his book on the Chinese Army was being studied by another committee of university scholars who recommended that it be published in book form. On his way back to Plymouth he planned to stay over a few days in New York. He telephoned to Plymouth to find out how his mother was. Karen told him she was dying; he'd better come right home.

The house was fixed for Christmas, tree and gifts and wreaths and holly. On the twenty-first Joetta Carlson died, and the moment came when Carlson felt older than his father.

"What does God require of thee?" asked Tom Carlson, her husband, silently to himself, silent in the forest of grief in which he found himself lost. 'Do justly, love kindness and walk humbly with Thy God.'"

He walked in the forest by himself.

Everyone came to the funeral. The neighbors came already in the conspiracy to cook and clean for their pastor and neighbor during the mourning. The selectmen came, the parishioners, the towns-people, the country people from outside the town. They wanted to walk with the great, tall tree of a pastor into his church where he had preached and had often mentioned his wife, and with him up to the cemetery on the hill.

In the White House that day, Franklin Roosevelt pushed aside some papers, very important ones, and wrote a letter of condolence to his friend, Evans Carlson.

After the funeral Thomas Carlson walked back into his house. She whom he had loved so wholly, the hero of his ministry, had left him.

Evans Carlson went to work on a book.[15] In February he had met Raymond Bond of Dodd, Mead and Company, publishers, at a meeting of the Dutch Treat Club in New York. Bond asked him to write a book about his experiences in China. Carlson said he wasn't sure he could or had the time. But Bond pressed him, and sent Carlson a contract and an advance of 500 dollars. The deadline for delivery was June 1, 1940.

He had his diaries and his notes and an extraordinary memory. But there were problems to be faced. He did not want it to be a book with all "I" in it; his shyness, secretiveness and pride rejected that approach. Yet, it would be ridiculous to eliminate the "I," for the worth of the book was derived from his experiences.

In his introduction, he wrote:

> For the use of the first person, I apologize to the reader. It is not pleasant to write of one's personal feelings and experiences, and I have done so only because I believe that I was privileged to witness events which are little known, and which have considerable historical significance. If this book possesses any merit, it lies in the honesty with which I have attempted to portray the people and events I observed.

He read it aloud that night to his father and his sister, Karen. They agreed that it was a good way of putting it.

He typed all morning, read what he had written to his father and Karen at lunch, banged the piano afterwards, worked again until around five, walked along the elm-shaded streets, into the country. After dinner he read aloud again what he had written in the afternoon; then worked on until two or three in the morning. He was in a hurry to finish. The winter and spring of 1940 were the

[15] *Twin Stars of China.*

seasons of disaster. May started with the surrender of Norway and
ended with the Belgian surrender and the despair of Dunkirk. He
had to hurry.

There were other problems in the writing of the book which had
to be faced. The united front of Chiang Kai-shek's Kuomintang
and the Communists was still in effect. And with all its strains and
tensions, Carlson anticipated that it would remain in effect, at least
until the war was won. He knew, too, that the Generalissimo was the
only man in China who could hold the country together. For
these reasons he refrained from offering any direct arguments
which might be used to create further conflict between Chiang Kai-
shek and the Communists. For example, he did not criticize Chiang
Kai-shek's failure to help the guerrillas of the Eighth Route Army,
but rather found excuses for him. He spoke of Chiang's Olympian
self-possession, the inscrutability which gave the "impression to each
political group that he secretly sympathizes with the doctrines of
that group." He said he felt that a mutual confidence obtained between the Generalissimo and the Communists (which he did honestly feel at the time), but to explain the continuing friction he
added: "The minds of bourgeois officials had to be adjusted to this
idea (unity) gradually." He spoke of Chiang Kai-shek's conversion
to Christianity and though he seemed to think it was a genuine
conversion, his own integrity forced him to say more about the
Generalissimo's religious faith.

> I will not attempt to reconcile the Generalissimo's Christian
> faith [Carlson wrote on page two hundred and seventy-seven
> of his book] with his action in causing the execution of thou-
> sands of people of Communist persuasion during the civil war,
> except to point out that down through the ages men have
> placed varying interpretations on Christian doctrine. . . .
> Perhaps Chiang reasoned that Communism was an evil
> which justified the use of un-Christian practices to eliminate it.
> I have known American missionaries who were violent and
> uncompromising in their denunciation of the Chinese Com-
> munist leaders. And yet I found those same leaders unostenta-
> tiously practicing Christian doctrines more punctiliously and

with greater consistency than many professing Christians of my acquaintance. Ideas sometimes do strange things to the human mind . . .

The reasonableness with which Carlson dealt with Chiang Kai-shek came from his recognition that a united China was more important than expressing his own straightforward opinion that Chiang Kai-shek was neither a Christian nor a democrat; that the Kuomintang, at the top, was more a party of corrupt freebooters than the representatives of the people. He was willing to acknowledge the possibility that Chiang Kai-shek might be changed by the conditions of peace, especially if the United States did not throw its weight around in China on his behalf.

During the writing of the book he kept lecturing on China.

In Washington he spoke on a program with Senator (later Secretary of Labor) Schwellenbach. "Embargo war shipments to Japan," he pleaded.

While he was in Washington, he saw the President.

"What are you doing these days, Evans?" F. D. R. asked.

"Trying to get our people to stop helping Japan, Mr. President."

"I'm trying too," the President said, "I think we're going to get something through this Congress."

"And if not, Mr. President?"

Franklin Roosevelt's face became solemn. "It may take an executive order," he said slowly. He looked up at Carlson from his desk. "What are your plans for the future?"

Carlson hesitated even as he answered, "I guess I'll continue working for good causes." He felt that Roosevelt's question indicated that he hoped Carlson would have some definite government job in mind. But he hadn't anything in mind. He'd given up a government job to be free to talk.

The President, seeming a little disappointed, changed the subject.

Carlson spoke to Foreign Policy Association groups in Boston, Philadelphia, New York, Pittsburgh, Springfield, Hartford.

He spoke to the Hudson River Valley Conferences of Methodist

Churches: "These Chinese of the Eighth Route Army," he said, "were not professing Christians but they were practicing Christian doctrine. . . . I have seen the doctrines of brotherly love work. . . . In the words of Christ: 'If you love only those who love you, what credit is that to you? . . . If you help only those who help you, what merit is that to you?' "

To the League of Nations Association in Baltimore, he said that if we stop appeasing Japan now, she will not attack us. If we continue to appease, sooner or later she will turn on us. . . .

On Memorial Day the selectmen of Plymouth asked him to speak at the services. They listened to him on the elm-bordered green which the Plymouth people called "the park."

He talked very briefly. He reminded them of Shiloh and Cold Harbor. "Democracy," he told them, "is a state of mind, a conviction which flows from within, and it can endure only so long as a majority of the people are determined that it shall be kept alive."

They were wading out into the channel from Dunkirk as his words fell on the soft Connecticut day.

"It means the freedom to think, act, write and speak as we feel, as long as we do our neighbor no harm; it means that we claim the right to share equally with all men the rights, privileges and opportunities which our way of life may provide."

They were being strafed on the beaches, on the roads, in the fields. The sun was warm and clear in Plymouth.

"Let us pledge ourselves. . . . Let us prove ourselves the worthy stewards of the golden heritage. . . ."

He wrote the whole one hundred thousand words of the book during April and May. He worked in his father's study, and the floor and tables and desk were cluttered with papers, notes and the photographs which he had taken in China and which would illustrate the volume.

When it came time to end the book, he was uncertain how to do it. He had already vaguely described his resignation from the Marine Corps by indicating nothing of his own feelings, but rather attributing it to the necessity of disembarrassing the Naval Service by his separation from it. This, therefore, would not be a good end. It would be too personal. After searching around for the right note, he finished his book by saying that there was hope for China; that national independence, democracy and an economic sufficiency for all its 450,000,000 people would come.

(In 1927 China to him was a mob that had to be taught respect for foreigners. In 1933 China was not so much a people as a high and esoteric culture. And now, in 1940, China was what she had always been, though he had not always known it, a yearning for freedom from feudalism and intervention.)

On this he had come far.

But he added still one more paragraph:

The key to this pattern (of progress) is the element which alone can be the key to any successful society of human beings: the practice of selflessness by its members and vigilant regard for the rights and feelings of others.

In this thought he had not traveled much. He had learned it from his father.

He might have dedicated his book to his father, but his mother was dead and, in her death, he realized that much of her he had never seen; that she, with his father, was the shadow of his home which followed wherever he went.

And so the dedication was written:

TO THE MEMORY OF MY MOTHER, WHO BEQUEATHED
TO HER CHILDREN A RICH LOVE FOR MANKIND
REGARDLESS OF RACE, CREED OR COLOR.

12

Jen jen wei wo, wo wei jen jen

When Carlson finished *Twin Stars of China* and attended a second Institute of International Relations at Mills College, he was ready for another trip to China unimpeded by officialdom. He wanted to gauge her war potential as our first line of defense. President Roosevelt in July had issued an executive order embargoing the shipment of certain important war materials to Japan, and Carlson felt that part of his job was done. In his heart he felt that Roosevelt had been too late. France had collapsed, England was against the wall of her home islands. Everyone was appeasing Japan. The Burma Road was closed. F. D. R. had waited too long.

En route to China, Carlson stopped off at Manila and met an old acquaintance, a man with an odd name who was to write the next chapter in Carlson's life, Rewi Alley.

Rewi Alley was the son of Irish and English pioneers who had moved into the New Zealand wilderness because they wanted to make a world. Two of his great-uncles fought with General Grant's armies in our own Civil War, and one of them was a founder of a city in Nebraska which he called by the name of his great hero, Lincoln.

The Chinese called Rewi Alley, *Kao Pi-tzu Gung-Ho Jen,* "the big-nosed work-together man." The name fitted. His nose thrust out from his face like an angry hawk's. It was bigger and more powerful even than Carlson's own. And like Carlson's, his eyes were burning blue, transparently mimicking the shifting phases of his temper and most frequently reflecting a wild indignation at poverty. All reports say that Alley's tongue was violent, his strength prodigious and his integrity unscalable.

In 1937 Rewi Alley gave up his job as chief factory inspector with the Shanghai Municipal Council when the government asked him to become chief technical advisor to the Chinese Industrial Co-operatives. The C.I.C. had nothing when he came to it, not a lathe or a single chisel. Alley was its total staff. But a Chinese industry had to be built, for Japan might win through her sale of goods in China what she could not win with her armies. China had to fight back on this front as well.

By 1938, when Carlson first met Rewi Alley in Hankow, the C.I.C. had already organized 1500 small co-operatives all over China. It was a guerrilla industry, portable, to be picked up and moved wherever Japanese armies came close. This vast decentralization saved it from attack by air and the hazards of transportation of raw materials. Wherever the raw material was, and wherever the Jap was not, there was built a co-operative factory. The slogan of the co-ops was Gung Ho. No slogan could better match the spirit of the C.I.C.

Although by August 1940 the C.I.C. had three thousand co-operatives and the sponsorship of such men and women as Mrs. Franklin Roosevelt, Madame Chiang Kai-shek, Madame Sun Yat-sen, Robert and Clark Millikan, Vincent Sheean, Henry Luce, Admiral Yarnell, Episcopal Bishops, Catholic Monsignors, scientists, statesmen and scholars, it required a great deal of monetary help.

Rewi Alley was in Manila for hospital treatment of his old World War wounds, malaria, malnutrition and overwork. When he met Carlson, he saw in him a man who would help. He asked Carlson to make a tour of inspection with him. Carlson promptly agreed.

By October they were in the heart of the Chekiang province, about four hundred miles west of Shanghai. They had already covered four provinces and several dozen co-operatives, but it wasn't until they had come to this place in Chekiang that Carlson saw the full drama of the co-operatives' contribution to China's war.

He and Rewi Alley and about twenty Chinese were sitting in the wing of a sprawling Buddhist temple. Near them was a triangular sign with the Chinese characters of Gung Ho, the slogan of the Chinese Industrial Co-operatives. Below it was another: *Jen jen wei wo, wo wei jen jen.* It meant, "All men help me, and I help all men."

The meeting had been called to discuss the danger of an imminent Japanese advance into their area.

At the opposite side of a huge round table sat the Regional Director of the co-operatives, Meng Tso-shun, his tall slender frame rising above those of the others.[16]

"The enemy is only thirty miles to the east," he was saying. "Our troops are now holding well and I believe the enemy drive has run its course, but it is wise to take precautions. At least those units which are located within the city should be moved to the rural sections to the west, and I have already selected tentative locations. But I want your advice." As he spoke a burr of r's slipped off his tongue at the end of a word now and then, betraying his Peiping origin.

The chairman of a co-operative which made steel helmets and canteens spoke:

"Our co-operative can move in two hours," he said. "I propose that we evacuate to the locations you have selected and wait there for future developments. If the city falls, there will still be time to move farther west into the mountains."

"I second that motion," boomed the chairman of a blanket-making co-operative — a refugee from Shanghai. "But the move will entail additional expense, and we should carry a reserve of food. Our co-operative has just started and we haven't much money."

The Regional Director looked at Rewi Alley. "I have some special funds," he said, "provided for bringing in the families of some of our workers from Shanghai."

"Use them," barked Rewi. "This is an emergency. First things first. Industry must be preserved at all cost. Here, I'll assume responsibility for diverting that money to this evacuation job." He scribbled a short note to the Regional Director, using the back of an envelope.

Towards nightfall Rewi Alley and Carlson went down to the river to see how things were going. A motley column of men, women and children, all bearing on their backs or on shoulder poles part

[16] Carlson reported this scene and his entire experience with the C.I.C. in *Amerasia*, March, 1941.

of the machinery of a weaving co-operative, was crossing a pontoon bridge. Behind them were leather workers carrying their huge hides, and down the river bank streamed the members of an iron works co-operative bent low under loads of metal and lathes. It was a great hegira of working people with their tools of production.

"There's the answer to the future of China," Rewi Alley said. "The working people. If they only had a chance to work out their own destiny."

In Kanchow on the first of November, Carlson received clippings of reviews of his book which had just been published. No one had thought of sending him a copy of the book, and it wasn't until January that he saw one in a bookstore in Hongkong. It was priced at $18 Chinese ($5 American) but his pleasure at seeing it prompted extravagance and he bought it.

His book was well received considering that this was 1940 when few people had any interest in China and fewer sympathized with the Chinese Communists. In a very long review in the *New York Times* R. L. Duffus praised the book's honesty and its lack of affectation. He remarked at Carlson's failure to make his heroic trek sound heroic and, in contrast to other reviews, he described him as anything but "a bright-eyed visionary." Lewis Gannett in the *Herald Tribune* thought he was too uncritical in his estimate of both Chiang Kai-shek and the Reds, and he wished that Carlson told more about himself. "He sounds like a good sort." Freda Utley reviewing the book for the *Saturday Review of Literature* tried to strike a balance between her respect and admiration for Carlson and her passionate and irrational detestation of anything Red. All the critics of his book, however, agreed that Carlson had opened their minds to the advantages to our country in a unified China.

It was this note which made him feel that his book had succeeded.

In Kanchow, too, he was delighted to hear from a Father Maguire of a nearby mission that Franklin Roosevelt had been elected for a third time.

At Christmas he was in Chungking where he met old friends

and talked once more with Chiang Kai-shek who was no more helpful than before. Chou En-lai was in Chungking too, to work out,
if possible, new tensions arisen between Chiang's Kuomintang army
and the New Fourth Army which had some Communists in its
leadership.

Chou En-lai told Carlson that Chiang Kai-shek had made a special
point of inviting Chou to dinner on the anniversary of the Sian
kidnaping. "He took my hand very tenderly in his and said, 'I
have never forgotten what you did for me at Sian.' He thinks I
saved his life there. He is a very grateful man. This is fine, except
that politics are never solved through gratitude."

Before January came around, he had traveled through nine provinces, four thousand miles, and had inspected about six hundred co-
operative shops for the manufacture of textiles, matches, leather
goods, shoes, paper, sugar, soap, alcohol, building materials, muni-
tions, tobacco, candles, umbrellas, flashlights, batteries, spare parts
for trucks, and shops producing machinery for all the other shops.

In this trip he learned the strategies of China's economic guerrilla war against Japan. He realized that without this prop, the political and military war could never be consummated in victory.

There was one thing more he learned: that the Japanese war
against our country would come upon us soon. With information he
gathered from Japanese prisoners, from Chinese military men and
statesmen, he concluded that the war would come sometime in
1941 by a surprise attack on the Philippines, and possibly Guam and
Wake.

He felt the need to return to the States quickly to put his findings
before the President and the State and Navy departments.

13

"This is no drill"

In a letter home from Hong Kong on the sixth of January 1941, he wrote:

> My last week in Chungking was hectic. Talked with officials daily: Chiang Kai-shek, Chen Li-fu, leader of the extreme rightests, Tai Li, chief of the Chinese Gestapo, who rarely sees foreigners, and Chou En-lai. As a result I have as good an understanding of the situation as it is possible for a foreigner to obtain, I believe.
>
> I cut short my trip because of a hunch. I feel that events in the international field are moving rapidly towards a point where it will be necessary for America to participate actively in the war. With such a prospect it behooves me to return before the break comes so that I may place my information before the authorities. I must also be in a position to offer my services for active duty.

He flew to Manila and talked with Francis B. Sayre, Philippine High Commissioner, who listened carefully to Carlson's prediction. General Douglas MacArthur also listened. But the General was not at all sure that the Japs would attack. And if they did, he was certain that they would be thrown out of the Philippines. To Carlson the General's military theories were as orthodox as the High Church. MacArthur did not take kindly to the idea that it might be wise to prepare the Filipinos for guerrilla warfare.

"Put in ammunition and food dumps in the hills north of Manila, General," Carlson suggested. "Train men for jungle war; how to hide, how to infiltrate, how to stop the Japs from infiltrating. Guerrillas will be able to attack Jap bases once they are established, and can cut their lines of communication."

MacArthur replied politely that in his opinion guerrilla warfare was indecisive, and turned the conversation back to the first World War when they had known each other in Germany.

But Carlson, free to speak his mind, spoke it unequivocally to reporters.

On January 30, 1941, ten months *before* the attack on Pearl Harbor, the Los Angeles *Times* ran an interview with Carlson headlined:

AMERICAN-JAPANESE WAR IN 90 DAYS PROPHESIED

United States Will Win, But It Won't Be Easy, Says Author Returning From Orient

On the same day, the Los Angeles *Daily News* headlined its story:

JAP ATTACK ON U. S. ISLANDS PREDICTED

In these interviews Carlson predicted a Japanese attack on the Dutch East Indies, French Indo-China, Singapore, and especially on the Philippine Islands. He figured the attack would be timed with Germany's blitz-invasion of England.

"Our first line of defense at this moment is China," he said.

He miscalculated only in the time of the attack. Instead of coming in three months, it came in ten months.

He went to Washington, saw President Roosevelt and told his story. Roosevelt was hopeful but realistic about the future in the Pacific. Among some of the Far-Eastern specialists of the State Department, Carlson found too great a reliance in the possibility of appeasing Japan into inactivity.

He presented his arguments for a loan to the Chinese Industrial Co-operatives, and was heartsick when he was told that there was no chance for it.

To secret sessions of the Foreign Policy Association and the Institute of Pacific Relations in Washington and New York he presented facts concerning the corruption and semi-Fascist behavior of much of Kuomintang China. He insisted on making these talks secret, for it was his belief that as long as Chiang Kai-shek continued to fight against Japan, open criticism of him would be harmful to our own interests.

In New York he worked with the American Committee for Chinese Industrial Co-operatives, urging it to make certain that its support went not to the Kuomintang-led co-ops which were not truly co-ops, but rather to those with democratic leadership, headed by Rewi Alley and Bishop Hall of Hong Kong.

And all this time he was putting his personal affairs in order so that he would be free to join the armed service again.

The time came, oddly enough, after a speech which he made in April to the Army and Navy Club in Washington. He had spoken for almost an hour on the possible tactics to be used in the eventual Pacific War. After he was finished, a Marine Colonel came up to him.

"Carlson," the Colonel said, "isn't it about time you came back?"

Carlson grinned. "Sure, it's about time."

"But when? The way you talk the Japs are going to attack us any day now."

"Well, I've been thinking of going over to talk to the Army one of these days."

"Why the Army?"

"Frankly, because I know what will happen if I put in my application for the Marines. My paper will come up to the Reserve board and someone will say, 'Carlson wants to come in again. What'll we do with the s.o.b.?'"

The Colonel laughed. "That's exactly what would happen," he admitted. "But we've called you s.o.b. ever since you resigned; it oughtn't to be news to you."

It was Carlson's turn to laugh. "It's hard to get used to, but maybe that's what will make me feel more at home in the Marines."

The next day he went up to see Major General Holcomb, Commandant of the Marines.

"General," Carlson said, "I think it's about time for me to get back in."

The light from the window sparkled in Holcomb's round glasses.

"I was expecting you, Carlson. Colonel Skinner told me he talked to you yesterday."

"Did he tell you what I said, sir?"

Holcomb smiled and nodded.

"Here I am, General."

"It's too bad you had to resign, Carlson," Holcomb said. "We won't be able to give you a commission in the Regulars."

"I know, sir."

Carlson, of course, expected this. It was not important. He knew that even in wartime, when promotions would come quickly to everyone, a Reserve officer rarely reached a grade higher than Colonel, certainly not beyond Brigadier. But he wasn't coming back to get a silver star on his shoulder.

Holcomb told him to report to Colonel Skinner who was the executive officer of the Reserve Division.

"If I have a choice of duty, General," Carlson said, "I'd like either a combat outfit or China."

It was almost as if he were back nineteen years in the Marine Recruiting office in Portland, Oregon. Physically he had not changed to match two decades. He was still erect, supple, youthful in body. His hair was only slightly gray, his cheeks lined only in the deep laugh lines which he had had for all the years.

Colonel Skinner wanted to know whether the General told Carlson what rank he was to have.

"I didn't ask him," Carlson said. "He didn't tell me."

Skinner called Holcomb's office.

"He says," the Colonel said, "that you are to be given the rank of Major, with rank as of today. That's a help, Carlson. The Old Man must like you." Skinner looked up an officer's register. "You've lost about 250 numbers on the Majors' list by your resignation," he said. "Too bad."

Carlson shrugged, signed his papers and left.

It is about this time that Etelle and Evans Carlson made a decision to separate.

They had been married for eighteen years. Etelle Carlson, in talking of her marriage, said, "I had eighteen very happy years. That's more than most women have in their lifetimes. I think I have been very lucky."

Etelle Carlson is a very sure-sighted woman. She had built her life on a fair reality and not on the awkward architecture of discontent or preconception. Her desires were not gigantic, and so perhaps this disappointment did not completely overwhelm her. She had, of course, genuinely enjoyed the life of the wife of a military man. She was with Carlson in Nicaragua, and in China in 1927 and 1933. The protocol and formalized grace of diplomatic and military society she had found particularly attractive.

Yet she knew during the last years that perhaps it would not go on. Carlson went to China in 1937 and in 1940 without her.

These were long periods of being apart.

Carlson's resignation from the Marines she understood only in part. For what she thought were his own best interests, she tried to dissuade him from the step. It seemed to her that he was striking out into an unknown world of "causes," where he stood alone against the tide of the time.

This decision to separate was not hers alone; for she and her husband worked out their states of mind and their proposed separation together. If Carlson wanted it, so then did she; if she wanted it, so then did he. It was the parting of two mature people who saw that it was not evil to part, nor necessarily good to remain together. Each might be happier in his own life. Both knew they might not be as happy together.

Carlson, of course, felt it would be better not to continue. As always, he had an intransigent romanticism which forced itself on him regardless of what he might lose. This romanticism which, in his green youth, took the form of feeling committed to marry a girl because he had kissed her, now in his maturity became an unarguable faith that a man can find absolute and lasting personal happiness.

As in the other parts of his life, his mind and heart could not feel alive with half measures. If he could risk a career because he would not compromise with an intellectual conviction, how could he do less in the profoundest segment of his personal life?

They parted, and in 1943 the divorce became final.

On April 28, 1941 his commission in the Marine Corps Reserve was forwarded to him at Plymouth; on May 2nd he asked for active duty, and by the twenty-fifth he was ordered to Camp Elliot, San Diego, to become Operations and Intelligence officer of the Second Regiment.

He was back in the green uniform of the Marines.

He was with his old friends, and those who were really friends like Major Bill Bales pretended that the resignation hadn't happened at all.

And it was good to be near his son, Evans, Jr., for the first time in years. Evans, Jr. was in the Marine Reserve, too, and would soon be stationed near his father. He had just been married to Jeanne Gaughan of San Francisco whom, in a letter to his father, Carlson described as "an unusually fine girl, tall, slender, attractive and possessed of a quiet, well-balanced judgment. Evans, Jr. is also more quiet and more mature now. He is a fine boy."

Father and son, both reserved, both saying little of their deepest feelings, treated each other as if nothing had intervened, no time, no distance, no age. They met like two good friends after a long separation. ·

At Camp Elliot Carlson began by sending memos to the Commandant volunteering for service if and when commando groups were to be activated. As a result, he was offered a chance to go to England to observe the British Commandoes. His reply was that he had already studied similar tactics in the *Guardia Nacional* in Nicaragua and with the Chinese.

He followed this up, as it has already been related, with a barrage of plans for setting up a special Marine Raider unit similar to the Commandoes.

During the summer and fall of 1941, he suggested several innovations in his own regiment. Noticing, for example, that on one maneuver it required the laying of three hundred miles of wire to maintain communications during an advance of a mile and a half, he argued that radio should be used. "In a war against the Jap," he said, "we won't have time to lay wire."

He also called for the manufacture of a compact ration. Men must be able to carry enough to sustain themselves without being burdened.

Some of his fellow officers, in those pre-Pearl Harbor days, thought he was mildly demented.

As for his Raider idea, it did not seem that he was getting anywhere.

On the morning of December 7, Carlson left his home in La Jolla, having nothing else to do on that Sunday, and drove over to Camp Elliot to see if there was any news. The Staff Duty officer said that nothing had come in. They talked a few minutes and Carlson got into his car and drove to the camp gates. The sentry stopped him.

"All leaves canceled, sir," he said, and his voice trembled. "The Japs attacked Pearl Harbor. This is no drill."

Carlson returned immediately to the Staff Duty officer, who showed him the dispatch which had come in a minute or two after Carlson had left.

Within a half-hour the camp buzzed with excited staff officers. The war plan which would tell them what to do was in a safe at the Marine Corps Base about fifteen miles away, and the safe was on a time lock and couldn't be opened until eight o'clock the next morning.

Confusion was augmented by the lack of knowledge as to who had the responsibility for defending Southern California. Local Army and Navy headquarters didn't know, and apparently weren't doing anything. By nightfall, Major General Clayton B. Vogel, Marine Area Commander, decided to act. He called in Army and Navy consultants, and within a few hours troops were on guard at the Consolidated Aircraft Plant in San Diego, in Coronado, along the Strand, and on the beaches as far north as Oceanside, fifty miles up the coast.

Later Major General Joe Stilwell took over the job. Carlson saw him for the first time since China when the General walked into Vogel's office. The two men, both old campaigners for a unified China and both early warriors against the Japanese, shook hands, said hello, and then, in a very human and bitter humor, laughed out loud.

Two months later, on February 5, 1942, word came that the First Separate Battalion, Second Marine Division, was to be organized immediately. That was what the Raiders were called at first.

In April the battalion under its right name, Second Raider Battalion, sailed for Hawaii. Four months later came Makin.

But Carlson's Raiders and Gung Ho were not yet fully tested at Makin. Not until November 1942 would Carlson himself be satisfied. Not until Guadalcanal.

Part Five

1

The Raiders tell their story

On November 4, 1942 a task force lay off the Solomon Island, Guadalcanal, in a heavy rain. In the officers' wardroom of a transport, Carlson, pipe in mouth, steaming up smoke like wet leaves burning, was writing a letter to his father and sister:

> Another one of these zero hours. First Makin. Now somewhere else. Always there is the same suspense — the wondering about the shape events will take when the landing occurs. From the standpoint of pure adventure there is nothing to equal it. But the issues at stake place this above sensational adventure.
>
> Well, the morrow will tell the tale. I never cross bridges till I come to them — and I try never to avoid a crossing when it faces me.
>
> I am really more at peace with myself now than I have ever been. Not that I am satisfied with my work — or that I feel that my work is done. Far from it. But — my conscience is clear. I have been honest in my effort. And I have tried to follow the inner light. My faith in Divine guidance is supreme. And so I await the outcome of each dangerous episode with a certain serenity. Planning and organizing are as thorough as I can make them. The men have been indoctrinated and trained. Thenceforth we are in God's hands. I must exercise patience and act according to His directions. You know I love and adore you both. God bless and keep

you. Sometime ago I sent you a letter marked to be opened
only in the event of my death. Please place it in a good hot
fire without opening it. I'm sending you another to replace it.

But before he had a chance to write it, word came from the Task
Force Commander to start loading the boats for the landing.

Raiders, talking of Guadalcanal, tell the story like this:

On August 7th, a few days before we left Pearl Harbor for the
Makin Raid, the Marine First Division under Major General
Vandegrift landed on Guadalcanal and quickly captured an air
strip which was soon re-named Henderson Field. For the next three
months the battle for Guadalcanal was like trying to plug eleven
holes in a dike with ten fingers. The First Division had to defend
Henderson Field against frontal assault, and at the same time keep
Jap artillery out of range of our transport, bombing, and fighter
planes that had no other place to land. In addition, they had to
destroy the enemy elsewhere on the island before his reinforcements
overwhelmed us. When our boys pushed out in one direction, the
Japanese moved in from another. If Vandegrift threw troops against
Jap landing parties at one end of the Island, he weakened his defense
of Henderson Field in the middle of the Island. If he tried to destroy
a strong enemy gun position one place, the Jap could land un-
opposed elsewhere.

August and September and October were rugged months. November looked brighter. Our fleet had somewhat cleared the seas
near by. The perimeter of Henderson Field had been enlarged.
Jap attacks, still furious, did not come with the old regularity. Yet
our command did not yet know what was going on in the interior
of the island, behind the Jap lines where as yet few or none of our
forces had penetrated. Our command did not know, for example,
how many Japs lay in wait behind the mountain ranges and in the
jungles; where the trails were which led east and west through the
backbone of the island and across which Jap reserves were moved;
nor just where were certain artillery positions called "Pistol Pete"
from which Henderson Field was still being shelled.

The dike was slowly being plugged, but no one knew where new holes might come, and how much of the flood might pour through.

During the months up to November we (the Raiders say) were biting our nails doing nothing at Espiritu Santo, about six hundred miles to the east. After Makin we had had a week of luxury at the Royal Hawaiian Hotel with the crews of the *Nautilus* and *Argonaut,* and then were sent to Espiritu Santo for more training as part of the floating reserve of Admiral Richmond Kelly Turner's Amphibious Task Force.

We thought we'd never see action again. Even the Old Man despaired. He'd come to the Friday night Gung Ho meetings and tell us he had seen Nimitz or Turner, and that things might cook up for us soon. But he'd say it week after week, and still we were doing nothing but train.

But one night, his lean face looking like a farmer's who had just won a prize at the State Fair, he told us that orders had come. It wouldn't be much doing. We were to land on Guadalcanal near the little town of Aola where Army engineers and Navy construction workers were to start building another air strip. We would secure the beach head for them — and then leave. It wasn't a big operation; we'd probably not meet any enemy and be back on the transports in twenty-four hours, and for that reason he would only take two companies with him.

His other four companies who did not go swore privately at the Old Man.

It was just as he said it would be — for a while. On November 4 we landed, carved out the beach head without opposition, and waited in an angry rain for Higgins boats to take us back to the transports the same evening.

But out of the rain hummed a scout plane, one of our own. It passed the beach several times, signaled with a beacon that it was going to drop a message; dropped it.

It was from Vandegrift. Jap reinforcements had just landed near the Metapona River, about fifteen miles to the west, and between us and Henderson Field. Other Marine forces were trying to destroy them; Vandegrift's orders to the Raiders were to push through the jungle and help. The other four companies of the Raiders at Espiritu Santo had been ordered to come to Guadalcanal to fill out the Battalion.

Now everybody was happy.

Lieutenant Jack Miller was happy. He had begged to go to Makin but an arm broken in training had prevented him. Now he was in it. "Transport" Maghakian was happy. The bullet hole in his right wrist punctured at Makin was almost healed, though he still wore it in a light sling. But he could do with his left hand whatever was needed to be done. Captain Bill Schwerin was happy, too. It was his father who in 1922 had sworn the Old Man in, and it was the workings of plain ordinary justice to be having duty with Carlson. But perhaps the happiest was Carlson's son, Lieutenant Evans C. Carlson, who had joined us a couple of months before. Now he could show what he was good for; now came the turn of the war when he could teach the Old Man that he was a soldier in his own right, to take, to give, to obey orders, and most of all, to win his father's approval. He would rather die, let the Japs get him, than not have the Old Man's okay on him (the Raiders say).[1]

Happy we were; yet "happy" is not quite the word. No one is happy going into a fire-fight with the enemy; nor glimpsing the strange green jungle, the thick hills behind them, the Solomon Island terrain, out of the mind, a faraway crazy spot on the map, the last place in the world to live and the last place in the world to die. But we were trained to the hair, volunteers for a suicide battalion; we felt we'd damned better get our action in quick and get it over. Espiritu Santo was worse, in the imagination, than any jungle or Jap ambush. It was the contrast that made the prospective operations a "happy" thought.

We who lived through Guadalcanal (the Raiders say) remember it as a kind of wild fantasy which lasted thirty-one days.

First, there was the jungle, the Siamese-joined trees, the thickness, the damp, rotting smell, skeins of rootless branches, spider

[1] Carlson's son won the Silver Star for bravery.

webs of brush tying us up like flies as we passed, the grasping vines running after us like beggars who won't be turned away. And the jungle noise; the crazy, nameless birds, the cracked grunts of rotting wood breaking and falling, the sharp senseless break of a branch in the night when the same sound meant an enemy sniper. And the jungle crawlers — the six-inch land crabs, the foot-long lizards.

Day after day we marched warily along the broken trails, walking as if every piece of earth beneath us had been mined. Five paces ahead was a Raider, five paces behind was another Raider — and all else, everywhere, on the top of your head in the trees, underfoot, down at the sides in the screen of brush, in your thighs and back and on your neck that suddenly grew as large as a horse — was the enemy. You held your breath until your chest ached. And then suddenly on some days you smelled something wonderfully familiar — the thin smoke of a pipe still drifting in the humid air. The Old Man's pipe; the wonderful, stinking, large-bowl pipe. We could imagine him way up front — he was always up with the point — stalking ahead like an Indian scout, taking a single puff every couple of paces, the smoke dribbling slowly out his pressed-together lips, curling up over his head, down the line to us. The god-damned smoke made us feel good. The Old Man was out of sight but not out of mind.

He never rested. That's what made us wonder. He marched with a full pack like the rest of us, but when we rested he stood up studying a map or talking with the company commanders or he walked off to do a little scouting of his own.

We never heard him say he was tired, so how could we complain?

Private Al Flores told us a story.

Flores was carrying a bag of grenades when the word came through to withdraw. Flores left the bag against a tree and joined his platoon. The next day they moved ahead again, and Flores saw the bag where he had left it. He wasn't sure he ought to pick it up. It might have been booby-trapped. He asked the Old Man's permission. Carlson looked at Flores as if he were trying to read something on his face. Then he said never mind. And while Flores watched, feeling ashamed of hesitating, the Old Man went over to the bag and looked at it closely, then picked it up and gave it back to Flores.

"If you want to know how we did Guadalcanal," Al Flores said, "it's because of the Old Man's absolute fearlessness."

He was always cool as lettuce (the Raiders say). When the man who leads you has no fear, you feel safe. We loved him because so few of us were killed.

The awful hunger was a bad dream of its own.

We had started out from Aola with four days' rations, rice, bacon, tea, salt, sugar, raisins. New rations were brought up to us or dropped by plane — but the variety of food was not changed, except that from the tenth day on, each man received a daily bar of vitaminized chocolate. Twice a wild steer was found and butchered for the whole Battalion, but most of us vomited out the meat. For a month, it was raisins, tea, bacon, salt, sugar, rice. Ah, rice! That was a worse dream than the running pain in the empty belly. Polished rice, unpolished, coarse Jap rice, rice boiled, rice fried, rice raw, rice mixed with salt, rice with sugar, rice with bacon, rice with chocolate, rice with tea, rice with rice!

"God damn rice, Colonel!" we said to him when he came by. "We're hungry!"

He would talk to us for a while, telling us the old things we had heard before. Gung Ho; the reason for being here; that he had promised nothing but privation. "I told you the day would come when our only food would be the rice we took from the bodies of dead Japs." Then he informed us that Vandegrift had sent word that we were to clean up the Japs who had succeeded in filtering through our lines at the Metapona River. "And we've got to find the trail that runs from east to west on which the Japs shuttle their reserves; and maybe, if we're lucky, we'll find and knock out 'Pistol Pete.'" He told us of the importance of winning Guadalcanal; where it fitted into the strategy of the Pacific offensive, with our campaign in North Africa, with the Russian defense of Stalingrad.

When he left us one of the men said, "Goddam! Here we are hungry as hell, and the Old Man gives us speeches."

"Second only to a good square meal," another man said, "I'd just as soon hear him speak."

A few laughed at that but many of us were thinking back.

"Ethical indoctrination . . ." one of us said slowly, playing with the words and their meanings. And as if finding a new truth, he added, "We damn well have to be indoctrinated to like *this* business."

A heavy rain started and the men grunted and shivered and tried to find dry places under the trees.

Some of us huddled over a small smoking fire to keep it going. We wanted some hot water for tea and coffee. The rain beat on the roof of our backs.

When Armistice Day came along, it went by pretty much like all the other days. Some of Captain Dick Washburn's company ambushed Japs swimming in the Lunga and killed about thirty. The rest of us killed about a hundred and thirty elsewhere.

But we didn't know until much later that on that day across the world a man named Raymond Swing was talking about us through a microphone in a Washington, D. C. radio station. The whole country heard him.

Mr. Swing told about the Old Man's life, how he talked around the country before the war asking for understanding of China. He had a personality so sincere, Mr. Swing said, that it filled a room, so that he awoke confidence and made friends, not by his gifts but with his character.

And he told about the Raiders, and how there was no other group of fighting men more inspiring because we knew why we were fighting. He said that we could have a genuine Armistice Day if all the civilians back home had some of our Gung Ho.

About six weeks after the broadcast hundreds of the boys got letters from their folks telling how proud they were to hear Mr. Swing talk about us that way. It made us feel good because we were not being forgotten.

Once there was something mighty precious stolen. A tin can. That's all. But that's everything. For with a tin can a man could make coffee at the same time he was warming his rice and bacon in his helmet. A tin can was a million dollars in the jungle.

"A tin can has been stolen," the Old Man said.

We were silent. One terrible son-of-a-bitch wasn't Gung Ho. Only one stinking, bad apple!

"Here's what I am going to do," the Old Man said slowly. "The next man accused of stealing a tin can I'm going to bring up before the men in his company. I'm not going to court-martial him. You are. We'll get the facts and the evidence. If you tell me to shoot him, I'll shoot him."

The Old Man stopped there and looked at us. We were still feeling angry. It was our war, our battalion, our Gung Ho. He'd put the responsibility on us.

The Old Man went his way, and we were alone. The rain beat down like a rat race.

There was no more of anything ever stolen again.

With the hunger and the Jap ambushes and the jungle and the rain and the festering sores and the nerves on edge, went diseases. Malaria moved in on us (the Raiders say) like flies on a dead horse. Two hundred and twenty-five men got dengue fever, dysentery, malaria, ringworm and other illnesses which the docs and corpsmen call jungle rot. We got most of that kind sleeping in soggy mud or crawling through a half-dozen rivers every day. When we were sick, so sick we couldn't stand, we reported it — and were sent back to Aola. The Old Man kept telling us: "If you can't make it, don't go on. We'll send you back. There's no disgrace."

We crossed behind the Japs from Aola to Mombula, into and through places with Solomon Island names that sounded like jungle noises: Binu, Reko, Asamana, Gegenda, Kema, Tasimboko, Malimbu, Tenaru, Lunga, Mombula. We met the enemy at least once a day. Sometimes twice; fought in rivers and on riverbanks, grassy knolls, behind trees, in the mud, ambushed, were ambushed, enveloped the enemy, were enveloped by him, and enveloped the envelopers. We fought in the dark and in the rutted jungle, and we might have killed our own men if we did not keep yelling, Hi, Raider! Hi, Raider! to say who we were.

Day after day we followed the Old Man's jungle-guerrilla tactics, putting into practice his theory of the mobile fire team. The team worked wonders. Toward evening we'd make a base; then next morning fan out patrols to find the enemy as well as the site of a forward base. The Old Man would okay it, and we'd all move up to it. The next day would be the same.

On the night of the twenty-eighth a runner from Captain Schwerin's company told the Colonel that they thought they had found traces of "Pistol Pete" on a sharp ridge between the Tenaru and Lunga Rivers. This was the artillery which kept shelling Henderson Field and which Naval guns and dive bombers had failed to find and destroy. The next day the Old Man led the whole battalion over the ridge. We needed ropes to pull each other up over the slippery muddy sides of the ridge. When we got to the top some of us followed a Jap telephone wire down a narrow ravine which came out into a large enemy bivouac on the bank of the Lunga. It was deserted. But we found what we had been looking for — "Pistol Pete." There were two .75's, plus an anti-tank .37 mm., with about sixty-five rounds for both. We destroyed everything. It was worth the jungle and the rain and the damned rations and the fellows we left buried on the trails.

On December 2 we were at the foot of Mombula, or as it was called by us, Mount Austen. It wasn't really a mountain, perhaps no more than fifteen hundred feet, but with sides like cliffs. It overlooked Henderson Field and it was in enemy hands and a constant threat.

The Old Man called all of us together, the remnants of our battalion, about six hundred half-starved, sick men with layers of mud on their combat dungarees from the swamps they had crossed or slept in. We were tired; we wanted to get the hell out of the jungle; we thought he was going to tell us that the time had come for us to return to our base; that it was all over.

He looked like a scarecrow when he stood up to talk. He looked like we looked. We suddenly remembered that pipe smoke we had caught on the trail. He was smoking it again.

We waited for the Old Man to say, "Now we go home."

"I've just received an order from General Vandegrift to return our battalion to Henderson Field," he said.

We cheered a little bit. The jungle deadened the sound.

"There are two ways of getting to Henderson Field from here. We can go back the way we came, across the Tenaru River. Or we can climb over Mount Austen, and then climb down again right onto Henderson."

We wondered what way he was going to take. The mountain was the tougher route; we would've wanted the Tenaru.

"A patrol has just reported to me that on the top of Mount Austen, in a spider web of ridges, is a very strong Jap position."

Somewhere near by a tree limb cracked sharply. We grabbed our weapons like a drowning man grabs for a raft. Someone called out softly that it was a tree.

The Old Man waited until we relaxed again.

"The Jap position is *unoccupied!*"

The way he underlined the words tipped us off.

"If we get up there in a hurry, we can take those positions; we can relieve the pressure on Henderson Field. We can find out how strong the enemy is there. This will help our command to make a more accurate estimate of the situation. It may mean cutting down the time it will take to finish up Guadalcanal. It would be a good thing, wouldn't it?"

We were tired. Sure, it would be a good thing, but why us? Why not some of the dogfaces from the 164th Army? Why not Edson's Raiders, the so-called First Raider Battalion? (We never forgave them for being called the "First," when we were the First. But Headquarters gives even numbers to all West Coast units, and odd numbers to the East Coast. Edson formed his battalion after us but in the East; so we were the Second and they were the First.)

"It is a good thing," the Old Man went on quietly. "We're going to do it because it's important, because we're fitted to do it and in a position to do it. C, D and E Companies, under the command of Captain Washburn, will return the Tenaru way. They've been out the longest. The other Companies, A, B and F are still pretty fresh."

He smiled when he said that. We all looked beaten down, no matter what company we were in. But it was true that A, B and F had had the fewest casualties and sick men. We knew that it didn't make any difference what companies he picked. We'd all have gone if it had been a volunteer job. Some of us had heard the Old Man tell Washburn that he'd go over Mount Austen alone if he had to.

The Old Man talked a few minutes more, thanking us for doing a fine job. It seemed a little funny. It was almost a Friday night Gung Ho meeting right in the middle of a Solomon Island jungle. The Old Man must have felt that way, too, because as the three companies that were to go the Tenaru way formed ranks, Carlson called out, "Let's sing 'Onward, Christian Soldiers.'"

It was right. That's what we wanted.

"Onward, Christian soldiers," we sang, "marching as to war . . ." We didn't care whether or not the Japs heard us. We felt good singing.

The columns separated, and in the thick brush were soon lost to sight. But we could hear each other sing for quite a while to come.

There wasn't anything harder than the climb up Mount Austen, for we were climbing up almost at ninety degrees into enemy country into certain enemy terrain. The rain made the earth slippery and the brush hard to hold; but on top was the Jap position we hoped was still unoccupied. We had to get there in a hurry to win surprise.

Near the top the Old Man saw some footprints. He whispered to the rest of his patrol led by Lieutenant Jack Miller to take a look. They were Jap footprints.

"We've got to hurry," the Old Man told Miller.

A few minutes later Jack Miller's patrol found the Jap positions at the top, a series of emplacements running out along the ridges like spokes from a hub.

We moved in and took the positions. Then up from the other side we saw Japs. They didn't know we were waiting for them. Suddenly their leading men stopped, and started to deploy. One of our men opened fire and killed three in the first burst. After a while they set their mortars on us, plus machine guns and automatic rifles. The Old Man ordered a double envelopment with a squad on each flank of the enemy. But the Jap infiltrated and soon our flankers were outflanked. The Old Man ordered a platoon to flank the enemy flankers, but not being satisfied with that, he told them to move to the rear of the enemy and surround them. As the battle report put it: "This was accomplished in due course."

But the battle reports say nothing about the darkness of the brush when you don't know who is behind the next tree and if there is a suspicious shadow or noise, you try to cut the tree down and the man behind it with a saw of bullets.

There were some casualties.

"Transport" Maghakian came bouncing down to the side of the ridge during the early part of the fire fight.

"I got hit in my —— arm!" he yelled disgustedly.

"In the same arm again?" the Old Man asked.

"No. The other one! Why don't I learn not to point!"

It wasn't funny, but those who heard him laughed.

Jack Miller was badly hurt. The Old Man was worried about him, but the docs thought he'd live.

We made a dry camp that night, meaning that we had no water. But we had the enemy position.

The Old Man spoke to Miller a little, encouraging him.

Early the next morning, Company B took the point, and only five hundred yards down the mountain were ambushed. Three men killed, and one mortally wounded. The wounded boy was Steve Van Buren from Chicago, a nice lad, skinny and blonde and too young.

On the way down, after the ambushers were flanked and beaten back, Jack Miller died. We buried him off the trail with the smell of Japs all around us. The Old Man took out the small American flag he carried in his pack and put it on Miller's body and said the prayer:

"Father, accept this body of Jack Miller to Thine own . . . Thou knowest he knew the reasons for which he fought. Give him peace. Amen."

There wasn't much time for a long prayer.

We finished the descent without further contact, though there were signs of the enemy all the way down.

When we marched into the Division Area at Henderson Field, some of the security guard saw us first and yelled, "My God, walking skeletons!" We marched right by them and through the Area, and five miles beyond to our base. They could've given us trucks, but they didn't — and we marched. Everyone who saw us said, "There goes Carlson's Raiders." We felt very tired — but also very good.

This is what we had done. We had spent a month in the jungle, had marched one hundred and fifty miles, met the enemy daily, captured and destroyed his guns and ammunition and food and medical supplies; we reassured the command that nothing important was going on in the Jap interior; we mapped out his east-west route; we destroyed "Pistol Pete," and finally we killed officially 488 Japs, but the Seabees who went in later to bury them said we killed 700. For all this, we lost 17 men, and 17 wounded.

And that's why we loved Carlson — because we could kill the enemy 40 to 1.

But we did more. We proved that we could live on the land, independent of the usual supply lines. We proved that we could get along with each other and with our officers. We proved that it was right for the Old Man to warn us it would be hard, for then we expected nothing but the worst. We proved that we would get along with the natives. At times we had as many as fifty to a hundred of them working as guides and scouts. We went Gung Ho together even though they were black-skinned and strange to us. We shared our food and sleeping places. We were men and they were men. And this Gung Ho between us saved our lives, for during the month when we marched along trails that were too complicated for our own scouts and primitive maps, these Melanesians took our hands and led us. Only twice were we surprised and ambushed. On Guadalcanal that was extraordinary. And perhaps the test of it all was that out of a thousand men only one — only *one* — got combat fatigue, was a psychiatric case. And on Guadalcanal that too was extraordinary.

And we learned the enemy. His tricks, his faults, his strength. And we proved that the Raiders — Gung Ho Raiders — could do any job that had to be done in the Pacific.

So the Raiders tell their story.

There is more that the Raiders say.

As we did after Makin, the Old Man went over our operations with us and we told him what we thought about improving the battalion, and he told us what he thought about improving ourselves.

And as before, we held a memorial for the seventeen comrades we buried along the back-country Solomon Island trails.

It was held at our base in Espiritu Santo. The Old Man looked thinner than ever. He read us his speech, his voice coming out slow and deep. It made us feel like hell.

"It is not given to us," he said, "to know the process by which certain of us are chosen for sacrifice while others remain. We can only rest our faith in the infinite wisdom of the Supreme Being who guides our destinies. As I ponder the names of those we honor it seems to me as if the most worthy among us are selected for separation in this way. These comrades of ours also loved life. Only yesterday their voices were heard among us as they joined in our songs, rejoiced over letters from home. . . . They knew the nature of the risk they took. But they knew also that human progress inevitably entails human sacrifice."

God, we thought, can nothing ever come easy? Do we have to go on making human sacrifices, being killed, being taken away from our people?

"What of the future for those of us who remain?" the Old Man asked for us. "The war is not yet won; the enemy is still strong; there are incontrovertible signs that he realizes he has met his match, but his power has still to be utterly crushed before we can count our job done and our institutions secure. Our course is clear. It is for us at this moment with the memory of the sacrifices of our brothers still fresh, to dedicate again our hearts, our minds and our bodies to the great task that lies ahead. The future of America — yes, the future condition of all peoples, rests in our hands.

"We must go further and dedicate ourselves also to the monumental task of assuring that the peace which follows this holocaust will be a just and equitable and conclusive peace. And beyond lies the mission of making certain that the social order which we bequeath to our sons and daughters is truly based on the four freedoms for which these men died. Any resolution less than this will spell betrayal of the faith which these staunch comrades reposed in us."

The Old Man turned to the Generals and Admirals who were his guests and then back to us.

"As a token of our affection and admiration," he said, "and as an earnest of our intention to so dedicate ourselves, let us rise and repeat in unison the final Raider benediction:

"We salute you, comrades . . ."

"We salute you, comrades," we said softly. Across the field a bulldozer man started its motors; raced them for a moment; then cut them off.

"As Raiders, as Marines . . ."

"As Raiders, as Marines . . ."

"As Americans, as men . . ."

"As Americans, as men . . ."

The Old Man seemed to be looking into all our faces. "God bless you."

"God bless you."

And some of us underlined the word *you,* for we felt that way then about the Old Man.

Later we were proud to hear that the Old Man was given his third Navy Cross by Admiral Halsey. We felt he ought to have received the Congressional Medal of Honor but three Navy Crosses are all right too. We were proud, too, when so many others of us received Navy Crosses, Silver Stars, Bronze Stars and so on. We were a much decorated outfit. Perhaps we were proudest of the citation which the whole battalion received from General Vandegrift, Commander of the First Division. The Old Man read it aloud to us and said that the only kind of reward which meant anything was when everybody got it.

A few weeks after that word came to us that the Old Man's eulogy had made quite a stir. Newspaper correspondents told us that Admiral Nimitz said it was the best sermon he had ever heard. The *New York Times* wrote an editorial, quoting it at great length. And the Office of War Information broadcast it to the troops overseas in a recording done by Frederic March, the actor. This broadcast was then translated into German, Italian, Spanish, French, Portuguese, Afrikaans, Arabic, Greek and Jugoslavic, and beamed to all the world to show them that we knew what we were fighting the war for. At least some of us knew.

But things were much too good for us after Guadalcanal. Everybody made a fuss over us and we were crossing our fingers. Sooner or later, the payoff must come. We had crowded our luck too far.

It did happen to us; we got a bad deal, a really bad deal. We and the Old Man. And some of us who didn't understand the whys and wherefores blamed the Old Man for it.

2

"Throw away your boots and knives . . ."

With thirty-one days of combat behind them, and with malaria, jaundice and dengue fever having cut down many of his men, Carlson requested from the High Command a long period of rest for his battalion. And so they were sent to New Zealand with the understanding they would be there for at least a month. And with that understanding, went another: that the Battalion *might* be sent back to the States for further training and replacements.

No one could stop the men and officers from making the understanding seem like a promise.

They all believed that they were going home soon.

When Secretary of the Navy Knox addressed them before they left for New Zealand, and began his speech with: "Now I must take you back —" they cheered. The Secretary, a little puzzled, continued: "I must take you back with me to the days of Teddy Roosevelt." There were few cheers after that.

Down in Wellington the boys made up for lost time. But Carlson didn't like the idea of being a Commanding Officer when he was on vacation.

> I can't have any fun [he wrote to Karen in the early part of 1943]. Everyone stands off as though I were untouchable. Gosh, my officers and men are having a swell time while I sit around the lobby or my room talking to old ladies and chambermaids. Oh yes, I ate with the General, and everyone was terribly nice and congratulatory, and said how proud they were of us. My thought was, "Nuts." Up in Guadalcanal the Marines talk of what they call the "George" medal. To be awarded to those who fall in the category of "George." You know, "Let George do it." A highly exclusive club.

They had counted on a rest in New Zealand for thirty days. And then someone in the rearmost echelon of the First Marine Amphibious Corps, headquarters of all the Marines in the Pacific at that time, forgetful of the Raiders' depletion, thought they could be used for a spearhead attack on New Georgia.

At the end of seven days the Battalion was ordered back to Espiritu Santo.

There was hell in the ranks. The one thing which shattered the men most was that it seemed to them that other outfits who had done less than they were getting *their* periods of rest. They felt the normal grievances of combat soldiers against their officers, the high command, and the highest command. They were convinced that their right to rest was being taken from them for discriminatory reasons. No one liked the Raiders, they concluded, because the Raiders had done so well and therefore had received more publicity than other units. Their record, their fame, their spirit, their morale, their Gung Ho was being held against them.

That was their complaint, and most of it was justified.

They didn't really know how justified.

Already word had gone back and forth from Washington to the Pacific that something had to be done with Carlson's Raiders. They were being made too much of; it was getting so that people in the States thought of Carlson's Raiders instead of the Marine Corps. Too much publicity; too many editorials; too many radio speeches like Raymond Swing's in which it seemed that without Gung Ho no Marine outfit could be any good.

None of this was official. No one sat down in Headquarters and wrote a report to the effect that Carlson's Raiders had better be "handled." But the word got around nonetheless. Carlson and his men knew that word was getting around. They had heard officers say that the goddam Raiders were getting too goddam arrogant; that they thought they owned the Corps; that they were all a bunch of publicity hounds, and sooner or later they would have something done to them.

On a higher level the complaint went: All Marines should be as good as Raiders. It was not conducive to the efficiency of the Corps to have specialized outfits. If Headquarters doesn't watch out, the whole Marine Corps will be a confused collection of prima donna battalions.

Carlson saw it coming. He was certain that soon he might be deprived of his battalion, and his battalion of Gung Ho.

First, there was the matter of new Raider battalions. Roosevelt was sent back to the States to organize one; this would make the fourth . . . Colonel Merrit Edson and Colonel Harry Liversedge had their own. There was nothing, of course, that could be said against forming new Raider outfits. But why were they being activated at the same time that ranking officers were outspoken in their demands that all special units be dissolved?

Second, there was the question of the A and B motors. After

Makin Carlson recommended again that the B be substituted for the A. Nothing had been done except that a new series of tests of both motors was ordered, as if they had not already been tested countless times. This seemed to Carlson to be a tragic ignoring of the experiences of field commanders, and he protested strongly in a letter to Major General C. B. Vogel, Commander of the First Marine Amphibious Corps and the Senior Marine General in the Pacific. Carlson stated that he was deeply disturbed by the way Headquarters, Marine Corps, was continuing to resist change in matters which affected the battle efficiency of Marine units and jeopardized the lives of men. He mentioned specifically the question of the motors, naming names and giving dates as to their trials and failures. He reminded General Vogel that he himself had recommended to Headquarters that one motor be given precedence over the other. General Vandegrift of the First Marine Division had also made a similar recommendation. Yet, despite these, Headquarters continued to delay the delivery to the field of reliable motors and asked for further tests.

Carlson went on to criticize the delay in getting a satisfactory portable radio for combat units which would increase their mobility and coördination.

Other examples of Headquarters' proscrastination, he pointed out to the General, were its reluctance to increase the fire power of infantry units and to work out a satisfactory ration for mobile combat groups.

"It is my belief," Carlson wrote Vogel, "that any officer, having knowledge of obstacles or conditions which militate against the vigorous and intelligent prosecution of the war, is remiss in his obligations as an officer and as a loyal citizen if he does not do all within his power to remove such obstacles and correct such conditions. It is in this spirit that I write. Pride, prejudice, sentiment and even considerations of personal security cannot be permitted to stand in the way of an efficient and economic war effort."

He said that he was prepared to make any sacrifice, even to accepting a court-martial, if by so doing the necessary results could be obtained.

No one took him up on his offer.

He knew that such protests and such offers were not looked upon with favor.

Third, there was the question of supplies essential to the health of his men. For almost a year they had been fighting or living under field conditions. No one minded. But now in Espiritu where they were to live indefinitely, the New Georgia campaign having been postponed, Carlson requested certain "comforts" for his men. He wanted lumber to make a semipermanent mess hall, and floors for tents, screening for openings, modest plumbing for "heads," pipe for water, showers and so on. He requisitioned these items only after he noticed that other units, recently arrived from the States, were being issued them. In addition, he had put in for Post Exchange supplies and a moving picture machine. None was forthcoming. Finally, it was always necessary to find and persuade a paymaster to pay the men. No other outfit seemed to have the same trouble.

Requisition after requisition was sent to Headquarters, but nothing resulted. Carlson was forced to conclude — and he said so in writing — that his battalion was being discriminated against for undetermined causes. He admitted that he had been unable, for reasons outside his control, to get for his Raiders what other outfits received as their due.

During February and March Carlson felt that he was fighting for the life of his battalion against enormous and ever-increasing odds.

It was during February that Carlson addressed his men on the first anniversary of the organization of the battalion. In this speech he referred obliquely to the problems which confronted them:

> We humans are weak in faith, [he said]. Lack of adequate faith is the real cause of our failure to bring the Gung Ho spirit to its highest perfection. We lack faith in each other; we lack faith in the ability of the human being to discipline ourselves. Believe me, boys, faith can move mountains. Do you suppose these past months since we first came together have been without discouragement for me? I hesitate to tell you how low my spirits have been at times, or how thin my faith has worn. But never has it been completely extinguished.

Many of you have been a great trial to me, both officers and men. But always, even in the darkest moments, my faith in your ultimate ability to master yourselves, my faith in your desire to do the right thing, has remained with me. My faith in the rightness of the patterns for life and conduct which I have emphasized for you so frequently has kept me on the course. And time after time you have confirmed that faith.[2]

The men, beset by frustration and justifiable grievance, did not hide their feelings. Some of them began to use Gung Ho as a term of derision, and some began to accuse Carlson of being no different from other brass hats.

There were words about Carlson spoken in the tents during this period which had never been spoken by his men before. Many of the men were convinced that all his talk had been a trick to get them to give more, work harder, sacrifice more. They held him responsible for their disappointments.

In one sense Carlson deserved their bitterness. Because of a tough, almost irrational, loyalty to the Marine Corps he did not admit to his men that his requisitions and protests had gone unheeded. He resisted washing the dirty linen of the higher command in public. He should have told his men at the Gung Ho meetings what they were up against. And yet so strange and perverted is the indoctrination of officers that even Carlson, at this time, felt that he would be reducing the general morale and dignity of the Corps by criticizing the higher echelons of command to his men. This was a mistake. He realized it too late.

The Gung Ho meetings were bitter.

"Why isn't something being done?" the men demanded.

Carlson, who might have given them the detail of what he had tried to do, answered only in generalizations which seemed like evasions.

"Some s.o.b. or a collection of s.o.b.'s," shouted a man, "are tryin' to ruin all our work. They talk big but they don't do anything. They make promises but they don't keep 'em."

[2] *See* Appendix 1.

"Corporal," Carlson replied, "you express my sentiments exactly."

But his reply was not enough. The men wanted facts and relief. Carlson, depressed because he could not help them, protected the reputations of those who could.

And now the open moves were being made. Carlson was called to Corps Headquarters and informed that a Raider Regiment was being organized to comprise the four Raider Battalions. The commander of the Regiment would be Colonel Harry Liversedge. Carlson was to be his Executive Officer. Lieutenant Colonel Alan Shapley would take over Carlson's Raiders.

How simple it was. With Shapley in, Gung Ho would go. And Carlson's job as Executive Officer of the Regiment would mean that he would no longer have direct command of men, and would be in the unhappy position of executing orthodox policies over which he had no control and through which he would be contravening everything he had taught his men and had observed to be effective in training and battle.

At Pacific Corps Headquarters, many officers expressed their sympathy to Carlson. "The high command is afraid of you, Carlson," they said. "You're too independent."

Carlson took orders. He made no protest once they had been given to him. His heart was sick, his spirit rebelled, but no one heard him complain.

Many of his men were off in submarine maneuvers at this time, and with them was Sergeant Jim Lucas, a Marine Corps combat correspondent and formerly a reporter on the *Tulsa Tribune*. Lucas had spent several weeks at the Raider camp and had become very close to the men. He had attended several Gung Ho meetings and heard the men debate such topics as, "The Kind of Social Order We Want after the War." He fell hard for the Gung Ho idea and Carlson.

In his book, *Combat Correspondent,* Lucas describes what happened when the men returning from their exercises heard that Carlson was going to leave them:

Tragedy awaited us. On shore, we learned that Colonel Carlson had been promoted to a more important command

and was to leave his men. I stumbled with them up the beach, tears in their eyes, and heard them curse the fate that had robbed them of their old man. I sat in their tents and heard them cry like babies.[3]

On a clear day, it was April 1, the Battalion was called together to witness the change of command.

Carlson rose to speak to his men. For the first time since they had come together he did not feel like talking to them. Partly because he was feeling physically ill. He had had a fever for several days running; malaria was returning. And partly because there was nothing he could say to his men other than the whole truth — a truth which would reduce their respect for their high leaders, he thought. This could not be done.

Shapley was standing at his side as Carlson spoke.

"I have been relieved of my command here," Carlson said. "I am taking over the job of Executive Officer of the Raider Regiment which will be headed by Colonel Liversedge. I am taking with me Captain Davis and Captain Plumley and Sergeant Schofield. Later there may be others."

He paused. He wanted to say a few words about Gung Ho, asking his men to keep it alive, but he was no longer their leader. He had no further right to ask them to do anything. Shapley was their commander now. He could not presume on Shapley. He could not commit his men to any act or thought while they were under another commander. The responsibility of command was something he held to scrupulously.

"Lieutenant Colonel Alan Shapley will be your new C.O.," he said firmly. "I hope you will give him the loyalty you gave me."

Carlson stepped down. This was farewell. He would never command these men again, never share experiences with them as he had shared Makin and Guadalcanal. His eyes burnt with the dry tears of pride and regret. Much that he loved he was leaving.

Shapley said a few polite words, praising the record of the Bat-

[3] *Combat Correspondent,* by James Lucas (New York: Reynal and Hitchcock, 1944).

talion, and then added that he had a few ideas of his own which he would communicate to the Battalion some other time.

The next day, when Carlson had left for the hospital, Shapley called the men together. His speech was brief.

He told them that he didn't know much about this Gung Ho business. If it was good, he'd keep it. If not, out it would go. He said that in all fairness he wanted them to know his own point of view. He wasn't going to have a boy-scout outfit. He expected his men to be Marines, to salute, to go through regular channels of command, and to abide by the Marine Corps regular setup. He was going to do away with the fire team as it now was organized and go back to the conventional squad.

He finished up by telling the men that he wanted the tent rows straightened. "I want this camp to look like a Marine camp!" he said.

"Gung Ho is dead," someone whispered in the ranks.

The men went back into their tents. They had heard the payoff. All complaint against Carlson vanished. In its place sprung a hate for Shapley — the awesome drunken hate which only enlisted men can have for an officer they despise. They hated Shapley, and even more they hated the authorities who put him in command.

"Boy scouts!" they muttered.

"Saluting!"

"Straighten up the tent rows!"

"Shapley can go —— himself for my money!"

"Gung Ho is dead, good and dead, I mean."

In one tent an amateur balladist began putting together words. Others in his tent added their own.

> Throw away your boots and knives,
> We're giving up our Raider lives.
> They're doing away with the best they got.
> And throwin' him in with the common lot.
>
> Give up your Raider schemes.
> Give up your Raider dreams . . .

Someone, in a pause, began to sing softly:

> In the memory of men there were those
> Who were brave . . .

"Shut up!" came a shout from across the tent.

"You ain't kiddin'. 'In the *memory* of men!' The Raiders are dead."

"Gung Ho is dead!"

"The Old Man is dead!"

"For Chrissake, shut up!"

There was a long silence.

The balladist started again:

> Throw away your boots and knives,
> We're giving up our Raider lives . . .

It must be here stated in all fairness that there is no conventional evidence that Carlson and Gung Ho were victims of the short-sightedness and timidity of Headquarters. The organization of the Raider Regiment — transformed within a year to regular G.I. status — the withholding of supplies, the difficulty of finding a paymaster, the appointment of Shapley instead of an officer from the Raiders who might have continued Gung Ho may all have been the result of red tape and accident. They may be circumstances which can be explained one way or another.

But there is one circumstance which cannot be explained away. From the day in 1943 when Carlson left his Raider Battalion until his retirement from the Marine Corps in 1946, he was never again given direct command of men. He would be at Tarawa, Kwajelein and Saipan; he would be a staff officer, a planner of campaigns, an inspector of divisions, but never a commander who could speak to Marines directly, teach them the principles of Gung Ho, or lead them into battle.

His career as a military leader of men was over. Other officers would be promoted rapidly, but not Carlson.

In the minds of the Marine High Command his record as a successful commander who had won much at a miraculously low cost in life was forgotten.

Perhaps the High Command was justified. Perhaps the morale

of the Corps as a whole was diminished by one battalion and one leader who made a profession, not only of fighting well, but also of preaching and trying to live the spirit of a democratic army.

Carlson became a very sick man. His malaria was complicated by jaundice and complete nervous exhaustion. The loss of his battalion and the defeat of Gung Ho depleted him more than did Makin and Guadalcanal.

The doctors advised that he be sent to New Zealand for a more complete examination than they could give him on Espiritu Santo.

A group of Raiders came down to see him off.

"How're things going?" he asked.

They made sour faces.

"There ain't no one preachin' Gung Ho to us any more, Colonel," one of them said.

"But you can practice it, can't you?" he said. "Among yourselves. If what we did together has any value, you oughn't to have to be constantly reminded."

"Sure, we practice it."

"But it ain't as easy as it was, Colonel. We see a lot of things done that ain't right, but we can't get up at a Gung Ho meeting and yell about it."

"What of it?" he said angrily. "Make sure you practice Gung Ho among yourselves. Do your jobs well. Work together. Stand by each other. Colonel Shapley'll come around. He's a good man. He may not see it at first, but he'll see it later, if you never let him forget that Gung Ho makes men better citizens and better fighters."

The men said that they'd try.

"We got some clean clothes for you, Colonel," Larry Peeples said. Laundry was always a problem in the Pacific.

"Wonderful! I was afraid I'd have to go to New Zealand naked."

"But it's not *your* laundry."

"What did you do — steal, Larry?"

The men laughed. "We just got some of the boys your size to contribute," Peeples said.

Carlson laughed. "Thank them for me."

On the ship he opened his laundry bag. There were socks and shorts and skivvies and shirts and pants, and on them were the name labels of their original owners. It was almost the roll call of the Headquarters Company.

At Auckland he was examined and ordered into a hospital for a two months' rest. The doctors gave him his choice of hospitals, Auckland's or San Diego's.

No less than his own men, he hungered for a sight of the States. He chose San Diego.

When he reached the San Diego Naval Hospital, he requested that no one be permitted to see him for the first two weeks. He wanted time to be alone, to think things through, to figure out, as if he had been coming from a battlefield, where he had made his mistakes.

While still on sick leave he went to Washington. He had decided to take his fight to Headquarters. He saw General Holcomb, the Commandant. The General turned him over to the Plans and Policies section, commonly known as Pots and Pans, and there he talked on the advantages of Raider training, organizations, tactics and orientation.

They listened, asked him questions.

But nothing was said about sending him back to the Pacific. In short, he had lost the final round for the Raider idea.

Holcomb saw him again and suggested that perhaps General William J. Donovan of the Office of Strategic Services might have a task for Carlson. He conferred with Donovan, with Dr. Stanley Hornbeck and John Davies of the State Department, then General Stilwell's adviser in China, and a job was offered to him, the details of which are still, and may well be for a very long time to come, top secret.

Carlson, however, saw that the mission had certain political aspects which were repugnant to him, and he begged to be relieved. "I'd rather go back to the Pacific," he told a friend, "and get a good clean bullet right in the heart."

While he was in Washington, he stopped in to see Brigadier General Robert L. Denig with whom he had served in Nicaragua.

Denig was now chief of Marine Corps Public Relations. In his office at the time was Lucien Hubbard, a journalist and screen writer. Hubbard had brought a script of a moving picture with him for Denig's approval. The script was the story of the Makin Raid, to be called "Gung Ho." Walter Wanger, one of Hollywood's most progressive and thoughtful producers, was to make it.

Denig thought it would be a good idea for Carlson to act as technical adviser to the film. Carlson agreed, providing it would not interfere with whatever duty he would be assigned to after his sick leave had terminated.

General Holcomb approved the arrangement.

Carlson liked the script of "Gung Ho" although he felt that it showed him off to be too heroic, and he asked for several changes. He rewrote the speeches which Randolph Scott, who played the part of Carlson, was to make to the Raiders. Carlson realized that through the medium of the screen the Gung Ho message would reach many millions of Americans. Perhaps such popular opinion might help, not to restore the Marine Raiders — he saw that that was pretty hopeless — but it might encourage other officers in all the armed services to pursue democratic leadership with greater vigor. He knew from letters he had received that there were many of them around who had the intention and needed only the incentive.

In June the Institute of Pacific Relations held a luncheon in New York in Carlson's honor for an audience consisting of many of America's foremost bankers and industrialists. And with that luncheon goes a tale of tragic irony.

Three years before, in the winter of 1939-40, after his resignation from the Marine Corps, Carlson went to New York to seek out some of our leading financiers and businessmen, particularly those who were responsible for loans and the shipment of raw materials to Japan; men from the National City and Chase National Banks, executives from Standard Oil and Texas Company.

"My purpose, gentlemen," he told them individually, "is to warn you that you are helping a nation which one day will turn against us and bring great losses in lives and wealth to our country."

One of the industrialists looked at him inquiringly. "You predict a Japanese-American war?" he asked.

"Yes," he said.

"When?"

Carlson smiled without humor. "It's impossible for me to guess at the exact date. But I'm convinced that it will come within the next decade."

It was now the turn of the other gentleman to smile without humor.

"My dear Carlson," he said. "We're not interested in a war in the next decade. We're not interested in a war next year or next month. We're interested only in returns on our investments today."

Carlson never forgot that conversation. Whenever he thought in the larger terms of what social order must come to in our country, he realized that it must exclude the power of men to risk the national fate for purposes of "returns on investment." Such "returns" were justifiable in both a moral and economic sense only when no large segment of people could be hurt by their existence.

He had that conversation in mind when he arose to speak at the luncheon in his honor. He saw around him the rich furnishings of the Downtown Association, the private club of Wall Street aristocracy, and he saw in front of him the fine clear skins of wealthy men, the parted silvering hair, the firm eyes and aggressive lips of leaders who had long practiced the art of quick decisions. There was something almost military in their faces, for just as the conventional military man is supposed to disregard the calculation that many men may die or be crippled by his order to enter battle, and therefore thinks of them merely as nonhuman elements which may be risked or not risked as strategy demands, so bankers and industrialists force themselves to ignore the personal and individual suffering which so frequently results from *their* strategies and manipulations.

It would make no point to list the members of his audience at that luncheon, except merely to say that there were executives from the main office of the wealthiest private and public banks in the world, and from the oil, communications, airplane and steel industries.

Edward C. Carter, head of the Institute of Pacific Relations, a fervent and honest student of international affairs, had introduced Carlson.

Carlson looked around him, and he felt an enormous anger. He thought of whom he had left behind at Makin and Guadalcanal. He thought of the rotting bodies, the drowned men of Makin, the dengue fever, the jungle sores, the vomitous meat.

He moved his hand across the table in front of him and pushed away a dessert dish as if it were poison.

When he looked up again his face was angry.

"I don't know precisely why I am here," he said, "because I stopped talking December seventh largely out of a feeling of frustration occasioned by the fact that I had talked to many of you gentlemen in 1939 and 1940. Then I told you of what I was convinced — that the Japanese intended to war on us. And I pleaded with you to stop the stupid practice of arming Japan. You did nothing about it."

He stared back at those staring at him.

"But my friend, Ned Carter, asked me to speak. And I'm glad to accommodate him."

Someone coughed; someone accidentally hit his spoon against a demitasse cup; someone sighed.

"Let me tell you about the return on investments at Makin and Guadalcanal."

And he told them.

During July, before he received new orders, Carlson worked as technical adviser to the Wanger company of "Gung Ho." Randolph Scott played the part of Carlson, J. Carroll Naish played Le Francois, Sam Levene played "Transport" Maghakian. Ray Enright directed Lucien Hubbard's screenplay.

To this day the stagehands, extras and bit players used in that picture remember Carlson, not so much for Makin and Guadalcanal, but for what he did when they all went out on location at San Clemente, California. The company manager had reserved hotel rooms for the principal actors, the director and Carlson. The others were given bunks in one of the temporary buildings which had been put up for some guayule workers. When Carlson found out about this, he told the company manager that there oughtn't to be any discrimination. Everybody ought to bunk together.

"If the picture is going to be about Gung Ho," he said, "the people who make it ought to try living it."

When the word passed around, the hotel rooms were given up, and stars and stagehands and extras shared the bunkhouse.

On the back lots of Hollywood they still talk of it.

Finally the time came for Carlson to return to duty. He was assigned to a staff job with the Fourth Division at Camp Pendleton, Oceanside, California, as divisional planning and operations officer. Major General Harry Schmidt, the Division Commander, and Colonel Walter Rogers, the Chief of Staff, greatly respected Carlson and appreciated the value of his ideas and efforts. But a staff job was not to his liking. He would have preferred to be with his Raiders who, at this moment, were fighting in New Georgia.

He was restless and still depressed. Only when he received letters from some of his old men, or read some article which plugged Gung Ho, did he feel that he had not failed completely.

3

Men under stress

In October word reached the Fourth Division staff that the Second Division then overseas was soon going to be used in an assault on an atoll in the Gilberts in the Central Pacific. Our war strategy called for the establishment of a base there from which to move into the Marshalls and Marianas beyond, and thus to clear the sea flank for our return to the Philippines.

Carlson volunteered to join the Second Division as an observer. Its success or failure in the attack on the atoll would determine, to some extent, the future training and tactics of his own division.

His request was approved, and on the first of November he and the other observers left Camp Pendleton. One of the other men was Brigadier General James L. Underhill, Assistant Division Commander of the Fourth, and an old China mate of Carlson's.

Twenty days later a cyclorama of transports, battleships, carriers and destroyers slowly appeared against the Pacific horizon. On the deck of one of the transports Carlson swept the distance through field glasses. In the haze was the dim green of an atoll. Over his head in an almost visible arch streamed trains of Naval shells. Below on the water were the beetle-like landing barges. And in the barges were the men of the Second Marine Division, Major General Julian C. Smith commanding, sweating and holding their weapons in a tight clutch of fear.

He heard the number of his boat over the loudspeaker, put away his glasses, took out of his pocket a letter and hurriedly dropped it into a mail sack near by.

> Dear Dad and Karen,
> When the call came this time, there was no time for lengthy farewells. I climbed in a plane and flew half the world. We're headed for another Great Adventure. Unless my logic is far amiss, this will be tougher from the standpoint of pure combat than anything that has gone before.
> Last Sunday was met with reverence by all on board. I saw three services being held — and each was packed with earnest-faced men . . .
> I have said to you before all the things in my mind. I love you. God bless you.

He climbed down the net into the boat of Regimental Commander Colonel David Shoup whose men were to lead the assault. In the boat were Gilbert Bundy, the artist, and Lieutenant Colonel P. M. Rixey, the son of Carlson's old commander at Peiping.

The battle for Tarawa was to begin, a terrible and tormented seventy-six hours, with few parallels in the history of war.

In the slaughter of Tarawa Carlson saw with sick heart the tragic confirmation of the correctness of Gung Ho theories of training; and he saw also in the victory an affirmation of his faith in the ingenuity and fortitude of the enlisted men, if they were given the chance.

One thing more came to him.

Carlson had achieved a reputation for fearlessness. Whoever had shared danger with him — Edgar Snow and Colin McDonald in China, Roosevelt and the Raiders in the Pacific — testified to his utter lack of fear as they would to a miracle.

Yet fear is the ever-present, volcanic companion of men in battle. Carlson was no exception. At first he managed it the way many others have done. In Nicaragua and China he concentrated on the task at hand, and there was no room for fear in his mind. This "technique," by no means a conscious or deliberately contrived thing, was transformed at Makin and Guadalcanal into something more substantial. There he was able to function without fear because of his deep knowledge of the issues of the war and his conviction that the cause he served was just. This was his greatest strength and the strength he gave to his Gung Ho battalion.[4]

And now at Tarawa his management of fear took on again a different shape. It came to him in the middle of the battle in the

[4] In *Men Under Stress,* a study of neuroses in World War II by two psychiatrists, Drs. Roy R. Grinker and John P. Spiegel, the point is made that while fear derives from the thought of losing something loved intensely, nevertheless "if a man is passionately devoted to an abstract idea which is in danger, such as his country or his political creed, he will give his life to protect it with little apprehension." Thus we see that some of the things which create fear may also create fearlessness. *Men Under Stress* is published by Blakiston, 1945.

In *Fear In Battle,* a Yale Institute of Human Relations study written by Professor John Dollard and Dr. Donald Horton, Carlson's *unconscious* management of fear is confirmed statistically. Of 300 veterans of the Abraham Lincoln Battalion who fought against the Fascists in Spain, 84 per cent said they were less afraid during the battle when they concentrated on their tasks, and 77 per cent said that a "belief in war aims" was the most important element in overcoming fear. This report was published by Yale University in 1943. Orientation officers in this war would probably endorse these percentages.

guise of a faith that men who act unselfishly are somehow protected.

Of course he knew that he himself was not a saint — and that good men were killed by the same shell that killed bad men.

"It is not given to us," he had said at the Guadalcanal memorial, "to know the process by which certain of us are chosen for sacrifice. . . . We can only rest our faith in the infinite wisdom of the Supreme Being . . ."

At Tarawa and later at Kwajalein and Saipan, Carlson held stubbornly to that "infinite wisdom" and to the idea of God as ultimate justice.

As other men went into the battle wearing their silver crucifixes and Stars of David, he went in believing that selflessness, too, can be an amulet; a way not only of avoiding the consciousness of imminent death, but also a device to protect a man from it.

And now came the moment of Tarawa when he needed protection.

Toward a heavily armed fortress, a little smaller than New York's Central Park, Marines walked in from the open sea; walked across a six-hundred-yard open coral reef whose shallow green waters, bubbling with enemy bullets, was slowly turning red with their blood. On the shore a little strip of white beach had already become the cemetery of five hundred men and the terror of a thousand more who lay huddled and leaderless and demoralized. For four hours in the equator's sun they lay there, with no place to hide, no place to retreat to, no purchase of ground from which to advance, their only ammunition what they could take from the belts of their own dead. The besiegers had become the besieged.

For four hours other men lay out to sea in their landing boats, beyond the range of Japanese fire, hysterically begging their officers to give the order to go to the aid of their comrades.

The order did not come for a long time. It could not come. Not enough boats could live through the shellfire and reach the reef to disembark the men; and not enough men could live to cross the six-hundred yards of mortar and machine-gun fire to get to shore.

Past the men in the boats dead bodies floated face downward, trailing blood.

The loudspeakers of the fleet, four hours after H-hour, announced: "The issue is in doubt."

There was a pier which jutted out from the beach about five hundred yards through the coral reef. Under that pier of cocoanut log and coral, part trestle, part solid, was the only protection for the men walking in. Even so, it was open to enemy cross fire from the beach, from a half-sunken hulk of a Jap ship near by, and from the shore end of the pier itself.

At 9:45 in the morning, thirty minutes after H-hour, Colonel Shoup's boat with Carlson and other men and officers in it stood off at the end of the pier.

Shoup could not determine which were Marines and which were Japs, so intermingled were both sides on the beaches. It would be stupid to land and be captured, and he decided to set up a command post under the pier, and make contact with his land forces from there.

Strung out under the pier were men afraid to leave its sanctuary for the open. Many of their officers and squad leaders lay dead in the water near by. And although they were needed on the beach, terror transfixed them. They did not move.

At about this time men of a fresh battalion were being disgorged from their landing craft at the edge of the reef and were beginning the long Golgotha into the beach. In excellent deployed formation they advanced slowly. But Japanese mortars and machine guns quickly got their range, and men fell into the water like grain rows under a scythe.

Carlson and Shoup yelled to them to come over to the pier. Some men heard, some were confused, and some, stricken with terror like the men already under the pier, stood rooted in the water.

Shoup was busy giving orders into his walkie-talkie. He had thrown in his regimental reserves, and was now calling for more plane support and Naval gunfire. Other officers were carrying on their own duties. Carlson, being an observer with no special task, left the protection of the pier, and moving up and down in the shallow bullet-splattered water, directed the new battalion to places under the pier and through to the other side where he had dis-

covered that the Japanese fire was not so intense. Then he ran up
and down the reef, from its seaward edge to the beach, leading
men in, pulling the half-drowned wounded out of the water, and
carrying orders from the command post. All around him men were
hit, some blown to pieces within reach of his arm. His trousers had
a hole in them from a sniper's bullet which passed between his legs
and burnt the flesh of his left thigh. Elsewhere, on the beach and
in the water, other officers and men were doing what he was doing, for at that moment in the assault he who had the baton of
Napoleon in his pack had the bitter opportunity of using it.

Earlier that morning, on his first trip down the length of the
pier, Carlson had thrown his gear and sleeping bag on the top of a
wrecked Japanese barge. The next time he passed it he thought that
he ought to go over, pick his gear up and carry it to the beach
where, by this time, Shoup had set up another command post. He
would need his sleeping bag that night.

He stopped near the barge to catch his breath. "Shall I get my
stuff this time?" he asked himself.

No, the next trip.

Then he suddenly remembered — odd flicker of thought in the
midst of being shot at — the offer which Donovan of the O.S.S.
had made to him. He had turned it down because it involved a kind
of politics he had no stomach for. He had said he would rather
meet a clean death in the Pacific. But there was something else about
the offer. The plane which had carried the man who had taken it
had gotten into trouble over Burma. The passengers had to bail
out. The man had been hurt.

"This time, Evans?" he asked himself again when he passed
close to the wrecked barge.

No. Not this time. Nor the next. He decided that to go over for
his gear would be an act of selfishness. If he had escaped death so
far on Tarawa, it was because he was doing something for others.
He could not expect to be protected if he dared bullets to do something for himself, for his own comfort.

He turned away from the barge. If he lived through the day, he'd
sleep in an open foxhole that night without a sleeping bag.

Later he returned to the beach where in the midst of intermingled Marines and Japanese, living and dead, Colonel Shoup had set up a command post at the side of a concrete pillbox still held by the enemy. Shoup needed someone to go out to General Smith's headquarters' ship with the facts of the situation as it then stood. Carlson volunteered.

Someone who saw him go by through the enemy mortar and machine guns, and who knew how often he had chanced it, said, "I'd go, too, if I could walk right behind Carlson."

This was the moment of Tarawa; after seventy-six hours of desperate fighting, three days and four hours without cease, every one of four thousand strongly entrenched enemy was dead.

When the word was passed that the island was secured, one could almost hear a deep sigh of relief rise above the dead like signal smoke. It seemed to Carlson as if the trees, broken by shellfire, were grieving.

Tarawa was not won by competent strategy or the skillful manipulation of troops or by the steadfast belligerency of some of the commanders on the beach, although all these were true.

Ten days after Tarawa was captured Carlson and the other observers of the Fourth Division, having been flown back to the States, addressed a meeting at Camp Pendleton of one thousand officers, anxious to hear the details of the Marine Corps' bloodiest battle.

"Tarawa was won," Carlson told them, "because a few *enlisted* men of great courage called out simply to their comrades, 'Come on, fellows. Follow me!' And then went on, followed by men who took heart at their example, to knock out, at great sacrifice, one Jap position after another, one after another, slowly, until there were no more. Tarawa is a victory because some *enlisted* men, unaffected by the loss of their officers, many of whom were casualties in the first hour, became great and heroic commanders in their own right.

"But — " He paused for a long time. "But with all that courage and fortitude and willingness to die on the part of some of the men, too many others lacked initiative and resourcefulness. They were not trained to understand the need for sacrifice. Too many men waited for orders — and while they waited they died. What if they had been trained not to wait for orders?"

He was deeply angry. Lives could have been saved. It was this very matter he had mentioned to Robert Sherrod of *Time,* who was on the same transport en route to Tarawa.

"Marines," he had told Sherrod, "have a great deal of *esprit de corps,* and that's all to the good. But that last ounce of sacrifice takes more than *esprit de corps.* Our great weakness is the calibre of our officers, and that, of course, is a reflection on our system of education and training." [5]

Tarawa cost the American people 3056 killed, wounded and missing, about one out of three men engaged. No other battle in the Pacific was to cost that many men in so short a time.

"What if they had been trained not to wait for orders?" Carlson had asked. And how extraordinary was the resourcefulness of the few! They had, for example, used bulldozers to pile up sand to cover the open ports and vents of enemy pillboxes making them ineffective. But if all had been trained to act by themselves . . .

"Our leaders did not give them that chance," Carlson told the thousand Marine officers at Camp Pendleton.

His citation for Tarawa mentions merely that:

> He volunteered twice when the situation was extremely critical to make the hazardous trip, even though the route was under enemy fire, to Division Headquarters with vital information of the progress of the operations ashore. He was instrumental in securing and directing the landing of badly needed reinforcements and supplies where they were needed the most, and at points where landings were possible.
>
> Colonel Carlson did much to aid the assault units in the final capture of the atoll, and his actions were in keeping with the highest traditions of the United States Naval Service.

[5] Robert Sherrod is the author of *Tarawa,* a classic of battle exposition, published by Duell, Sloan and Pearce. Sherrod reports this and other conversations with Carlson in his book.

The citation was signed by Major General Julian C. Smith, commander of the Second Division, which is credited with the victory.

4

"My mission is still not completed"

In a long letter about Tarawa to his father and Karen, he said:

> I traveled about 13,000 miles by air and a couple of thousand by ship on this last trip. When one thinks of it in retrospect it seems rather silly to travel that far solely for the privilege of being shot at by the Japs. But there was a sounder purpose, of course. This was to be the first attack on an atoll, so I requested permission to go in with the 2nd Division.
>
> It was truly a tough job. . . . I did not condition myself for this battle. Thought that I would go ashore with the regimental commander as an observer, take a few notes and that would be that. But I never worked so hard in my life as in those first three days. It was a case of every man who was still on his feet having to pitch in . . .
>
> I have been in many battles now, and I've had a lot of lead and steel thrown in my direction. But I don't believe that more lead was ever flowing around me at one time than during the first two days at Tarawa. How I got through is a miracle. The same holds true of the others who emerged in one piece in the initial landing.
>
> The fact is none of it worried me too much for I was confident, as always, that when my time comes there is nothing I can do about it. No point in dodging, for there is as much chance of dodging into one as away from it. *My mission is still not completed.* [Italics author's.]

After Tarawa, Marine Corps and Army units suddenly flooded Carlson with requests for lectures on tactics and training. He was allowed to understand that he could talk freely and without restraint, and wherever he went he repeated what he had told the officers at Camp Pendleton. He received hundreds of letters asking for more information about Gung Ho training, and petitions from Army, Marine Corps and even Navy personnel which said in essence: "We understand that you are going to organize a new outfit. How can we join it?"

But there was no new outfit being organized.

> I am still without a great deal of authority [he wrote home at the end of December, 1943]. All hands come around for advice and frequently it is accepted but I'd much prefer to run the show myself. My present role requires a considerable amount of self-discipline.

In the same letter he mentions a flight to Pearl Harbor to attend an important strategy conference.

> I saw George Marshall for the first time since the GHQ days at Chaumont. He and Nimitz are without doubt the brainiest and most apt men of the Army and Navy, respectively. Keen, modest, kindly.

He refers also to the fact that he had been receiving a great deal of public attention. *Liberty, Life* and *Fortune* had run stories on him and the Raiders. Of all the articles written on him, the one of which he was proudest was published in *Fortune:*

> Psychiatrically [wrote *Fortune*] the American Dunkerque was Guadalcanal. Lieutenant Commander E. Rogers Smith, a psychiatrist at the Mare Island U. S. Naval Hospital, said last Spring, "Never before in history has such a group of healthy, toughened, well-trained men been subjected to such conditions. . . . The strain and stress experienced by these men (at Guadalcanal) produced a group neurosis which has not been seen before and may never be seen again."
>
> Some of the Guadalcanal Raiders [*Fortune* went on to relate] were sent into battle psychologically well prepared. They were the famed and heroic "Carlson's Raiders" . . . . *In this group of a thousand men . . . only one case of traumatic war*

neurosis occurred, despite the fact that the Raiders fought under the same conditions as the other Marines [author's italics].

Carlson believes that because he prepared the men for what they might expect; because he considered their opinions and feelings; because they were convinced he would never sacrifice a man needlessly; because he provided an outlet for terror and tension; because his men understood what they were fighting for; because the Raiders trusted him implicitly — they suffered virtually no psychiatric casualties.

Despite the success of Carlson's methods, no steps have since been taken to use them elsewhere in the Marine Corps, or in any other unit of the armed forces for that matter. . . . Carlson himself has been kicked upstairs. . . . Thus there would seem to be no field command for an officer with Evans Carlson's proven qualities of leadership and with his respect for the dignity of man.[6]

When a Philadelphia churchman was quoted as saying that Carlson had done more for religion in this war than any other single individual, Carlson wrote about it to his father:

It made me feel good to hear it. I have always hoped that I was doing something to restore faith in Christ's precepts.

I feel humble about all this publicity. But I recognize two things about it: it is evidence that people are interested in the fundamental values which I continually stress, and two, that people like to personalize their war fervor.

I do not take this as a personal tribute — it could not be that — people do not know me well enough in the first place to evaluate me with any degree of honesty, and in the second place, I would be violating their intelligence if I thought they were seriously trying to endow me with virtues which human beings do not have.

No, I am merely the vehicle for disseminating ideas that have sound basic value and which people instinctively respect but, to a large degree, have lost faith in. They want to believe in them but the circumstances of their environment have constrained them to accept the doctrine of rugged individual-

[6] *Fortune:* "Psychiatric Toll of Warfare" (December 1943).

ism in order to preserve themselves. Probably my own contempt for convention and orthodoxy, when they stand in the way of honesty and truth, gives them courage to try anew the doctrine of faith and tolerance and co-operative effort.

At this time his personal life became enriched by the translation of a friendship into a love.

A few months before, he met Mrs. Peggy Tatum Whyte, a cousin of one of his Raiders, Larry Peeples. Mrs. Whyte had been divorced in 1937. When Carlson met her she was living with her mother and her six-year-old son, Tony. From the beginning they liked each other. Tony especially liked Carlson. It was no small thing to have as a friend a Marine officer with all those medals.

Mrs. Peggy Whyte was the daughter of an Army Cavalry Colonel of the old school who died when she was twenty-six. Her impressionable years were spent on Army posts all over the country. While she recalls with a glow certain happy memories of Army life — the parades, the flag formations, the fine bugle music of Retreat — she recalls with distaste the lickspittle system of rank which determined how the children were to be seated in the school bus, and the size and priority of parties.

The wildness of Army children is notorious. For some reason Army parents have a hard time getting their children to obey. Perhaps this comes because Army children live in a closed system of commands which they rebel against from the very beginning.

Peggy was as tomboyish as all the other girls at the Presidio in Monterey or at Fort Bliss or Fort Leavenworth. But underlying her indiscipline was a native sense of justice which, after a while, turned her into an unconscious radical.

She married when she was twenty-three, after a variegated education which intensified but did not clarify her resentment of the *status quo*. Her marriage quickly fell apart, and she was left alone to support herself and her son.

When she met Carlson Peggy Whyte was a rebel without a cause. Intelligent and sharp-witted and highly articulate, nevertheless she needed a focus to her life, some magnet of idea which could catch to itself her intellectual energy, now diffused and turned inward.

At this time also Mrs. Whyte was depressed at the way life had gone for her. She needed not only to experience affection and loyalty again, but faith in human beings as well.

Carlson had enough faith in human beings to carry two. He had an integrity to which she could give herself unequivocally. And he, too, needed at this time someone to break into his loneliness. Although Carlson was a secretive person, almost rigid in maintaining the privacy of his personal life, he felt lost without a woman in whom he could confide all his private doubts, his failures and his mistakes. Women had always been his best friends and confidantes.

In Mrs. Whyte he found a woman whom he could trust; but more than that, he found someone whom he could teach, for he was at heart always the teacher. Her disillusion inspired him to "save" her, so to speak; and her swift grasp of new ideas, which she tested with a deeply honest skepticism, stimulated him.

Their need for each other was strong; the undecipherable elements of mutual attraction even stronger. They fell in love. Carlson was sure that he had found, at last, the woman he had been hoping one day to find. In this he was like most romanticists. But with Peggy Whyte he was luckier than most. She matched his romanticism and she was equal to his maturity. Both, however, had the great quality of youthfulness — the pure willingness to adventure anywhere, any time, in place or idea.

With more certainty and less illusion than he had ever had before, Carlson proposed marriage and was accepted.

But before they could get married, the Fourth Division packed its baggage and left Camp Pendleton for its first combat — the attack on Kwajalein atoll in the Marshalls.

On January 20, 1944, Carlson wrote still another precombat letter to his father and sister:

> As I go out this time, as always I have the feeling that I have ill-expressed my love for you. I repeat it again and again.

Kwajalein was perhaps the most successful of the Pacific atoll assaults and Carlson deservedly received some of the credit, for it was

he who had most of the responsibility for the planning of the
Marine Corps part of it.

His plan was to move in to the outlying islands around Kwajalein,
so that land-based artillery could be used for the attack on the main
island. It also called for the use of two-thousand-pound bombs to be
dropped by planes on Kwajalein's strong points. Bombs this size
had been promised for Tarawa, but for some reason had not been
delivered.

When the atoll was secured, he wrote home again:

> Things clicked. We really put the lessons of Tarawa to work.
> I rate this operation a success because we were able to keep
> casualties low.

Carlson requested a stateside leave after Kwajalein. His division
would be in a rest area for a while, and he wanted to get married
before another D-Day came around. His request was granted.

They were married in the La Jolla Union Congregational Church
on February 29. "With malice aforethought," Carlson said later.
"We like the idea of having a wedding anniversary only every four
years." Mrs. Whyte's seven-year-old son, Tony, was best man.

Before his leave was over Carlson flew to New York to address a
Sun Yat-sen memorial meeting at which Paul Robeson, the great
Negro, and Admiral Harry Yarnell spoke. He saw his old friends,
Ed and Peg Snow, and his father, brother and sister. He told them
all about his new wife who, unfortunately, had been unable to make
the trip with him.

Carlson was happy to see how well his father looked. He was
seventy-seven now, and almost two years had passed since he had
resigned his ministry of the Plymouth Congregational Church after
fifty years as a preacher and sixteen years in the little Connecticut
town.

A day after Carlson returned to California and his bride he left
for the Pacific base where the Fourth Division was being prepared
for its next combat. This time it was to be something bigger than
Kwajalein. Two islands; not atolls. Saipan and Tinian. Carlson, as

planning officer, was given the task of working out the tactics of the assault.

He was tired. The last two years — it was now the end of March 1944 — had depleted him. He had been through Makin, Guadalcanal, Tarawa and Kwajalein. He had crossed the Pacific eight times, the continent four times. Malaria still fevered and froze him. He had had no rest, little chance to recapture the ceaseless outflow of energy. And now on him was placed the heavy responsibility of helping to plan an invasion. He felt it was absolutely necessary for the Division to gain a tactical surprise in order to avoid heavy casualties. As he studied the beaches of Saipan and Tinian, especially Tinian, he realized that to achieve that surprise it would require a very radical departure from the standard operating procedure of an amphibious attack. On Tinian, for example, the available beaches for landing a large force would obviously be those on which the Japanese would expect landings and therefore would place their heaviest defenses. But there were other beaches, inconvenient and small, certainly not the kind that anyone in his right mind would recommend for a landing. They were hard to approach and were too small to permit a force larger than two hundred and fifty men to land on. These beaches, of course, would be lightly defended, if at all. The Japanese command, if Carlson knew it right, would discount them.

Carlson proposed that the Fourth Division land on these small and inaccessible beaches; land thousands of men on beaches that could only hold hundreds. "We can shoulder our way in through the enemy's back door," he said. "It's the only way to surprise him."

Major General Harry Schmidt of the Fourth and Colonel Walter Rogers, his Chief of Staff, heartily approved Carlson's plan.

Harry Schmidt, now a Lieutenant General, was always one of Carlson's defenders in the ranks of the Marine Corps brass. In a letter to the author, General Schmidt wrote: "I found Colonel Carlson always diligent in the performance of his duties. He is a man of fine character, a soldier of distinction and intensely loyal to those over him and to the Marine Corps. He contributed greatly in our efforts in the Pacific and as my planning officer he did outstanding work."

Later, General Schmidt told the author: "Carlson made a good-sized contribution to the winning of the Pacific war."

The assault on Saipan began June 14.

President Roosevelt, just the week before, had prayed with his fellow citizens for the success of D-Day in the invasion of Europe. "These men . . . fight not for the lust of conquest, but to end conquest," he had said. "They fight to let justice arise and for tolerance and good will."

The Russians were into Czechoslovakia in the great offensive from the East, and the accord of Teheran had seemed to signal, once and for all, the unity of the Big Three.

And now once again an armada filled the Pacific. There were the same fleets as before, only larger; the same aerial and naval bombardment, only heavier; the same beetle-like landing boats, only more.

It was as if Carlson were seeing a moving picture he had seen many times before, except that now it was filled with double exposures.

Carlson sent one more "last" letter home to Plymouth, and he had wondered whether or not it might be his truly "last."

> God be with you, Dad and Karen, and make His light to
> shine upon you . . .

His thoughts were on Plymouth, and on his brother Tom who lived with his family in a little New Jersey town, commuter's distance from New York. He always remembered Tom with affectionate irony. Years ago, when Tom was just out of college and Evans was a by-the-book Marine, they had had long, bitter arguments on politics. Tom was then the liberal, Evans the conservative. Now their arguments were still bitter, but their opinions were reversed.

He thought, of course, of his son, Evans, Jr., who was in the States preparing to go overseas again; and he thought of Edgar Snow, doing wonderful work as a war correspondent, of his old friends,

Agnes Smedley and Chu Teh and Mao Tse-tung and Chou En-lai and the five boys he had traveled with. Now they were all fighting the enemy together.

And he thought of Peggy Carlson. Not the last in his mind, but the first. He felt deeply the wrench of their separation so soon after marriage. He was glad he had remembered to write his father earlier, to send Peggy the letter he had marked "Not to be Opened Except in the Event of My Death." If anything happened to him, there would be little enough for Peggy Carlson to have; the few months of their courtship, the few weeks of their marriage. Neither of them had questioned the advisability of getting married during the war. They had loved each other and they wanted to marry, even though the risks were great.

He was a little afraid of Saipan. He had a premonition.

In an earlier letter to his father dated May 4th, five weeks before Saipan's D-Day, he mentioned, for the first time since the war, the possibilities of his death in battle. And he added:

> If I live through the war, God willing, I hope that in the turbulent period that will follow I will be able to work for the happiness and welfare of all men and women of good faith.

But the scent of trouble ahead was clearly in his nostrils. He told the author before departing Camp Pendleton for the Saipan operation that he wished he did not have to go. For every other operation he had been eager, and had volunteered for most of them. For Saipan, he was reluctant.

How long could he last? he asked himself. Makin, Guadalcanal, Tarawa, Kwajalein . . . How long?

On June 14, as he stood against the bulkhead of his landing boat, watching the smoke from high explosive shells bloom from Saipan up ahead, he made a vow. If he lived through this that was forthcoming, he would give his whole life from that time on to the cause of a progressive and people's peace.

Eight days later, on the 22nd of June, Carlson, Lieutenant Colonel Justice Chambers and Pfc. Vic Cassara, a radioman from

Brooklyn, New York, were moving up the flank of Mount Tapot-
chau where a fiery battle was going on. Cassara was carrying a
walkie-talkie, and every now and then Carlson or Chambers would
give him a message detailing the battle situation to Division Headquarters.

"We were moving up a little to the rear of the main body of
troops," Cassara reported later. "Suddenly there was a burst of
machine gun fire from behind, and I fell with a bullet in my thigh.
I couldn't crawl out of the line of fire because of the heavy radio
apparatus on my back, so the two officers rushed over and helped
me to cover behind a small dirt bank.

"Then the machine gun opened up again and bullets zipped into
the dirt inches above my head. Colonel Carlson realized that the
cover was not adequate so he picked me up to remove me to a safer
place.

"The Colonel hadn't carried me more than a few yards when
there came another burst and he was struck. It seems almost miraculous to me that I was not hit again.

"A corpsman and stretcher bearers arrived seconds later. They
started to remove Colonel Carlson first until he instructed them to
take me because I had been wounded first.

"They don't come any better than the Colonel. He has won the
respect and admiration of all who have served with him. I know if
he hadn't carried me away from that spot I would certainly have
been hit again and probably killed. That gunner really had my
range." [7]

As the stretcher bearers carried Cassara away, Colonel Chambers
moved Carlson over to a wooden shed near by and put him down
gently to wait for the bearers to return. Carlson had been hit in the
right arm and left thigh, and was bleeding badly. Chambers made
a makeshift bandage, and gave him a handful of sulfa tablets.

When the bullets had hit him, Carlson felt as if hammers had
fallen on him. He recalls that the first thing he thought of was that

[7] An interview published in the Marine Corps *Chevron,* San Diego,
California, in July 1944. The interview was given to Sergeant Ellsworth
A. Shiebler, Marine Corps combat correspondent.

he was not killed. And then gratitude. And then he thought that the wound meant he would be out of combat for some time to come, and he might live out the war and into the peace.

Later, lying in the little shed, with the insane sounds of the near-by battle filling his ears, he could not help feeling a deep joy. He thought back on the past. Everything seemed to fit together. He had been led from his father's house, and through all the seeking, to this moment, and from this moment on he would remember his vow.

When the stretcher bearers returned, his pain was coming in fast but he was still conscious. They carried him to an aid station in an old stable. The Japs had zeroed in their mortars on the stable and the terrain all around was being chewed into pieces by the bursting shells. Doctors and medical corpsmen and the wounded expected a direct hit at any minute.

"I remember thinking at that time," Carlson says, "that if the Japs couldn't hit me up front, they weren't going to hit me back there."

The doctors ordered him back to Pearl Harbor, and after a few harassing days in the Naval Hospital there, he was shipped to San Diego's.

One year before he had entered the same hospital. His Raiders had been taken from him. He had been depressed. He had wanted to see no one.

Now, though weak and troubled with his wounds, he was ready to see the world.

5

"Gon-Hoe"

He saw the world. Mrs. Peggy Carlson came first, of course, but soon he numbered among his visitors the President and Mrs. Roosevelt and Colonel James Roosevelt. Mrs. Roosevelt mentioned the visit in her column, and referred to him as General Carlson. This created a flurry among his admirers in the Marines and outside who had been claiming that with his record Carlson should have been given a general's stars long ago. But Mrs. Roosevelt, unfortunately, was in error. Marine Corps Headquarters quickly informed the United Press that "whatever his deserts, (Carlson) still has two jumps to make before becoming a general officer." In this connection, it might be well to record that Carlson never received his stars. Carlson himself was considerably surprised when he was promoted to full Colonel in March 1945, to rank as of November 1942. He did not think he would ever get that far.[8]

He gave many newspaper interviews. His estimate of Saipan was that "Tarawa was a side show compared to it." He figured that the Japanese were far from beaten and the war would last at least two years more. And, as for the home front, he praised the contribution to the war of trade unions. To him they were the spine of democracy.

Letters for him flooded the hospital, from strangers, old friends he hadn't heard from in years, Army and Navy men, and of course, his Raiders.

"Dear Sir," began one Raider, and ended: "Your pal."

Another commenced: "Knowing the kind of fellow you are, I feel as though I can write to you without going through all the regular routine."

"Your loyal follower," said another Raider. Then added a P.S.: "Sir, if you ever need a man for any kind of job — and I mean anything — just call on me. I just had to say that!"

From a Master Sergeant ex-Raider:

> In a few days I am to go overseas again but just couldn't go without writing to you. Believe me, Colonel, how often we talk of the old outfit. Those days were the happiest I ever had in the Marines. I'll remember you in my prayers. God bless you.

[8] He was retired for wounds and disability in the summer of 1946 as a Brigadier General, an automatic promotion given to men who had received high battle honors such as the Navy Cross.

A pharmacist's mate who served with the Raiders on Guadalcanal:

> I saw your picture and read about the wound. . . . I will always cherish the days I had duty under you.

From a "Sergeant by your own hand":

> This Gung Ho business is above most people's heads but even though I don't get it across verbally, they still seem to appreciate it in practice.

The personnel officer of a PT boat squadron in the Pacific wrote of how, after reading descriptions of Gung Ho in *Fortune* and in *Life,* he tried to instill it in his own men. He wasn't getting results. "How did you begin, sir?" he asked. "How can I get it to work? Where did I make my mistakes?"

From the chief surgeon of the Army 102nd Infantry Division came a request for Gung Ho material. He had read a brief summary in the *Reader's Digest* and thought it might be a way of preventing neuropsychiatric casualties.

From the American Red Cross in Brooklyn, New York, came word that a man whose name was unknown to Carlson had made a blood donation in his honor.

From Saipan came letters. They were missing him. His plan had worked.

"Evans, your back door plan really fooled 'em. Thanks for your ideas," wrote Colonel Walter Jordan from Tinian in August.

Second Lieutenant Harry McCabe, assistant to Carlson, told him what was going on in Saipan. Carlson had come to have great affection for Mac. He was the only one, apart from the Division Commander and the Chief of Staff, to whom Carlson could talk over top-secret material. He found in Mac what Carlson had always needed, responsiveness and loyalty. "Mac was pure Gung Ho," Carlson says. And beyond that he can praise no higher. The broad-faced, earnest Pittsburgher was killed on Iwo Jima. In his pocket at that time was a letter from Carlson telling him to be careful. "Never go into a danger area, Mac," the letter had said, "unless it's your duty. Never hesitate if it is." Mac's friends on Iwo say that he was eternally dragging out that letter, using it as a guide to decision. McCabe found it was his duty to go forward into a quarry, the center of a fierce fire-fight. He was wounded in his shoulder, refused evacuation; was wounded a few minutes later on the side of his head, refused evacuation again. The third bullet went through his head.

No loss in the war meant as much to Carlson. The two men, twenty years apart, were friends, and Carlson has few close friends.

There is a story about Carlson which throws some light on McCabe's loyalty to his leader and to the principles of Gung Ho even in the smallest detail.

Sergeant David Dempsey, a Marine Corps combat correspondent, who had been with the Fourth Division, wrote the author the following:

> When our division was returning from the Marianas campaign, the Merchant Marine vessel on which we sailed served the troops but two meals a day. (They were lousy meals, too, I can assure you.) However, the officers got the usual three feedings per day. This is hard to believe, but men actually asked for mess duty in order to get enough to eat; others bought food from the crew, or traded souvenirs for it; some even stood outside the officers' mess and "begged" for it. There was a great deal of bitterness about the whole thing, especially in view of the treatment the officers got. The story got around — and this is the part I cannot verify — that Col. Carlson voluntarily limited himself to two meals a day in view of the situation. Even though it may not be true (although I rather suspect it is) it is significant that the troops would spread a story like this and believe in it. In other words, they believed in Carlson.

In commenting on Dempsey's story, Carlson said: "It happened — but on the trip back from the Marshall Islands on the S.S. *Young America*. I had forgotten about it. As I recall, both McCabe and I voluntarily skipped the noon meal. To the best of my recollection McCabe thought of it on his own, and only later did we find out that each of us had done it."

*　　*　　*

More letters came to him at the hospital. Admiral Yarnell, now retired, wrote him:

> Much has happened since you were in North China and saw what troops could really do if they were trained for it. Your experience has borne rich fruit, since I feel that you have really been responsible for the commando type of soldier.

He heard from Yong Hak Park, and Ching Lee, the Mr. "Gung" and Mr. "Ho," their Korean guides of the Guadalcanal days, and from Schofield, Le Francois, Nelson, Bulgar, Maghakian, Peeples, Hermanek, Peatross, Plumley and Coyte. They all wrote, as one of them put it, "in the faith."

And there were the sad letters: "Do you remember Wiseman, the tall red-headed fellow; Studer, the small, weaseled, bald-headed guy? They were killed. Remember Tony Rilja — killed. Out of two hundred Raiders left, seventy-five were killed, one hundred wounded."

There were letters from some of his old corporals and sergeants, now master sergeants and officers commissioned in the field, who wanted to know how soon they could figure on joining him in a new outfit.

"We hope we meet again some day — Wake, Philippines, China. Who knows! Gung Ho will see us through as it has done before."

One Raider wrote him a history of the Battalion after Carlson had left.

> If you remember, sir, some of our weaker men blamed you for our short stay in New Zealand, but most of us were 100% loyal to you and your teachings. You had no sooner left us than any one of us would have done anything to get back under your command.
>
> Most of us thought you would be coming back to us after your rest in the States. So we bided our time and waited for that day. Colonel Shapley made a bad start by reverting to the ten man squad set-up but the fire-team system had become a part of the Raiders so we saw to it that all the new replacements were properly indoctrinated and the training was largely along your lines. At least, we made it so.

You understand, of course, that these are mostly my impressions of the general trend among your old men.

Of course there were some few who aren't capable of understanding such a philosophy as Gung Ho but then those men weren't able to stand the tests of Guadalcanal either. It wasn't their fault but they didn't belong with us who had the spirit, will and determination to suffer any and all sacrifices.

Shortly before we left for Bougainville, a new Colonel took charge — Lt. Colonel McCafferty and he gradually let us drift back into your training methods and Gung Ho came to life again! Unfortunately he was killed on the beach and Major Washburn took over (Washburn was an original member of the Raiders) and once more things ran like a well-oiled machine. You would have been proud of our spirit! We done jobs there that it took the 3rd Raiders and 3rd Marine Regiment days to do. We done it in a few hours. Some of us died, but we knew we'd end the opposition with a minimum loss of life & we did.

In the days that followed we thoroughly proved once more that your teachings & methods were sound for we done every job we were supposed to do with minimum delay, loss of life, and willingness. We sort of felt like we were doing it for you.

When the old men all came home in Feb after 21 months overseas they all hoped you'd meet them at the dock. It's very hard to be content in any other service after serving under you.

That's why I am writing this & for the other fellows. If there is ever a chance of us getting together again we'd like to know it so that we could once again do what is dearest to our hearts. In my small way I feel like the part of a Crusade! Perhaps some day we can make *enough* people listen!

A Methodist minister from Thomaston, Connecticut, who was a Chaplain with the Air Transport Command, wrote:

Please let me take this occasion to tell you how much of a source of inspiration you have been for me during the last few years. . . . Your attitude is making a real contribution to the ideal of democratic understanding . . .

From an Army man who had also fought with the Spanish Loyalists against Franco:

> It is heartening to know that we have men like you, and surely there must be many others, who are fighting for a better and saner world.

But of all his letters, the ones that meant the most came from the parents of his boys.

From Chicago:

> Our son left us over two years ago a normal intelligent youngster, just out of prep school. He returned to us an even finer man than our fondest dreams had hoped, for which I wish to thank you and a Providence who placed our boy under your command. You are his ideal. To be as you are, his ultimate goal.

From parents whose son had been killed:

> We hate saying things like this but feel you will understand. There never would have been so many of our lads dead had you been their leader. I can hear our darling saying he would rather eat a bowl of rice with the Old Man than the finest chow with anyone else. I can see you smile for I know you have heard that often. Of course the lads didn't think you did.

From Puyullup, Washington:

> I was listening in on the radio and heard what you had to say about Gon-Hoe. My son, of your Raiders, was wounded on Guadalcanal. Then gave his all at Tarawa. Can you not write and tell me how he met his death — was he taught Gon-Hoe — did you know him to talk to?

From Omaha, Nebraska, from Hornbeak, Tennessee, from Anahuac, Texas, Tortilla Flat, Arizona, Sterling, Colorado, Baker, Oregon, Concord, New Hampshire, Perry, Oklahoma, Springfield, Massachusetts — the letters came. They were typed; they were handwritten, some with Palmer method grace, some in the stubby awkwardness of the untaught. They told their stories of loneliness for their never-returning boys and of a gratitude that was more meaningful for having come out of sorrow. They invited him to "come by and stay with us"; to "please make our home your home when you come to Chicago"; they told him he was being prayed for daily; they quoted sermons their preachers had given with excerpts from the Guadalcanal memorial. And they congratulated him on his marriage and wished speedy recovery from his wounds. They sent him fruit and flowers and printed greeting cards with notes attached.

To the fathers and mothers of his dead Carlson wrote letters of condolence.

In one letter, Carlson wrote:

> I know what the loss of your son means to you. I wish I could say or do something to alleviate your grief. I know this is not possible; that your strength and consolation must come from your faith in the righteousness of the cause for which your son fought with all his youthful vigor and determination. We who survive must work for the objectives for which he died; that tolerance and understanding and harmony may be established in human relationships. Only through an honest regard on the part of each individual for the welfare of others can we hope to obviate the tragedy of war. Then only will your sacrifice have a measure of justification.

In another letter, he said:

> Those of us who remain must elect men and women to public office who will use their positions honestly to advance the welfare of all the people.

Carlson knew that when the war was won the same fight in a different guise would continue at home. To him the "lost loved ones" as he put it in a letter to a mother, might be forever lost — if the war-in-peace were not fought and won in the city council as well as in the Congress.

6

December distaste

His arm wound was troubling him. After a month in the hospital the doctors decided it was time for a bone graft. However, when the surgeons got into his arm they found infection still present and the wound still draining. It was no time for a graft. They removed the wire joining the broken bone, and broke adhesions which, owing to the immobility of the arm, had formed in his elbow and shoulder.

To his father he wrote:

> Another two months must elapse before the graft can be made. But I feel human for the first time in many months. My jaundice is just about out of my system, and despite the shock of the wounds and the debility caused by the jaundice and malaria, lying in bed for the last three months has really rested me.

The doctors permitted him to rest at home, and he and Mrs. Carlson rented a house in the country, about three miles northwest of Escondido, California, and only an eighth of a mile off Highway 395 which he had helped survey in 1916, and where he had once promised himself he would like to live one day. It was good living on a hill with groves of fruit trees on all sides, with fine pines and sycamores and peppers on his own land, with high dry air and temperate sun. His neighbors were generous, industrious and friendly people. Carlson had his books and, for the first time in many years, a chance to loaf and read and think slowly.

The days went by, and he was happy.

In January 1945, he made a trip to Chicago to talk over a national radio hookup for Wrigley's "Front Line" program. When he was asked what his fee was, he replied that he wanted only railroad fare for himself and his wife and their hotel expenses. To the somewhat shocked advertising man, he explained what he was going to talk about, and he didn't want to make any money off Gung Ho. Years before, he had decided to avoid "cashing in" on his convictions. In 1939–1940, when he had lectured around the country for the Stimson Committee against participation in Japanese aggression, he turned back to the committee all his fees, many of them large, and accepted a wage which came to $200 a month, "enough to live on."

In Chicago he was also to address the Union League Club. He couldn't figure out why they wanted him. Didn't they know he was a very progressive Democrat? But they gave him carte blanche and with it he would talk to the Devil himself.

When he arrived, he found that a room had been reserved for him at the Union League Club. He told the committee which met him at the train that he would prefer to go to a hotel. "There are lots of people I would like to see while I'm here," he explained in a friendly way. "Negroes, Chinese, labor leaders. They might be reluctant to come to see me at the Club." He did not add that the Club might be reluctant to have them come to him there.

He stayed at a hotel.

Another committee called on him: the parents and relatives of men who had served in the Second Raider Battalion. They had organized a "Carlson's Raider Family Club." Would he honor them by attending a dinner?

Would he honor them! He would have come to Chicago for them alone!

The club had been started when Raiders wrote home sending messages to their parents for other parents. Members of about forty families in Chicago met each other this way. After a while they got together to see newsreel films of Guadalcanal in which their sons appeared, and the idea of a club came into being. Gung Ho was its slogan.

At the dinner Carlson was presented with a hand-inscribed memorial, signed by the parents, relatives and friends of local Raiders. When Thomas J. Hermanek, the club's president, handed the memorial to him, Carlson was deeply stirred. He could not prevent his tears. When he spoke, he spoke as one of them, telling them what he had tried to do and how much their sons had done. Simply, he repeated the plea, for which he had vowed his life, not to permit the peace to mock the war.

In March Carlson was sent overseas again to act as Deputy Chief of Staff for the Fifth Amphibious Corps. This passage of time was marked for him by the death in April of a man he dearly loved, Franklin D. Roosevelt.

In a letter, he wrote:

> The news of the President's passing has hit me hard. For ten years he has been my inspiration and my ideal. I was privileged to serve him and was honored by his friendship and confidence. To the world he is a great man but only his family and friends knew how truly great he was.
>
> At the moment I feel like a ship without a rudder. I know of no one else whose leadership I could follow with the supreme confidence with which I followed FDR. I was so certain of his integrity, of his concern for the welfare of all the people. How tragic is his passing at this time, only history can discern and record.
>
> Perhaps in death his influence for an equitable and lasting peace will be more profound than if he had lived. At any rate, his great heart is now at peace. God rest him.[9]

By June 1945, he had to be returned to the States for another operation on his arm. The bones were not knitting together as they should. At Escondido he found his father and his sister. They had driven across country from Connecticut. From now on California would be their home. The family was together again, and Carlson was overjoyed at how warmly his father and sister accepted Peggy, his new wife, whom they were meeting for the first time.

Peace had come — now what was he going to do?

Carlson had once made a talk before the faculty of California Institute of Technology, and out of it had come the suggestion that

[9] To the author.

there might be a place for him there to teach the politics of the Far East. From Occidental College, acting President Arthur Coons, an old friend from Peiping days, talked about a teaching job. From the New School for Social Research in New York came still another offer. Carlson liked the idea of teaching. He had practiced it successfully in the Raiders. He looked forward to time for study and writing, and to the friendship of young men who must some day be our leaders.

There was still another prospect. Some California friends proposed that he enter the 1946 primaries for the United States Senate.[10]

Carlson was quite reluctant to enter politics. He did not want to "make deals" or play the required game of compromise and deceit which, unhappily, is the lifeblood of our politics. If the politicians and the voters would accept him as he was, knowing in full that he was strongly pro-labor, anti-Big Business, opposed to our supporting Chiang Kai-shek against the Chinese Communists, in favor of our sharing our atomic discoveries with the world; why, then, he would run. He did not want to have anybody write or rewrite his speeches for him. He wanted to say what he believed. He wanted all to know, politicians and people, that he was for full employment and for the Fair Practices Employment measure; for a Federal program of education. He wanted the veterans to know that he did not consider them a special part of the citizenry. What benefited all, benefited them. He was, of course, for the G.I. Bill of Rights which he wanted even more liberalized. But, "The welfare of any single citizen is inseparable from the welfare of the whole," he wrote to the American Veterans' Committee of which he was a member. He urged veterans to get into politics, but to keep politics out of the Veterans' Administration. He was particularly bitter against the lobbies which tried to get Veterans' Hospitals in their communities for pork-barrel reasons.

If he was acceptable to the politicians and the people on these principles, he would fight for the nomination. It was not an easy decision to make, for he knew it would mean the end of privacy and

[10] Carey McWilliams, in an article in the *Nation* of December 1, 1945, describes the genesis of this proposal.

the end of time to study and write. And although he did not say this, his wife knew that he had not overcome a fatigue which was bone-deep.

While still on sick leave after the operation on his arm in which the bones were reset, he made many speeches. These were not political campaign speeches, for he was still in uniform. But in another sense they were campaign speeches; for he was using whatever forum was available to speak out, as he had done in 1939–1940, to the good sense of the American people. There were Makins and Tarawas to be won at home.

December 1945 was the high point of this activity. It almost led him to disaster.

On Monday, December 2, he flew from California to New York to speak before the American Veterans' Committee, and to a meeting of the Independent Citizens' Committee of the Arts, Sciences and Professions at Madison Square Garden. The subject was "Atomic Energy and Foreign Policy." Speakers were Henry Wallace, Senator Tobey of New Hampshire, the famous scientists, Harlow Shapley, Harold Urey and Julian Huxley, Helen Keller, R. J. Thomas, President of the United Automobile Workers, and others. It was a magnificent meeting, attended by 22,000 people. As Carlson was introduced they rose to their feet with roars of "Gung Ho! Gung Ho!"

His tall, spare, uniformed figure stood out sharply in the spotlights; the battle stars on his ribbons glistened; he stood for a moment in front of the microphone and with his good arm waved thanks for the applause. It kept coming. He grinned happily. He felt the powerful wave of kinship which flowed to him through the cheers and the handclaps. He thought that there is nothing in all of the emotion of man which is more exciting than brotherhood.

When the applause died away, he put on his silver-rimmed glasses and read his speech.

"We must direct our thinking," he said in part, "toward building a world organization which will have as its objective the harmonizing of human relations and the satisfying of human needs among all the peoples of the earth."

On Wednesday he spoke at a meeting to raise money for the dissemination of information about democratic China. Thursday, he flew from New York to San Francisco to speak before the State C.I.O. Convention. (The month before he had received a special medal from the National Maritime Union for his war services.) While in San Francisco, he talked to the Press Club on China. "The best interests of China are served by withdrawing our troops from there," he said. "Let the Chinese people decide for themselves who shall be their own leaders."

Friday, he flew to San Diego to spend a few hours at home. On Sunday he went to Bakersfield where he addressed the District Convention of the 20–30 Clubs. Monday night, he was back in Los Angeles to join Congresswoman Helen Gahagan Douglas and Thomas Mann, the author of *The Magic Mountain,* in a public discussion of atomic energy and peace. Tuesday, he drove down to San Pedro to talk to the tenants of the Channel Heights Federal Housing Project. To an audience of laboring men and women — for him an audience in which he found himself most at home — he spoke of the necessity to place human needs on a par with profits.

Wednesday, in Los Angeles, he spoke by remote control to a New York meeting honoring returning servicemen. At the radio station he met for the first time ex-Sergeant Bill Mauldin, the cartoonist and gadfly of the brass hats. Mauldin was overheard to say that of the brass only Eisenhower and Carlson had the respect of the G.I. Carlson spoke privately to Mauldin encouraging him in his fight against home-grown Fascism. "It'll be real rugged as the time goes on, Bill," he said. "Then you'll need all your wits and all your courage against all kinds of pressures."

"Hell," Mauldin said. "They're calling me a 'Red' already."

That Wednesday night he spoke on atomic power politics to a meeting at the Hollywood American Legion Stadium. Here he discarded a prepared address and spoke extemporaneously. He let himself go. He delighted and inspired the audience. Of all his talks — many of them suffering from too many generalizations — this was his most effective. This one was warm, affectionate, salty, humorous — a little like Will Rogers, a lot like the Yankee of tradition. Referring to the chairman's remark that Carlson was fifty-two, he said: "He has placed me among the wise old men of fifty-two, when I'm really only an adolescent of forty-nine. Where you and I will be on my fifty-second birthday depends on what we do about this atomic bomb."

Thursday, San Francisco again, to appear before the famous Commonwealth Club; and on Sunday a dinner for Bill Mauldin in Los Angeles.

Late Sunday night, tired and with his arm hurting him, he drove home to Escondido.

In the meantime some of the professional politicians in the state, realizing Carlson's progressivism, his appeal to the citizen, and his unwillingness to talk "deals," had started a "Stop Carlson" movement. Others, not so professional, were building organized support for him. At a conference of California Democratic Party leaders, the pro-Carlson forces were strong enough to prevent the caucus from coming out in support of the machine candidate.

Carlson's candidacy looked very promising. A number of prominent Californians, among them James Roosevelt, now retired from the Marine Corps, announced themselves publicly for him. Hundreds of others, veterans and citizens, flooded Carlson with letters and telephone calls, asking what they could do to help.

Then depressing news slowly came out of Escondido. Carlson was sick. Carlson had heart trouble.

The rumor was true. Carlson was sick. During that strenuous month of December, he had been feeling deep pains in his chest. For awhile he hid this from his wife. He reasoned that they may have been deferred pains from his wound, or were a result of a chest cold. But a few days before Christmas he could not hide them from his wife any more. He had his first heart attack. The campaign for the senatorship was over. If he was to live, the Naval doctors at San Diego told him, he must rest for at least six months.

"I've fallen apart like the one-horse shay," he told his friends.

His illness came as a great shock to him. For a while he was really frightened. And there were some things he felt he wanted to get said. He wrote a letter to his old friend Agnes Smedley which shared the temper of his "last" letters before H-hours.

In his brief experience as a possible candidate for the senatorship from California he had his first intimate contacts with professional politicians and old-line labor leaders. Some of these experiences had outraged him — and he wanted to go on record, if, perchance, he did not live through this last battle with his heart.

> My meager experience with politics and politicians [he wrote] has convinced me of several things with regard to this country. 1) There is need for a political party which will truly represent the people and will have machinery which will permit the people to select individuals of their own choice for public office. Both existing major parties have too many self-seeking racketeers who don't give two cents about the people. 2) There are too many racketeers among the leaders of organized labor. The members of labor unions will never get more than the cow's hind tit until they organize and clean house in a democratic manner and put in leaders who will work in their interests. The only hope for progress in America is a strong united labor movement. The bar to such a movement is the presence in the ranks of labor of many leaders who place their own selfish interests ahead of the welfare of the people; many of these leaders stand in the way of the education of union members which would give them the knowledge and understanding of democratic objectives and processes.
>
> Well, I'm just beefing, Agnes, I burn up when I see people stupidly working against their own interests. I burn up, too, when I think of all the good guys who went out and got killed to protect the rights of a handful of s.o.b.'s to make more money for themselves.
>
> Don't worry about me. I have just got to keep down until some of these blood vessels are healed. I know a lot of people, including yourself, living with heart ailments for a long time. I'm sorry this came to me at this time, but probably some other time would have been no better.

With his friends he tried to joke at his illness, but beneath he was bitter and frustrated. The redemption of his vow taken at Saipan seemed hopeless now. He thought he had found a way of making it good — and the way had been taken from him. Not since the loss of the Raiders had he felt so utterly helpless.

But after a while the first shock wore off. He was used to discipline — and he forced himself to accept the prospect of six months to a year of complete rest. In this he was sustained by his wife, for with her to help he came to see ways and means of continuing his fight and confirming his vow. In a few months he could begin to write and talk with people; he could give his name in sponsorship of those organizations whose aims were the same as his. Whatever influence he had could still be used.

In a few weeks he came to think of his illness as a kind of tactical withdrawal forced on him by conditions beyond his control, but by no means beyond overcoming in the end. His belief in Ultimate Justice had not wavered. He was yet a young man. Destiny must still have a part for him to play.

7

"Who is this man?" we asked

If you were to walk into Carlson's room, during his convalescence, at his house at Escondido, you would find him dutifully in a bed surrounded foot-high with newspapers, magazines, Government reports, and books. His hair, almost entirely white, is still close-cropped. His thin face with its strong jutting nose and *Norsk* blue eyes seems less thin. The enforced rest has put a little weight on it. He greets his friends with perhaps more demonstrativeness than ever before, with an arm around shoulders, perhaps with a quick clasp — a rough, manly embrace. It is almost as if he were eager to feel people as well as see and hear them. After a while he might ask you to listen to the recording of Earl Robinson's "The Lonesome Train," his favorite. Or, if you had heard it the last time you were there, he would ask his wife to put on a new Tchaikovsky or Bach album. He listens to the music like a child at a circus, reflecting his delight with broad expressions on a face which is always quick to reveal likes or dislikes. When the music is over, he might talk about the latest news, and when he gives an opinion, he invariably asks earnestly, "Do you think I'm right?"

When it comes time to eat, he is at the table. (He's permitted to get up several times a day.) The family and guests join hands and Carlson, bowing his head, says a grace which his father taught him at Peacham. If you have a good joke to tell, you have a perfect audience, for Carlson's laugh is quick and full-bodied and loud. Nor is he averse to laughing just as loudly at his own jokes.

If the talk — as it usually does — turns to public enemies, you find yourself startled at the vehemence with which he expresses himself — a vehemence combining opinion and a good sprinkling of expletives. But the "goddams" sound more like a Jeremiah's curse than easy vernacular.

When the time comes to go, you are thanked for coming in a way which makes you feel that you are the giver and not the receiver of a great favor.

"While we were aware," his father wrote in a letter to the author in May 1945, "that all through Evans's life as a soldier, he had done conscientious work, the significance of what so suddenly developed after Makin was not at once apparent to us. The mushroom, they say, does not spring up in a night, but in reality has a long undercover preparation. This seems to have been the case with Evans, and the full significance of it has only now come to light. I confess that I am rather stunned with the magnitude of his impact upon men of many classes, high as well as low. In the nature of the case, this only now has come to me . . ."

*   *   *

From Okinawa during a pause in the battle a Marine officer wrote a letter to a friend: "Being interested, I have asked around about Carlson. Frankly, if you want to hear good things spoken about him, you have to ask the enlisted men."

On May 27, 1946, James Forrestal, Secretary of the Navy, forwarded to Carlson his final and permanent citation for the Legion of Merit, given to him for Saipan. In this citation Mr. Forrestal said among other things:

> Schooled by grim experience in the art of countering Japanese strategy, Lieutenant Colonel Carlson . . . defined the most effective methods of attacking the objectives. Landing on D-day plus 1 under heavy mortar and artillery fire, he immediately volunteered to visit front line units in an effort to obtain information and, fearlessly moving into areas where the battle raged with savage fanaticism, he repeatedly risked his life during the critical days following the invasion. . . . Consistently sound in his evaluation of enemy positions and strength, he continued his determined efforts . . . persevering despite the mounting fury of hostile resistance and providing first hand information under increasingly difficult conditions, until he sustained serious wounds while engaged in a front line reconnaissance on 22 June 1944. A brilliant tactician and indomitable fighter, Lieutenant Colonel Carlson rendered services of inestimable value to his Commanding General prior to and during the assault and occupation of this fiercely defended Japanese base, and his dauntless initiative, outstanding professional skill and unwavering devotion to duty in the face of tremendous opposition were important factors in the ultimate seizure of the objective . . .

Yet somewhere in the higher echelons of the Marine Corps, there exists a stubborn resentment of Carlson.

In the official history of the Fourth Marine Division, published by the Historical Section of Marine Corps Headquarters, there is no mention of Carlson's name on the list of winners of the Legion of Merit. In the history of the Fourth Division all the leading staff officers are named except Carlson, although he was head of the

Planning Section which, according to the Fourth Division Commander, Lieutenant General Harry Schmidt, was a separate staff section equal in standing to the other sections. In substance, one could read through the entire history of his division and not know that Carlson was ever connected with it.

It is difficult not to conclude that the "brass" dies hard.

"I can still recall the feeling of exultation I experienced as a young man," Carlson told Dr. Dollard of Yale, "when I first read in Emerson's Essay on Self-Reliance the lines: 'In every work of genius we recognize our own rejected thoughts; they come back to us with a certain alienated majesty. Great works of art have no more affecting lesson than this. They teach us to abide by our spontaneous impression with good-humored inflexibility then most when the whole cry of voices is on the other side. Else tomorrow a stranger will say with masterly good sense precisely what we have thought and felt all the time, and we shall be forced to take with shame our own opinion from another.'

"The point is," Carlson went on, "that this essay of Emerson's made me realize for the first time that the potential power to conceive substantial ideas and to implement them lies within each human being."

Carlson's search through the whole of his life was to find, first, a world which would sustain his own confidence in his own ideas and his ability to make them work; and, second, he sought for a world which would sustain every man's confidence to express the rich potential of life.

Out of all that he has seen and learned, he has come to believe that the desire for great wealth and power stands between man and his contentment.

In the life of America Evans Carlson is its real promise. Stumbling, searching, growing out of the bony wisdom of deeds, he learned the full measure of the rights of man. He became drunk with democracy.

Evans Carlson is the absolute certainty that men can learn; that there is something irrevocably true in our country and in the sources of our life.

If Evans Carlson lived no more than these fifty years he would have proved the reality of his own deepest conviction. In 1944, in referring to China, he said, "As free men and women we have abiding faith in the ability of free men to fashion a society in which there will be justice, well-being and happiness for all."

It was for this he fought the war. And for it he will fight in the peace for as long as he lives.

"I'm afraid I have nothing of interest to add to the story of Evans's life," Rewi Alley wrote in a letter. "Evans belongs to the next age of creative man — man who will master his environment and tear a new furrow into the unknown. I hope Evans stays longer with us all."

Appendices

1

Address

[The following address was given by Lieutenant Colonel Evans F. Carlson, U.S.M.C., on the occasion of the first anniversary of the organization of the Second Marine Raider Battalion.]

One year ago the Marine Raider Battalion came into being, the first organization in the history of American armed forces to be organized and designed purely for raiding and guerrilla missions. Hereafter, this date will be known as Marine Raider Organization Day. It is a significant day in American naval-military history. In the years to come you members of this battalion who pioneered the work; you who proved to the world the value of democratic practices in connection with military operations, and who further gave proof of the practicability and deep significance of what we are pleased to call the Gung Ho spirit; you men will tell with pride of your part in this great work.

Our goal was to create and perfect a cohesive, smooth-functioning team which, by virtue of its harmony of action, unity of purpose and its invincible determination, would be able to out-point the enemy on every count. What were the requisites? First, the quality of leadership. Leaders must invariably be professionally competent; they must be honest, especially honest intellectually, admitting their mistakes when they make them and endeavoring to correct them.

It was necessary that officers live close to their men, studying them, encouraging them and teaching them not only military technique and maneuvers but basic ethical doctrines as well. They must cheerfully and willingly forego those superficial privileges which ordinarily insulate officers from their men and impair mutual sympathy and understanding. They must share the hardships and privations of those they lead and prove by their character and ability their qualifications for leadership. Only in this way could full confidence be engendered and a harmony of spirit prevail. The basis of leadership must be merit.

Then it was necessary to so organize tactical units as to enhance and perfect team work. We gave to military science the fire group, a balanced team which lends itself easily to control even when advancing by infiltration.

Most important, though, was the development of what we call the Gung Ho spirit; our ability to co-operate — work together. Not only was it imperative to understand this spirit; it was even more imperative to apply it to daily actions no matter how unimportant they might seem. This called for self-discipline and implicit belief in the doctrine of helping the other fellow. Followed through to its ultimate end it would mean that each while helping the other fellow would in turn be helped by him.

It was in the matter of Gung Ho that we made our slowest progress, though progress we have made. We were handicapped by our native background, that background in which greed and rugged individualism predominated. Human beings are creatures of habit. Human nature does not change its coat without a struggle. But Rome wasn't built in a day. The important thing was for each individual to have the *desire* to help the other fellow, the desire to achieve that mastery over his mind, his body and his desires that he might succeed in disciplining himself. This means tolerance of ideas, tolerance of personal eccentricities, the sweeping away of personal prejudices, concentration on an effort to see the good in human beings of all types and persuasions. What a task; what a task! As I say, we have made progress, great progress, but we still have a long way to go before we attain that degree of perfection which will rid this outfit of petty friction and will make us a living harmonious entity.

Hand in hand with Gung Ho goes the willingness to endure hardship and pain in order that the toughest job may be accomplished as economically in terms of human life and as effectively in terms of exterminating the enemy as possible. This will-to-endure is akin to the element of consent in our democratic form of government. In this particular application it transcends in importance the element of consent in government, because it makes possible the luxury of such a form of government.

Finally, it was necessary to the success of this military pattern of ours that individuals understand the reasons for which they fight and offer themselves for sacrifice. Hope for glory will carry some men a long way in battle; pride in the outfit and the desire not to let your buddies down is an even more potent force; but the force which impels men to carry on when the going is tough and victory appears to be remote is a deep spiritual conviction in the righteousness of the cause for which he fights and in the belief that victory will bring an improved social pattern wherein his loved ones and the loved ones of future generations will enjoy a greater measure of happiness and well being than was his lot. And so it has been an unfailing policy in this organization to articulate for you and constantly to remind you of the reasons why we endure and fight and sacrifice.

Let us pause for a moment to re-examine these reasons. Most pressing of life's problems are the need for sufficiency in food, clothes and cover from the elements. We want the assurance that these things will be provided in adequate quantity. Then there is the matter of education; we want our loved ones to be educated along the lines for which they have an aptitude. When school is over we want them to be able to pursue that line of endeavor in which lies their heart and ability. We want freedom; freedom to speak our minds as long as we do not defame our neighbors; freedom to worship whom and where and when we wish; freedom to influence the trend of government; freedom and the opportunity to have a voice in all those matters which affect our daily lives. We want just and sympathetic treatment by all men; we want love and not hatred to prevail among men. We want to assure for those who survive and for those loved ones to come the inalienable right to life, liberty and the opportunity to pursue happiness, each in his own way, so long as it does not impair the rights of others. Are these things worth fighting for? Our hearts, our most sacred convictions, tell us they are. The knowledge that victory means the realization of these things for us cannot fail to inspire and sustain us in those times when discomfort, boredom or even death are immediate realities. Only by pain and sacrifice can we win the right to these things our hearts cherish.

Perhaps the greatest benefit we derived from that grueling experience on Guadalcanal was an increase in faith in the power of a Supreme Being or of a Higher Destiny, however you please to describe it. We humans are weak in faith. Lack of adequate faith is the real cause for our failure to bring the Gung Ho spirit to its highest perfection. We lack faith in each other; we lack faith in the ability of the human being to grow and change; we lack faith in ourselves, our ability to discipline ourselves. Believe me, boys, faith can move mountains. Do you suppose these past months since we first came together have been without discouragement for me? I hesitate to tell you how low my spirits have been at times, or how thin my faith has worn. But never has it been completely extinguished. Many of you have been a great trial to me, both officers and men. But always, even in the darkest moments, my faith in your ultimate ability to master yourselves, my faith in your desire to do the right thing, has remained with me. My faith in the rightness of the patterns for life and conduct which I have emphasized for you so frequently has kept me on the course. And time after time you have confirmed that faith.

Now my hope is that this exposition of our goals and our accomplishments, of the character of our doctrines and the reasons why we do what we do, will inspire you to greater effort in the direction of making the spirit of Gung Ho your own. When you are on the verge of doing something you shouldn't do, ask yourself if it is be-

cause you lack the power to control and discipline yourself. The
most painful moments of my life with you are those minutes when
I am constrained to administer punishment for some thoughtless
offense. Always I think, "How unnecessary this all is. If this boy
could only be brought to see the value of self-discipline he would not
do those things. How can I make him see?"

I hope also that you will have a deeper understanding of your
duty to your Country, which means an unfailing effort to see this
war through to ultimate victory. Your contribution is not one battle,
or two. No, your obligation to yourself and to those loved ones you
desire to protect and preserve means that you must have the fortitude
and patience and determination to drive on until the enemy is
annihilated and a lasting peace is secured. Yes, I know what you are
thinking. There are men back home who serve in places of safety
and where conditions are more comfortable. What a hell of a war
effort we would make if each jockeyed with the other for the soft
jobs! We must be honest with ourselves and our convictions. And
remember this, the right to determine the pattern of life we shall
have in our country after the war belongs to those who have had
the courage to suffer pain and privation and who have persistently
offered themselves for sacrifice. It belongs to such as you. Our job,
yours and mine, is to see this thing through. By so doing we raise
ourselves to be peers among men. Ours is the satisfaction of having
done the job. No one, nothing, can ever rob us of this achievement.

Remember, too, that those who serve in factories and offices, and
on the farm back home are also making essential contributions to the
war effort. We on the firing line could not do our job without their
uncompromising effort to produce and transport to us the means
with which to fight. There is such a thing as division of labor in
war as well as in peacetime production. Each contributes according
to his ability and his talent; each receives according to his needs.
Gung Ho is the watchword for not only this battalion, but for all
units of the armed services and for all those who labor on the home
front.

Our contribution is to fight and win battles. In your ability and
willingness to continue to make this sublime contribution I have

the fullest confidence. May that Supreme Being who has guided us
with such infinite wisdom in the past continue to watch over, protect
and guide you, bringing us to victory and a richer fulfillment of
life's obligations.

2

Speech

[Excerpts from a speech delivered October 1943, at a congress
of writers sponsored by the University of California at Los
Angeles and the Hollywood Writers' Mobilization. President
Roosevelt, Vice-President Wallace and Wendell Willkie were
among those who supported this congress. The proceedings
have been published by the University of California Press,
1944.]

There is need for us to refresh our memories on the principles
which comprise democracy. Especially is there need for us to weigh
our own actions against these principles. Now that we are political
and moral missionaries to the world we must make certain that we
practice the precepts we preach. Are we individually working for
the welfare of our democratic society as a whole? Do we accept all
racial and religious groups as equals? Are we tolerant of ideas, encouraging their expression and choosing from among them those
which we can apply with benefit? Or are we unconsciously drifting
away from that stern sense of justice, that impartial equality, that
mellow tolerance and that inalienable right of liberty enunciated for
us by our forefathers? If we are, then democracy is on the skids,
for these principles constitute its lifeblood. Greed and prejudice;
intolerance and government by privilege; these are the precepts of
the Fascists whom we fight.

Furthermore, we cannot afford to be inconsistent in the application of democratic principles within the framework of our society. I have been strongly of the opinion, since first I began to reflect seriously on our way of life, that it is both incongruous and inconsistent for our armed forces to be organized and governed by aristocratic methods. For several years I accepted the explanation of recognized military leaders that the need for immediate and implicit obedience to orders justified the molding of members of armed services into automatons. It was obvious to me that obedience, particularly under battle conditions, must be prompt and complete. Perhaps intensive regimentation was essential to gain this end. But no such explanation could justify special privilege for leaders. Special privilege invariably invites self-indulgence. Under campaign conditions in the orthodox military setup the quality of living conditions of officers and men were practically identical. Why not under all conditions?

In due time I came to have a better understanding of, and a deep respect for, the basic decency, the honesty, and the quality of intelligence of human beings, especially humans constrained to work for their livelihood. There came a day when I realized that democracy itself was a way of life acceptable to, and workable by, only men of good intention, honest men, men of sound common sense.

3

Commendation

[Excerpt from General A. A. Vandegrift's commendation to the whole Raider Battalion after Guadalcanal. This was the second unit commendation given in the Pacific war.]

From the operational records of this division it appears that the Raider Battalion, while attached to this division, took the field against the enemy in early November, 1942.

For a period of thirty days this battalion, moving through difficult terrain, pursued, harried and by repeated attacks destroyed an enemy force of equal or greater size, and drove the remnants from the area of operations. During this period the battalion, as a whole or by detachments, attacked the enemy whenever and wherever he could be found in a repeated series of carefully planned and well-executed surprise attacks.

In this latter phase of these operations the battalion destroyed the remnants of the enemy forces and bases on the upper Lunga River and secured valuable information of the terrain and the enemy line of operations.

In these battles the enemy suffered 400 killed and the loss of his artillery, weapons and ammunitions, whereas the battalion losses were limited to 15 killed. For the consummate skill displayed in the conduct of operations, for the training, stamina and fortitude displayed by all members of the battalion and for its commendably aggressive spirit and high morale, the commanding general cites to the division, the commanding officer, officers and men of the Raider Battalion.

Acknowledgments

For this book, there are many to whom a debt is owed.

In all the confusion of American life, the promise and the patterns of its hope are frequently obscured, and complete defeats seem more common than even partial victories. I am most grateful, therefore, to Evans Carlson, for having lived the kind of life which makes an American gain heart again, and know that there is an endless inspiration deriving from our common people. Somehow, now that this biography is finished, the promises and the hopes are more visible than ever before.

Painfully overcoming his New England sense of privacy and his excessive secretiveness, he patiently went through countless hours of questioning and analysis. His memory of men and places was extraordinarily helpful. He gave me his private papers, orders, diaries and manuscripts. More than that, he has examined the facts in this book for errors, and if any remain it is no fault of his. All the thoughts and dialogue which I have attributed to him, he has confirmed, although he is not responsible for any of my interpretations.

Enormous help came from Reverend Thomas A. Carlson, who had kept all his son's letters from 1912 to 1944. There are about 350, and in them Carlson spoke to his father as he might have spoken to himself. For this, and for even more important aid, I have inadequately acknowledged my debt to Thomas Carlson in the dedication.

Mrs. Peggy Carlson — an extraordinary woman in her own right — contributed many insights and apt evaluations. Literally, she has given this book bed and board during the countless nights and days which I spent at the Carlson home.

Edgar and Peg Snow helped me formulate the idea for this book from the beginning, and I am indebted to them.

Among Carlson's Raiders who were almost menacing in their

concern that I tell the truth about the Old Man, I received much aid from James Roosevelt, Victor "Transport" Maghakian, Harry Reynolds, Tom Jolly, Al Flores and Chris Drake.

Mrs. Etelle Carlson very graciously filled in many details which I could have heard from no other source. Thomas O. Carlson and Karen Carlson were also very helpful. Ida Pruitt of the Chinese Industrial Co-operatives worked hard to get me information about that part of Carlson's China experiences, while Mac Fisher, Colin McDonald, Rewi Alley, Joris Ivens, Robert Capa and J. P. Marquand gave me impressions and information about other aspects of Carlson's life in China.

Lieutenant General Harry Schmidt, U.S.M.C., Major General James Ulio, U.S.A., Brigadier General Robert L. Denig, U.S.M.C., and Captain Warren Goodman, U.S.M.C., were kind enough to help me with material and estimates of Carlson's military life.

I want also to thank Agnes Smedley, Stuart Schulberg, Thomas Hermanek, L. H. Mattoon, Arthur Coons, Franklin Fearing, John Dollard, Samuel Ornitz, Kurt Lewin and Vera Caspary for their help.

To Albert Maltz and George Sklar I herewith offer my gratitude, not only for their friendship, but for their encouragement during the days when the going was toughest. And, finally, to Donald Angus Cameron, my thanks for his criticism and his faith that this book, as inadequate as it must inevitably be, would nevertheless communicate some of the spirit and substance of Evans Carlson's life.

Grateful acknowledgment is made to the following publishers and authors who have generously granted permission for the use of brief quotations of copyrighted books and articles:

The *New York Times Book Review* and Nathaniel Peffer; Doubleday, Doran & Company, Inc., for Vincent Sheean's *Personal History;* the *Eastern Underwriter* for a letter from Clyde Thomason; Raymond Swing; John B. Powell; the *Marine Corps Gazette* for Garrett Graham's "Back to Makin"; the *Nation* and Carleton Beals; Dodd, Mead & Company, Inc., for Evans Fordyce Carlson's *Twin Stars of China;* Houghton Mifflin Company for Robert Berkov's *Strong*

Man of China; the *New York Herald Tribune; Time* Magazine; Harbinger House for Henry Misselwitz's *The Dragon Stirs;* Little, Brown & Company for *The Letters of William James;* Harcourt, Brace & Company, Inc., for Hallett Abend's *My Life in China, 1926–1941;* Marine Corps Headquarters for Evans F. Carlson's article in the *Walla Walla;* United Feature Syndicate for Eleanor Roosevelt's "My Day"; the *Saturday Evening Post* for W. S. Le Francois's "We Mopped up Makin"; the *Hartford Courant* for Thomas A. Carlson's letter; Random House, Inc., for Edgar Snow's *Red Star over China* and *The Battle for Asia;* George Sixta for his Rivets cartoon in the *Saturday Evening Post; Fortune* Magazine for "Psychiatric Toll of Warfare"; Little, Brown & Company for Ilona Ralf Sues's *Shark's Fins and Millet;* Doubleday, Doran & Company, Inc., for Nym Wales's *Inside Red China;* Reynal & Hitchcock for James Lucas's *Combat Correspondent;* The Blakiston Company for Dr. John P. Spiegel's and Dr. Roy R. Grinker's *Men Under Stress;* Alfred A. Knopf for Agnes Smedley's *Battle Hymn of China;* the *Portland Telegram;* Louis Carrier & Company for Gustav Amann's *The Legacy of Sun Yat-sen;* Duell, Sloan and Pearce, Inc., for Robert Sherrod's *Tarawa.*

Index

Breinigsville, PA USA
12 February 2010
232394BV00001B/150/A